THE NORMAL PERSONALITY

In *The Normal Personality*, Steven Reiss argues that human beings are naturally intolerant of people who express values significantly different from their own. Because of this intolerance, psychologists and psychiatrists sometimes confuse individuality with abnormality and thus overdiagnose disorders. Reiss shows how normal motives – not anxiety or traumatic childhood experiences – underlie many personality and relationship problems, such as divorce, infidelity, combativeness, workaholism, loneliness, authoritarianism, weak leadership style, perfectionism, underachievement, arrogance, extravagance, stuffed shirt, disloyalty, disorganization, and overanxiety. Calling for greater understanding and tolerance of all kinds of personalities, Reiss applies his theory of motivation to leadership, human development, relationships, and counseling.

Steven Reiss was educated at Dartmouth College, Yale University, Harvard University, and the Massachusetts General Hospital. He has published scientific and clinical studies on the co-occurrence of intellectual disabilities and mental illness. His work has been recognized with five national awards, two for scientific research, two for national impact on clinical services, and one for national leadership, and he has received two certificates of recognition for volunteer work. In 1985, Professor Reiss and then–graduate student Richard J. McNally published the construct of anxiety sensitivity as an early risk factor for Panic Disorder. The anxiety sensitivity index has been translated into more than thirty-five languages and is used to help diagnose many thousands of patients throughout the world. Professor Reiss's theory of motivation is an expansion of the anxiety sensitivity construct to motives other than anxiety.

The Normal Personality

A NEW WAY OF THINKING ABOUT PEOPLE

Steven Reiss

Ohio State University

CAMBRIDGE
UNIVERSITY PRESS

CAMBRIDGE UNIVERSITY PRESS
Cambridge, New York, Melbourne, Madrid, Cape Town, Singapore, São Paulo, Delhi

Cambridge University Press
32 Avenue of the Americas, New York, NY 10013-2473, USA

www.cambridge.org
Information on this title: www.cambridge.org/9780521881067

First published 2008

Printed in the United States of America

A catalog record for this publication is available from the British Library.

Library of Congress Cataloging in Publication Data

Reiss, Steven.
The normal personality : a new way of thinking about people / Steven Reiss.
    p.   cm.
Includes bibliographical references and index.
ISBN-13:   978-0-521-88106-7 (hardback)
1. Personality.   I. Title.
BF698.R65   2007
155.2 – dc22   2007018965

ISBN   978-0-521-88106-7 hardback

Dedicated to my family, Maggi, Michael, and Ben

(and in memory of our dog, Rusty)

I call [a] mean in relation to us that which is neither excessive nor deficient, and this is *not* one and the same for all.

– Aristotle
The quotation is from the Doctrine of the Mean, Book II,
Nichomachean Ethics.

Contents

 **Acknowledgments**

The author would like to express appreciation to Dr. Mary Ellen Milos, Professor Barry Mitnick, Professor Kenneth Olson, school psychologist Maggi Reiss, and Dr. James Wiltz for their extensive comments on earlier versions of this manuscript.

Overview

Values, not unconscious psychodynamics, drive the human psyche.

– theme of this book

I advocate a new way of thinking about people called *motivation analysis*. Psychodynamic counselors and therapists ask, "What happened when this individual was a toddler? Deep down, how does this person feel about his/her parents?" These theorists explain adult personality traits in terms of early childhood experiences, anxiety, and defense; they regard many of life's common problems as mild forms of mental illness. In contrast, motivation analysts ask, "What are the individual's life goals and intrinsically held values? What is he or she trying to accomplish with this or that behavior? Do the individual's current work situation and relationships fulfill or frustrate his or her desires and values?" Motivation analysts explain adult personality as habits people learn to satisfy their life motives, psychological needs, and intrinsically held values. Motivation analysts explain many personal troubles as the result of unmet or frustrated needs, possibly including a conflict of values between the individual and his/her current career, social life, relationships, or family life.

The Abnormal Personality

Sigmund Freud (1963/1916) asserted three significant similarities between personality traits and symptoms of mental illnesses: (1) Both originate in childhood experiences; (2) both are manifestations of unconscious mental forces (called *psychodynamics*); and (3) both are motivated by anxiety or tension reduction. Based on these asserted similarities, psychodynamic theorists have used psychiatric terminology to describe the personality traits of ordinary people. When I was a student at Dartmouth College and Yale University, for example, nationally eminent psychodynamic theorists taught me that suspiciousness is a mild

1

form of paranoia; orderliness is a mild form of Obsessive-Compulsive Disorder; unhappiness is a mild form of depression; divorce results from unconscious forces similar to those that cause neurosis; ulcers are caused by an intense need for people (dependency); and obesity is caused by an unconscious wish for self-destruction. Today, I know of no convincing scientific evidence to support any of these teachings (Dolan-Sewell, Krueger, & Shea, 2001; Kline, 1972).

Psychodynamic theorists have regarded personality as those behaviors we engage in that most resemble symptoms of mental illness. To appreciate the extent to which psychologists have derived personality traits from theories of mental illness, please compare the following two lists. On the left are the original ten traits assessed by the Minnesota Multiphasic Personality Inventory (MMPI; Hathaway & McKinley, 1943). Notice the extent to which the MMPI personality traits read like a list of mental illnesses. On the right are examples of the "normal" personality traits discussed in this book. (The traits on the same line are not matched.)

Original MMPI	Reiss Motivation Profile
Hypochondriasis	Brave/Cautious
Depression	Secure/Insecure
Hysteria	Self-reliant/Interdependent
Psychopathic deviate	Honorable/Expedient
Masculinity–femininity	Saver/Spender
Paranoia	Formal/Informal
Psychasthenia	Willful/Nondirective
Schizophrenia	Organized/Spontaneous
Hypomania	Athletic/Physically lazy
Social introversion	Sociable/Introvert

Even a cursory inspection of these two lists shows the extent to which personality assessments of ordinary (normal) people have been focused on symptoms of abnormality. Although the MMPI has been updated (Butcher et al., 1989), it remains focused on clinical assessment and constructs similar to those put forth in the original version.

Many psychologists still regard personality and mental illness as closely connected constructs. The Society for Personality Assessment (SPA), for example, is a national organization of about four thousand clinical and social psychologists. The SPA is largely concerned with clinical assessment, as if personality assessment and clinical diagnosis were as closely related as Freud had held. According to Claridge and Davis (2003), for example, it is "self-evident" that "psychological disorders are intimately connected to personality" (p. 1).

Psychopathology of Everyday Life

Freud (1963/1916) regarded many common personal troubles – such as divorce, underachievement, unhappiness, and work–life imbalance – as mild forms of mental illness. He put forth the hypothesis of "psychopathology of everyday life." This hypothesis implies a fine line between normality and abnormality; psychodynamic theory encourages a broad definition of "disorder." Here is a partial list of what psychiatrist Norman Cameron (1963), who authored an influential psychiatry textbook, considered to be expressions of "psychopathology of everyday life": A businessperson who flies into a rage when his or her judgment is questioned; a man who feels misunderstood and the target of unjust criticism; people who live for approval and praise; a vague, perplexed woman who is preoccupied with the meaning of life; mystical experience; and a wealthy individual who wants even more wealth. Cameron presented no scientific evidence that any of these personal troubles are actually connected to mental illnesses such as Schizophrenia, Panic Disorder, or Obsessive-Compulsive Disorder.

When Freudians blurred the distinction between what is normal versus abnormal, estimates of the prevalence of psychopathology soared. Reading a newspaper in 2004, for example, I learned that a sports counselor had diagnosed 15 percent of a sample of NCAA athletes as clinically depressed (The Plain Dealer, 2006). I assessed 150 NCAA athletes, only a few of whom seemed to be clinically depressed. Most showed behavior inconsistent with depression such as cheerfulness, alertness, and pep. I suspect that the sports counselor confused "unhappiness" with clinical depression. Nobody would be surprised to learn that 15 percent of NCAA athletes are unhappy, but diagnosing them as mentally ill goes too far.

The hypothesis of psychopathology of everyday life remains influential. Freud may be dead in the halls of the United States' leading psychology departments, but he is still a significant force in marital counseling, personal counseling, and psychotherapy. Today many counselors try to understand their clients' personal troubles and personality using constructs developed to study mental illnesses. They believe that dark, unconscious mental forces that originated during childhood cause personality traits, personal troubles, and mental illnesses.

Although many psychodynamic experts regard personal troubles[1] as mild disorders, I think problems are a normal part of life. *I will make the case for the normality of personal troubles by showing the normality of the underlying motives.* I will show that many personal troubles are motivated by frustrated psychological needs, not by the Freudian constructs of anxiety or defense. When we learn what is normal, we will stop treating everything that goes wrong in life as a potential psychiatric disorder.

The Normal Personality

I believe that *values, not unconscious psychodynamics, hold the keys for understanding the personal troubles of ordinary people.* People should stop blaming their troubles on their parents or on their unconscious mind; they should stop thinking of themselves as victims of their upbringing. Instead, people should learn how their unfulfilled desires, unexpressed values, and conflicts of values get them into trouble. With greater self-awareness, people can make more fulfilling choices that lead to more meaningful lives and fewer troubles as the years pass.

Please don't get me wrong: I realize that mental illness exists, and I accept the reality of psychiatric disorders such as Schizophrenia and Panic Disorder. I take issue, however, with the psychodynamic thesis that such disorders have common causes with both personality development and personal troubles. *I am not rejecting the construct of mental illness; I am distinguishing between normal and abnormal.* I think it is normal to have troubles but abnormal to have a mental illness. *I think personality is about individuality, not abnormality.* I think Freud misunderstood motivation, and, therefore, he misunderstood what life is really about.

I reject the hypothesis of "psychopathology of everyday life." Freud held that personality traits are motivated by anxiety reduction; in contrast, I will show that personality traits are actually motivated by a variety of intrinsically held values. Psychodynamic theorists err when they claim, for example, that a dominant personality is motivated by anxiety reduction. Actually, the personality trait of dominance is motivated by stronger-than-average intrinsic valuations of competence, achievement, and will/influence. Psychodynamic theorists err when they claim that mystics are regressing to an oral stage of development to manage anxiety. Actually, mystics are seeking interdependence because they have stronger-than-average intrinsic valuations of oneness.

A number of previous psychologists have criticized psychodynamic theories of personality as being overly focused on abnormality. Abraham Maslow's (1954) humanistic psychology gave emphasis to the study of mental health. Today, positive psychology expresses a similar point (Snyder & Lopez, 2002). Previous theorists have yearned for a psychology of the normal personality. My aim in this book is to go far beyond constructs like "positive" and "normal" and put forth a detailed description of personality traits unrelated to mental illness.

Normal personality traits are habits people develop to satisfy their psychological needs (herein called *basic desires*). According to the results of research surveys of large groups (Reiss & Havercamp, 1998), sixteen basic desires drive the human psyche and potentially explain a wide range of human experiences, everything from relationships to values and culture. Everybody embraces all sixteen basic desires, but they prioritize them differently (Reiss, 2000a). How an individual prioritizes the sixteeen basic desires, called a *Reiss Motivation Profile* (RMP), reveals his or her values and personality traits. If I know how an individual prioritizes and combines the sixteen basic desires, I can predict with significant validity the individual's personality traits, values, relationships, and behavior in real-life situations. The RMP provides a detailed description of human motivation, showing in unprecedented detail the connections among motives, values, and many normal personality traits.

Motivation analysis is based on peer-reviewed, scientifically valid surveys of what motivates people (Reiss & Havercamp, 1998). More than 25,000 people in North America and Europe have taken the RMP. Most people do not realize this, but throughout history no prior scholar addressed the issue of what makes human beings tick by asking large numbers of people. Every prior scholar identified universal motives based on philosophical or psychological speculation or on observations of animals; in contrast, I surveyed large numbers of ordinary people. The results of our studies showed sixteen basic desires of life. The sixteen basic desires have been cross-culturally validated in the United States, Canada, Germany, and Japan (Havercamp & Reiss, 2003; Reiss, 2000a; Reiss & Havercamp, 1998). People all over the world regardless of culture seem to be motivated by the same sixteen basic desires, although they may prioritize or satisfy them differently. In a series of peer-reviewed scientific publications, the sixteen basic desires have been validated and shown to predict meaningful behavior. (See Table 2.1 for summary of results and citations.) *Our empirical methods, I suspect, may be why our taxonomy of sixteen basic desires seems significantly more valid than prior taxonomies.*

Motivation analysis is outside the mainstream of current psychological thought. Psychologists have studied the unconscious mind, behavior, and cognitions, but not motivation. From my standpoint, the great psychologists of the past failed to provide viable accounts of motivation. Freud held that all human motivation reduces to sex and aggression, which is invalid. Freud actually explained personality traits as motivated by anxiety reduction, which also is invalid. Since behaviorists made animals very hungry prior to experiments, they never observed the significance of psychological needs. A man might be extremely ambitious, for example, but you would never notice it if the man were starving and had to direct all his energy to finding food. Cognitive psychologists have studied thought processes as if thinking were unmotivated and occurred simply because they were rational. I regard motivation as the last frontier of scientific psychology.

To the extent to which psychologists have studied motivation, moreover, they have focused on situational motives that have mostly short-term influences. In contrast, motivation analysis is focused on the study of enduring individual differences in life motives (also called *basic desires*). These are motives that satiate only temporarily and, thus, influence our lives from adolescence through adulthood. I will make the case that life motives express intrinsically held values and drive personality development. I will show how normal personality traits can be ordered along continua of varying intensities of life motives. I will explain how personal troubles occur when we find ourselves in life circumstances, jobs, or relationships that frustrate our life motives and contradict our intrinsically held values. Many personal troubles can be avoided by smart living in which people choose situations where they can thrive and avoid those situations that frustrate their individual values and needs. In contrast, mental illnesses such as Schizophrenia and clinical depression arise from genetic or upbringing factors. The possibility of preventing mental illnesses is not discussed in this book.

Overview

CHAPTER 1. MY WIFE THINKS SOMETHING IS WRONG WITH ME. This chapter provides an initial, easy-to-read example of the differences between motivation analysis and psychodynamics. What makes people organized versus disorganized? According to psychodynamic theory, how organized we are depends on how much we embrace authority versus rebel with anger (e.g., Fenichel, 1945; White & Watt, 1973). According to motivation analysis, how organized we are depends on how much we value structure. I will make the case that the degree of valuation of structure explains the details of organized and disorganized behavior significantly better than does psychodynamics.

CHAPTER 2. THE SIXTEEN BASIC DESIRES. This chapter summarizes the scientific research evidence for motivation analysis. Sixteen basic desires drive the human psyche and motivate normal behavior and personality traits. I identify these desires and compare my taxonomy of psychological needs to those previously proposed by William James, William McDougall, and Henry Murray. The reliability and validity of each of the sixteen basic desires is summarized. All human motives seem to reduce to combinations of these sixteen, except for certain biological processes that have no relevance to personality, such as homeostasis.

CHAPTER 3. INTENSITY OF BASIC MOTIVATION. This chapter shows the normal personality traits associated with strong- and weak-intensities of each of the sixteen basic desires. Everybody embraces all sixteen basic desires, but to different extents. *How an individual prioritizes the sixteen basic desires reveals his or her values and personality.* Personality traits are associated with strong- and weak-intensity basic desires; average-intensity basic desires do not cause personality traits. Strong-intensity honor, for example, leads to the personality trait of righteousness, whereas weak-intensity honor leads to the personality trait of expedience.

Righteousness and expedience are "opposite" traits because they represent approach/avoidance of the same goal (honor).

CHAPTER 4. NORMAL PERSONALITY TYPES. In this chapter, I compare motivational and psychodynamic explanations for seven personality types: Workaholic, Competitor, Humanitarian, Thinker, Romantic, Loner, and Ascetic. I show how these personality types can be considered as results of normal variations in how people prioritize the sixteen basic desires. They are motivated by conditions unrelated to psychodynamic anxiety reduction and unconscious mental forces.

CHAPTER 5. OVERCOMING PERSONAL TROUBLES. Readers will learn how job coaches and counselors use motivation analysis to help their clients resolve a wide range of personal problems. Many personal problems result from value conflicts, as when an employee holds values that are in conflict with the work itself, the firm's culture, or the supervisor's values. Common examples of value conflicts at work include the high-achievement individual working for a government agency with a laid-back culture; an independent individual working in a culture that rewards teamwork; a person with a strong competitive spirit working for a school that devalues competitiveness; and a creative individual working in a job that expects things to be done the same way every time. Each of these examples is a conflict of values, not a mild mental illness as mainstream psychologists have said.

CHAPTER 6. SIX REASONS FOR ADOLESCENT UNDERACHIEVEMENT. Readers will learn six common motivational reasons for scholastic underachievement. They are lack of curiosity, lack of ambition, fear of failure, looking for trouble, expedience, and spontaneity. The Reiss School Motivation Profile (RSMP) evaluates each of these reasons based on standardized test scores.

CHAPTER 7. SELF-HUGGING AND PERSONAL BLIND SPOTS. I will discuss self-hugging, which is a natural tendency to think that our values are best (produce the greatest happiness), not just for ourselves, but potentially for everyone. Self-hugging motivates us to confuse individuality with abnormality. *When people choose values opposite our own, we think something must be wrong with them.* Sociable people, for example, think that something must be wrong with loners – maybe they avoid socializing because they lack social skills or fear being disliked. Most sociable people never appreciate that many loners may lack social skills because they want to be alone (intrinsically value solitude) and have no use for such skills.

CHAPTER 8. RELATIONSHIPS. Readers will learn how motivation analysis explains relationships. We are a species motivated to assert our values over and over again.

Individuality is so great, however, that others (including parents, children, siblings, and spouse) may assert values different from or even opposite to our own. *We are an intolerant species*; we naturally separate from people whose values significantly differ from our own. We tend to fight repeatedly with parents or children who have values different from our own, and we tend to divorce partners whose values are significantly different from our own. We bond to people whose values are similar to our own, and we have a successful life when career and relationships express our values.

The Reiss Relationship Profile (RRP) is an assessment tool that evaluates the compatibilities and incompatibilities of any romantic relationship. The RRP shows matched versus mismatched basic desires and values. In this chapter, I show how satisfaction within a relationship arises from matched basic desires and how conflict arises from mismatched basic desires.

CHAPTER 9. REINTERPRETATION OF MYERS-BRIGGS PERSONALITY TYPES. The sixteen basic desires provide a basis for reinterpreting and broadening the results of the Myers-Briggs Personality Type Indicator (MBTI). Although the MBTI was intended to assess individual preferences in collecting and processing information and in making decisions, the MBTI is really an assessment of a limited number of psychological needs and basic desires. The RMP assesses all of the personality traits assessed by the MBTI without using any Jungian constructs.

CHAPTER 10. THE SIXTEEN PRINCIPLES OF MOTIVATION. I summarize the theory of motivation analysis in terms of sixteen principles. Each principle is stated and briefly discussed. The sixteen principles provide a formal statement of the conceptual foundation of motivation analysis.

APPENDIX A. DICTIONARY OF NORMAL PERSONALITY TRAITS. This dictionary shows theoretically the specific motivational basis of the personality traits in a thesaurus. Although such detailed classifications are common in biology, chemistry, and physics, this is the first psychological effort to classify each and every personality trait in a manner that is fully testable empirically.

APPENDIX B. REISS MOTIVATION PROFILE ESTIMATOR. This questionnaire estimates the results readers might obtain were they to take the standardized Reiss Motivation Profile. The questionnaire shows which of the sixteen basic desires the reader places in high or low valuation.

APPENDIX C. THE SIXTEEN BASIC DESIRES AT A GLANCE. This concise chart is intended for use in seminars and classrooms.

1 My Wife Thinks Something Is Wrong with Me

We will compare psychodynamic versus motivational explanations of organized and disorganized personality traits. According to psychodynamic theory, these personality traits are determined by unconscious mental forces set in motion during early childhood. According to motivation analysis, personality traits are determined by intrinsically held values and life motives (variously called *basic desires or psychological needs*).

A Disorganized Person

Even the dullest observers of human nature notice that I am disorganized. My office is a mess: My files are on the floor with papers falling out of them, and my wastebasket is overflowing with paper trash. My coat is thrown on a chair, and my hat is misplaced where even I cannot find it. Every winter I need a half dozen pairs of gloves because I keep losing them.

My wife, Maggi, cleans my office whenever I leave town on a business trip. Instead of returning home and exclaiming, "What a wonderful wife you are – you straightened and cleaned my office," I complain, "I can't find my academic papers on anxiety! What did you do with them? Please make my office the way it was when I left."

I hate following schedules and have a tendency to arrive for appointments at the last second. I was at least 30 years old when I first bought an appointment book. Despite this major concession to organizing values, I continue to rush to appointments at the last minute just as I had before I used appointment books. Although part of my schedule is now written in my appointment book, I often forget to look in the book.

Both my wife and work assistants have learned to remind me of important meetings an hour beforehand. I guess you could say I am surrounded by enablers in my disorganized lifestyle. The reason they remind me is because the previous method – leaving notes in the morning – did not work. I read the notes but quickly forgot them after I moved on to something else.

Like other disorganized people, I hate plans. I believe people should learn how to adjust to whatever comes their way rather than lock themselves into a planned course of action. Before I had studied motivation, I had assumed that planners are the way they are because they lack the talent needed to respond effectively on the spur-of-the-moment. If only planners could be more spontaneous and creative, I figured, they would be like me and not make plans.

I hate planning so much that as a university professor I wrote few research grant applications. I figured that planning research destroys my creativity. What if I get an important idea after the grant is awarded? I would be locked into the plan of the grant and not be able to go where new thinking takes me.

I especially hate planning leisure activities. Our family vacations are decided at the last possible minute even though travel and lodging costs are less expensive when reservations are made in advance. I recall the time when my family and I packed up the car and pulled out of the driveway to go on our vacation. Michael and Ben, my two children, gritted their teeth and asked with obvious annoyance, "Dad, where are we going?" Since we were still two miles from the expressway intersection, which would force the decision, I replied, "We don't have to make the decision now. We still have a few minutes to think about it."

As a professor, I often fly around the country to give talks. Naturally, I almost never plan these trips. On one occasion I opened my invitation to speak after my plane to Philadelphia had taken off. I discovered that my talk was scheduled for Harrisburg, not Philadelphia. Oops! When I arrived in Philly, I rushed through the airport, rented a car, and drove the 140 miles to the Harrisburg hotel where I was scheduled to speak. I arrived at the podium two minutes before my talk was to begin. About 400 people were seated in the audience, and the sponsors of my talk were wondering nervously what had happened to me. I turned to them and quipped, "Guess I'm a minute or two early." I just had to point out that organized people worry needlessly.

I was about 40 when I first realized that many people consider details important, rather than annoyances. Many people told me details are important, but I thought they were just making excuses for being mired in trivia. I like to focus on the essence of a matter, or the so-called big picture. I had long thought that the big picture is so obvious it was no feather in one's cap to discern it.

When I was in elementary school, teachers told my parents I was brilliant but very sloppy. I figured it was terrific to be brilliant and that a little sloppiness shows I am a regular fellow. I had no idea why people wasted time with neatness. As a boy I worked on logical proofs to show that cleaning was unnecessary. I used to tell my mother, for example, that tomorrow the house will need straightening up just like today, so she can skip today and clean tomorrow. When it comes to my values, neatness was never one of them.

I can't stand paperwork. Filling out forms seems to me to be one of life's greatest displeasures. I give Maggi all the forms and ask her to fill them out for me. I resist filling out even the simplest form. I recall a conversation I had with a now well-known child psychologist, Susan, whom I have known since we were both graduate students at Yale in the 1960s. Susan has gone through life without a driver's license; she relies on public transportation or the generosity of friends. I once asked Susan why she did not get a driver's license like everybody else, and she said she did not want to fill out the required paperwork. I figured smart people think alike.

An Organized Person

My wife, Maggi, has long thought something is wrong with me. She is baffled as to why I have not learned to be more organized. I tell her I like being disorganized, but she dismisses such talk. She knows she feels comfortable when she is organized but not when she is disorganized. Since it is *her* nature to value orderliness, she thinks it is *human* nature to be that way. She is confident I would be much better off if I were more organized. Not only would I be more "efficient," as she puts it, but also I would be happier.

Maggi assumes everybody is born with the potential to be an organized person but that in my case something went wrong. She admits she doesn't know what went wrong, but she is confident *something* went wrong. Maybe I was dropped when I was a baby and have undiscovered brain damage. Perhaps I had traumatic experiences when I was potty trained. Maybe my parents were untidy and never taught me organizing skills. The solution, she thought, was to teach me how to organize my life. I didn't realize this at the time, but when we courted Maggi quietly figured I needed her to make me a better-organized human being. She didn't actually come out and say that she planned to change me after we married, but that is what she had in mind.

I tell Maggi over and over again that I like being disorganized, but she doesn't believe me. I tell her I feel comfortable in rooms that are a little messy (I call them "lived in"); I tell her I feel uncomfortable in rooms that are immaculate. "Being organized is better than being disorganized," she retorts. She seems to think that orderliness is a divine revelation. She thinks that deep down I am dissatisfied with my disorganized lifestyle but I am too proud to admit it.

Like most organized people, Maggi is very clean. After we got married, everybody in our circle viewed my wife as the gold standard for household tidiness. They would say things like, "I saw Sue the other day. Her house was incredibly clean, but of course, not as clean as Maggi's." I admit I came to appreciate the house being clean, but I am still more comfortable in rooms that haven't been straightened up.

The first spring after we married, Maggi hired a small army of helpers to clean our already immaculate apartment. That was when Maggi showed me her family's spring cleaning rituals. I couldn't believe it – a detailed set of spring cleaning instructions handed down from generation to generation. The Holy Grail of the family I married into was a manual for spring cleaning! I had understood the concept of cleaning things that are dirty, but it wasn't until after I married Maggi that I realized that some people clean things that are already clean.

Motivation of Orderliness and Disorderliness

The classic psychoanalytic analysis of organized people seems far-fetched even by Freudian standards. According to Freud, everybody naturally enjoys defecation, but organized people can't admit it. Organized people experience an unconscious "reaction formation," which means they are clean and orderly to disguise their true fondness for feces. Even they are unaware of their unconscious attraction to defecation. They unconsciously fear their parents would reject or punish them if they showed their natural enthusiasm for defecation. In contrast, disorderly people are more in touch with the natural joys of defecation.

Further, psychoanalysts have suggested that a child's experiences with toilet training can influence how orderly he or she grows up to be. Psychoanalysts distinguished two maladaptive reactions to toilet training, called *anal retentive* versus *anal expulsive*. As Millon & Davis (2000) described it, "Essentially the [anal-retentive] child reacts to the parents by 'holding back' and refusing to perform, leading to such adult traits as stubbornness, stinginess, and hidden anger. Anal-retentive types were also believed to be punctual, orderly, conscientious, and preoccupied with cleanliness . . . with everything in its place and no mess" (p. 182). In contrast, anal-expulsive types smeared feces to fight back at the parents and are supposedly disorderly, sadistically cruel, and destructive.

Erikson (1963/1950) and White & Watt (1973) suggested that toilet training is just one of a number of important situations in which the child's impulses come into conflict with adult authority. Children who learn to conform to authority may grow up to be orderly, whereas those who rebel may grow up to be disorderly. According to this line of thought, Maggi's parents are presumed to have been disciplinarians; she became a conformist; and in her desire to conform, she became the organized woman she is today. In contrast, my parents are presumed to have been permissive; I never learned the discipline required for conformity; and without adequate discipline, I became the disorganized man I am today.

Yet other psychoanalysts say that disorderliness is a disguised expression of anger motivating nonconformity or rebelliousness. According to this notion, I make others angry when I leave a mess in my office, do not make plans so my family can anticipate what they will be doing, or keep people wondering where I am before showing at the last minute for appointments. The hypothesis is that I make them angry because I am angry. Psychodynamic therapists would say I am really angry at my parents but I take my anger out on my wife, children, and colleagues. When I am under stress, they say, I may show symptoms of rage or perhaps a passive-aggressive personality disorder.

I reject the anger hypothesis because it does not explain the details of my disorderliness. Instead, I suggest that disorderliness is motivated by a strong need for spontaneity. I feel excited and alive when I experience spontaneity, but I feel uncomfortable in highly structured situations. I embrace a disorganized lifestyle as a means of decreasing my experience of order and increasing my experience of spontaneity. My desire for spontaneity is intrinsically motivated: The key to understanding disorganized people is to realize that they want to experience spontaneity for no reason other than that it is what they desire.

Please review everything I revealed about myself and notice how many details can be explained by a desire for spontaneity. Don't get me wrong – I do not want to experience chaos. Instead, I regulate my behavior to experience a high degree of spontaneity but stop far short of chaos. Even I organize a situation when I see chaos coming.

I like to follow my nose as a means of experiencing spontaneity. I dislike following rules, patterns, rituals, or plans because all these things reduce my experience of spontaneity by ordering my life and making me feel scripted. When I am following a plan, I am focused on *remembering* what the plan says I should do rather than on *mindfully deciding* what to do as events unfold. I become inattentive, bored, and mindless, unless the plan lacks detail so I can fill in blanks as events unfold. A vague plan lacking details keeps me mindfully engaged because I know I will need to make decisions rather than just follow the plan.

I do little planning for my professional presentations. When I have only minimal preparation, I am mindful of what I am saying and how the audience is reacting. I give my best presentations when I am minimally prepared because I am in a highly motivated state. By "minimally prepared," I do not mean totally unprepared. I have a general idea of what I am going to say, but I make up the specifics at the time of my presentation. Every time I give a fully prepared talk, I find myself mindlessly trying to remember what I am supposed to say instead of thinking about what I am saying.

Disorganized people tend to overlook details and focus on the big picture. With details absent from my consciousness, I experience the world as less ordered and structured than it really is. Further, my behavior makes a value statement that details are less important than the big picture.

Sloppiness is a more spontaneous and less-ordered experience than is neatness. When I was younger, I was very sloppy in my work. As I grew older, I learned to avoid being sloppy in business situations. Having developed my theory of motivation and gained greater self-awareness of my disorganized manner, I now make a great effort to pay attention to details in business situations. If I were stranded on a deserted island, however, I would return to being sloppy.

A common question I receive after I talk is how can I develop such a detailed, orderly analysis of personality and still say I am sloppy? The principle of a "greater motive" provides the answer. As much as I hate being organized, I hate even more being intellectually wrong. As much as I love spontaneity, I love even more the pursuit of truth. My love of spontaneity motivates me to be *generally* disorganized, especially when I am relaxing or vacationing, but when it comes to the pursuit of truth, my need for curiosity motivates me to organize my intellectual analyses. I am much more organized today than when I was younger because I have learned that I must be more organized in my thoughts to have any chance of communicating my ideas.

I like to keep my options open until the last possible minute. This way I experience spontaneity for as long as possible. I have a high tolerance for ambiguity and often do not need to know in advance what to expect. When the people I supervise ask to meet with me, I usually don't ask them what it is about because I pride myself on being able to answer almost any question on the spot. I especially do not like to make early plans for vacations because I feel I am entitled to enjoy my vacations and I do not enjoy making plans.

Behavioral psychologists would say, "Professor Reiss is disorganized because he lacks planning skills." In contrast, motivation analysts would say, "Professor Reiss wants to be disorganized and, thus, has little use for planning skills." *I lack planning skills because I am disorganized; I am not disorganized because I lack planning skills.*

Whereas disorganized people aim to experience a high degree of spontaneity, organized people aim to increase their experiences of order and decrease their experiences of spontaneity. By always putting household objects in the *same* place, for example, organized people create structure and unchanging stability in their homes. Whenever I need to ask Maggi where something is in our house, she always says, "It is in its place." I tell her things do not have a "place," but she disputes that. Everything was put in its place shortly after we married, and it remains there today. Yet after thirty-five years of marriage, I still have no idea where she keeps things.

Maggi imposes order on everything in our household. Our clothes are hung in our closet in accordance with a plan. Every day we sit at the same seats at the kitchen and dining room tables. We used to have a weekly meal schedule, but that broke down over the years because we both work and eat out often.

Organized people value unchanging rituals and routines. They become nervous when they cannot do things as they always do. Psychologically,rituals create a reassuring sense of order, stability, and predictability. Maggi has many cleaning rituals that have changed little as the years pass.She has the same cleaning rituals today that she had when we married, and those were the same cleaning rituals her parents had when they married, and so on all the way back to the Adam and Eve of her clan. Wars may come and go, economies may boom and bust, but in Maggi's family, the cleaning rituals do not change.

Straightening up and cleaning can be understood as efforts to restore order by reinstituting familiar patterns of objects in rooms. Clean environments offer more sameness from day to day than do messy environments. My office is usually messy and appears different from time to time; it always looks the same, however, when it is clean.

Organized people tend to dislike doing things on the spur-of-the-moment because spontaneity is the psychological opposite of order. They like to know in advance what to expect and be prepared for what they will be asked to do. They intrinsically value preparation and planning. Maggi, for example, hates going places on the spur of the moment. If I say, "Let's fly to Vegas this weekend," she replies, "If I told you once, I told you a million times. Trips like this must be planned! You cannot just take off and go to Vegas." When I ask why not, she just throws up her hands in frustration that I can't understand the need for planning.

Many organized people experience change as instability and impermanence. They dislike change and have difficulty adapting. Since they highly value permanence, they have a tendency to think things should always be done in a certain way; some organized people even may think there is only one way to do things. When trouble strikes, they are motivated to stay the course, not because staying the course is always a wise choice, but rather because they value stability and permanence.

Many organized people have difficulty distinguishing between important versus insignificant details. Organized people sometimes drive other people nuts with their attention to small details and trivia. They can be so focused on details they do not see the forest for the trees.

Motivation Analysis vs. Psychodynamics

Here are the points I would make in favor of motivational versus psychodynamic explanations of orderliness and disorderliness.

1. Orderliness Is Not a Mild Form of OCD. Psychodynamic theorists say that orderliness is a mild form of Obsessive-Compulsive Disorder (OCD; Cameron,

1963; Fenichel, 1945), which is an anxiety disorder. Yet researchers have found that OCD is actually associated with many personality traits and personality disorders (Claridge & Davis, 2003; Dolan-Sewell, Krueger, & Shea, 2001; Pfohl, 1996). Researchers have found little overlap between orderliness as a personality trait and compulsiveness as a symptom of OCD (e.g., Claridge & Davis, 2003). I suspect that orderliness is caused by normal variations in the universal need for structure, whereas OCD is caused by unknown abnormal, psychopathological factors.

2. Anger Does Not Motivate Disorderliness. Many therapists assume that disorganized people are angry because they leave messes for others to clean up or show up late for appointments, making others wait. This analysis erroneously assumes that disorganized people want their "messes" cleaned up. Disorganized people want organized people to lighten up and stop organizing, they want organized people to enjoy a "lived in" room.

Therapists are taught that if a patient makes them angry, the patient must be angry. I reject this unsubstantiated principle of psychotherapy. I think patients make therapists angry when they express values that contradict the therapists' values.

3. Annoyance Is a Two-Way Process. Not only do the habits of disorganized people annoy organized people, but vice versa. The fact of the matter is that organized and disorganized people hold opposite values – disorganized people annoy organized people when they leave a mess, and organized people annoy disorganized people when they pay attention to trivia. The anger in these examples arises from a conflict of values (order versus spontaneity), not from anal eroticism, reaction formations, psychopathology, and the like. The anger is not present until after one person has behaved inconsistently with the other's values.

4. Fear of Criticism Does Not Motivate Orderliness. Some therapists might suppose that orderly people are conformists to avoid criticism, rejection, or punishment from authority figures (Millon & Davis, 2000, p. 175). If this analysis were valid, however, organized people would give inconsistent effort. *People who fear failure and criticism hold back effort because failure and criticism hurt less when we do not try.* Since organized people do not hold back effort, I suspect they are no more afraid of being criticized than is the average person. Motivation analysis implies that a need for order/stability/structure, not fear of criticism, motivates orderly behavior.

5. The Anal Character Is Not Valid. Psychodynamic theorists have suggested the construct of an "anal character" (e.g., Fenichel, 1945, p. 278). They say that during toilet training some children react to parental demands with orderliness (motivated by anal eroticism), frugality (motivated by anal retention), and obstinacy (motivated by anal sadism). In contrast, I say that orderliness, frugality, and obstinacy are not as strongly related traits as Freud claimed. Maggi, for example, is orderly but not frugal.

According to motivation analysis (see Chapter 3), orderliness is motivated by an intrinsic valuation of structure and may have evolutionary links to cleaning rituals; frugality is motivated by an intrinsic valuation of collecting and may have evolutionary links to hoarding instincts; and obstinacy is motivated by an intrinsic valuation of individuality (autonomy) and may have evolutionary links to animal instincts to leave the nest and strike out on one's own. Perhaps these traits co-vary in OCD, but not in the normal personality. Freud's "anal character" is much less valid than experts have realized. Many organized people are spenders; many disorganized people are savers; and as Maggi would quickly tell you, I am much more stubborn than she is even though Freud would have predicted it the other way around.

6. *Mastery Does Not Motivate Orderliness.* Psychodynamic theorists have sug-gested that mastery motivates orderliness (Fenichel, 1945). They say that a child gains a sense of accomplishment by learning to go at socially appropriate places and times. This may be, but there is little connection between achievement moti-vation and orderliness. According to motivation analysis (see Chapters 3 and 6), mastery is motivated by intrinsic valuations of competence and influence of will. In contrast, orderliness is motivated by an intrinsic valuation of structure. There is little relationship between orderliness and achievement motivation: Some people with a high need for achievement are organized and others are disorganized. I have very high achievement motivation, for example, and yet I am disorganized.

Predicting Behavior In Natural Environments

Motivation analysis excels when it comes to predicting how people will behave in the real world. Suppose Mr. Smith's 2-year-old, Joey, is smearing feces and rebelling over potty training. Even Freudian theorists admit that nobody can predict that Joey will be disorganized when he is an adult. Freudians admit that knowing how someone was toilet trained is not a sufficient basis for predicting adult personality traits because many other factors are involved. Now suppose that Smith mentions to you that he loves spontaneity and values flexibility. I say you can bet your house that Smith is disorganized. *If you want to understand and predict traits such as organized versus disorganized and could ask only one question, ask how much the person enjoys spontaneity, not what happened when the individual was toilet trained.*

If you know what motivates someone, you can predict how the individual will behave. If a woman tells you she loves spontaneity, for example, you can predict that she dislikes making plans; tends to walk into situations with minimal preparation; overlooks details; and may tend to be sloppy. She may not show all of these traits, but she will likely show many of them. This method for predicting behavior may not work every time, but it works much better than what behavioral experts are doing now.

What determines who is motivated by order versus spontaneity? Unfortunately, nobody really knows. For centuries scholars have argued over how much we are molded by our upbringing versus genetics without deciding the issue. Although I do not know where our motives come from, I assume that universal motives have a genetic origin and are modified by experience. I realize this analysis lacks details, but I will move on anyway. I know a lot about motivation and how to help people with personal troubles and predict behavior in natural environments. I do not want to dwell on issues of causation, about which I know very little. Although it is very unusual for a psychologist to offer a theory of behavior while paying only token attention to causation, the fact is that nearly all of those detailed theories on causation previously proposed are arguably invalid. Nobody knows what causes personality and human motivation, but fortunately we can move on to issues we do know about.

If you are a disorganized person who has undergone counseling or psychoanalysis, you may have been told that you have a deep-seated anger toward your father that is motivating your disorganized behavior. You may have been told you arc a rebel or a nonconformist. I suggest you read this book and reconsider these views of yourself. Look at the details of what you actually do that makes you disorganized and ask yourself, "Is my aim to vent anger, as many therapists might say, or do I aim to increase spontaneity in my life, as motivation analysts say?" Learn motivation analysis and stop worrying that something is wrong with you just because you are disorganized.

If you are a highly organized person who has undergone counseling or psychoanalysis, you may have been told that you have a deep-seated fear of criticism or rejection or that you are a conformist or perfectionist. I suggest you read this book and reconsider this view of yourself. Look at the details of what you actually do that makes you organized and ask yourself, "Am I unconsciously avoiding criticism, as some therapists say, or am I aiming to increase structure in my life, as motivation analysts say?" Learn motivation analysis and stop worrying that something is wrong with you just because you may be a perfectionist.

Conclusion

Psychologists have discussed orderliness and disorderliness in terms of constructs used to understand mental illnesses, especially OCD. They have considered what it might be like for a 2-year-old confronted by parental demands for toilet training. In this context, they have invoked motives such as conformity, obstinacy, mastery, and rebelliousness. In contrast, I have suggested that orderliness is motivated by an intrinsic valuation of structure and that disorderliness is motivated by an intrinsic valuation of spontaneity. I have shown how these motives potentially explain the details of how organized and disorganized people behave.

Psychodynamic theorists realize that orderly people like structure, but they look for deeper explanations such as reactions to anal eroticism. They invoke theories of anxiety and defense, such as reaction formations. They say that orderliness is a learned means of managing anger or anxiety arising from toilet training and other experiences with authority.

In contrast, I believe we should stop looking beyond motivation and values to explain personality traits. Anxiety reduction isn't the universal motive driving personality development, as Freud had assumed. Orderliness can be explained by assuming that the desire for structure is an *intrinsic* motive, meaning the end of a psychological explanation. Life motives (psychological needs) are the keys for predicting the behavior of mentally healthy people in natural environments and for making smart decisions going forward.

2 The Sixteen Basic Desires

Sixteen psychological needs (herein called *basic desires*) drive the human psyche and potentially explain a wide range of human experiences, everything from relationships to values (Reiss, 2000a). Based on peer-reviewed studies with thousands of people from different backgrounds (Havercamp & Reiss, 2003; Reiss & Havercamp, 1998), I believe that everybody embraces all sixteen basic desires, but they prioritize them differently. How an individual prioritizes these basic desires, called a Reiss Motivation Profile (RMP), reveals his or her values. Since many "normal" personality traits are habits people develop to satisfy their strong-and weak-intensity basic desires, the RMP is a valid indicator of normal personality traits and types. The RMP is a detailed description of human motivation, showing specific connections among motives, values, and many normal personality traits. If I know how an individual prioritizes and combines the sixteen basic desires, I can predict with significant validity the individual's behavior in real-life situations.

Nature of Basic Desires

We know what motives are – wants, desires, strivings, and psychological needs. The construct of a basic desire, however, refers to a particular kind of motive. Here are the five defining qualities of a basic desire.

UNIVERSAL MOTIVATION. Basic desires motivate everyone. As William McDougall (2003/1908) observed in his landmark book, *An Introduction to Social Psychology*,

> Every man is so constituted to seek, to strive for, and to desire certain goals which are common to the species, and the attainment of which goals satisfies and allays the urge or craving or desire that moves us. These goals . . . are not only common to all men, but also . . . [to] their nearer relatives in the animal world;

such goals as food, shelter from danger, the company of our fellows, intimacy with the opposite sex, triumph over our opponents, and leadership among our companions.

McDougall called universal motives "instincts" to describe their genetic origin and automatically occurring nature. Although I will not use the term "instinct," I nevertheless assume that universal goals have evolved from lower animals. I believe that basic desires have a genetic component.

PSYCHOLOGICAL NEEDS (LIFE MOTIVES). Basic desires are psychological needs: Some basic desires must be gratified for survival, and others must be gratified to experience life as meaningful. Eating, for example, is both a basic desire and a survival need, whereas curiosity is a basic desire that gives meaning to life.

Satiation of a basic desire is always temporary – hours or days after the satiating goal is experienced, the basic desire reasserts itself and influences behavior anew. When we eat, for example, it is only a matter of hours before we become hungry again. When we satisfy our curiosity about one topic, sooner or later we become curious about another topic.

Why do basic desires reassert themselves after they are satiated? Because basic desires motivate us to seek certain *rates* of satiating experiences. The basic desire for eating, for example, motivates me to consume roughly 2,500 calories daily. When I eat significantly fewer calories in a given day, I experience hunger. When I eat significantly more calories, I feel bloated. When I eat approximately the right amount of food, I am satiated. My satiation is only temporary, however, because my rate of consumption automatically decreases as time elapses since my last meal.

All basic desires can be thought of as desired rates of experience of intrinsically valued goals. By definition, all basic desires can be satiated only temporarily. They all reassert themselves as time elapses from the last satiation.

Since basic desires can be satiated only temporarily, I refer to them as "life motives." Basic desires motivate us from adolescence through adulthood. Childhood motivation is possibly different – at least, I have not yet been able to show a continuity of what motivates people from childhood through adulthood. None of my comments, therefore, applies to children age 10 and younger. In contrast, I have been able to demonstrate significant stability of motivation from adolescence through adulthood (Reiss & Havercamp, 2005).

INTRINSIC MOTIVATION. People pursue basic desires for no reason other than that is what they want. The basic desire for order, for example, motivates us to organize our lives because we intrinsically value structure, whereas the basic desire for acceptance motivates us to avoid criticism because we intrinsically value acceptance.

Different basic desires can motivate the same behavior. When we organize our workspace because we value structure, for example, we are motivated by the basic desire for order. When we organize our workspace to avoid being criticized by our supervisor, we are motivated by the basic desire for acceptance. When we organize our environments for both reasons, we are motivated by both basic desires acting in concert.

INTRINSIC VALUES. We are a species motivated to assert our values. Whether cheering for our school's football team (which expresses the value of loyalty), or reading a book (which expresses the value of learning), much of what we do can be considered as an assertion of our values.

Motives and values are so closely connected we can infer values from intrinsic motives, and motives from intrinsically held values. If you know that I am intrinsically motivated by family life, for example, you can infer that I value parenting and children. If you know that Peterson is intrinsically motivated by honor, you can infer that Peterson values character.

Aristotle (1953/330 B.C.E.) understood the close connection between values and motives. His book on motivation was titled *The Nichomachean Ethics*. For many years, moreover, philosophical inquiries on motivation were classified as ethical philosophy.

PSYCHOLOGICAL SIGNIFICANCE. Some universal motives have no relevance for the normal personality. Although our bodies are motivated to maintain a constant body temperature, I excluded homeostasis from my taxonomy of basic desires because homeostasis has nothing to do with personality functioning. I deliberately excluded from my work those biological needs with little or no significance for psychology.

Scientific Validation of Sixteen Basic Desires

What are the basic desires of human nature? What are the fundamental strivings that guide our lives? Deep down, what do people want from life? Table 2.1 shows how some past scholars addressed these questions. Using philosophical analysis, Plato concluded that justice and goodness are life's greatest motives (Irwin, 1995). Charles Darwin (1859) thought that the greatest motives are survival and reproduction. Sigmund Freud (1963/1916) reduced all motives to sex and aggression, whereas behaviorist Edward Thorndike (1913) identified pain avoidance and pleasure seeking as the motivational basis of learned behavior.

Table 2.1. Some historical suggestions for greatest motives		
Theorist	Greatest motives	Method of discovery
Plato	Justice and goodness	Philosophical analysis
Charles Darwin	Survival and reproduction	Scientific study of animals
Sigmund Freud	Sex and aggression	Talking to psychiatric patients
Edward Thorndike	Pleasure and pain	Learning theory

In 1995 I asked diverse groups of people what motivates them. At first I asked people if they are motivated by sex, family, and achievement. When almost everybody responded affirmatively, I wondered how I would study individual differences in universal motives since science requires variations in responses.

I persisted with my research effort and eventually learned how to study universal motives. Instead of asking people, "Do you like sex?" I learned to ask people, "Is sex essential for your happiness?" Although everybody says they like sex, only some people say that sex is essential to their happiness. Some people say that sex is not "essential" to their happiness. By varying how extreme the suggested desire is, I learned how to develop a questionnaire that measures individual differences in the valuation of universal motives.

I constructed a questionnaire, called the Reiss Profile of Fundamental Goals and Motivational Sensitivities (hereafter *Reiss Motivation Profile* or *RMP*), to evaluate what motivates people. I began with a list of every possible universal motive I could imagine. I consulted a variety of reference sources and asked colleagues for suggestions. The initial draft questionnaire had more than 500 items. I pared the list to 328 items by eliminating redundancies and motives of little psychological significance.

Reiss and Havercamp (1998) asked a diverse group of people to rate anonymously the significance of 328 items in motivating their behavior. We relied on a mathematical technique called *factor analysis* to interpret our results. We conducted a series of studies (three exploratory factor studies and one confirmatory factor study), each with a different sample of participants. The combined total of 2,554 research participants included people of diverse ages (12 to 76 years) and stations in life (e.g., high school students, college students, military people, fast food workers, seminary students, human-service providers, nursing home residents). After each factor study, we shortened the RMP questionnaire until we had identified 120 items that assessed 15 basic desires.

Several colleagues suggested we should add a scale for "Saving," which became the sixteenth basic desire. In an unpublished study of 512 adults solicited from sources in urban and rural Ohio, Havercamp (1998) confirmed the sixteen-factor solution (the original fifteen plus saving) to the revised 128-item RMP instrument.

The sixteen basic desires are as follows (Reiss, 2000a):

> Acceptance, the desire to avoid criticism and rejection
> Curiosity, the desire for cognition
> Eating, the desire for food
> Family, the desire to raise one's own children
> Honor, the desire to behave morally
> Idealism, the desire for social justice
> Independence, the desire for self-reliance
> Order, the desire for structure
> Physical Activity, the desire to move one's muscles
> Power, the desire for influence of will
> Romance, the desire for sex
> Saving, the desire to collect
> Social Contact, the desire for friendship
> Status, the desire for prestige
> Tranquility, the desire for inner peace
> Vengeance, the desire to get even

As shown in Table 2.2, the RMP questionnaire has been validated as a scientific measure of the sixteen basic desires. The four-week test–retest reliability and internal reliability have been assessed. Three confirmatory factor studies have shown factorial validity for both American and Japanese samples. Concurrent and criterion validity also have been demonstrated for each of the sixteen scales. Social validity has been demonstrated with more than 25,000 professional administrations in Europe and North America. (Readers interested in greater scientific details of the psychometric studies are invited to consult the scientific journal articles listed in the reference section near the end of this book.)

Principal Emotions of Humankind

As shown in Table 2.3, basic desires are associated with both positive and negative emotions. Generally, the positive emotions are signals that a basic desire has been temporarily satiated, whereas negative emotions are signals that a basic desire has been frustrated or needs to be satiated.

We have the potential to experience principal emotions through both direct and vicarious experiences including imagination, fantasy, reflection, watching sports, and viewing shows (Reiss & Wiltz, 2004). When we watch or imagine our favorite team scoring a goal, for example, we experience self-efficacy,

Table 2.2. Summary of reliability and validity of the Reiss motivation profile of motivation 16 basic desires

Motive[a]	r[b]	a[c]	Factor validity[d]	Concurrent and criterion validity[e]
Acceptance	.80	.83	✓✓✓	Positively correlated with Big 5 Neuroticism scale ($p < .001$). Positively correlated with Negative Affect ($p < .01$). Students referred for evaluation in schools scored above average. Athletes scored below average ($p < .05$). Low-achieving high school students scored above average ($p < .001$). MRDD[f] version: Positively correlated with total score on Psychopathology Symptoms Scale ($p < .01$). MRDD version: Negatively correlated with relationship compatibility ($p < .001$).
Curiosity	.84	.82	✓✓✓	Philosophers scored very high for curiosity ($p < .001$). Low-achieving high school students scored below average ($p < .001$). Athletes scored below average ($p < .05$). Significantly correlated to Big 5 Openness to Experience scale ($p < .01$). Positively correlated with scales of intrinsic motivation ($p < .01$).
Eating	.82	.80	✓✓✓	Positively correlated with participation in dieting groups ($p < .001$). Positively correlated with extrinsic motivation scale ($p < .01$). Culinary students scored above average ($p < .001$). Negatively correlated with adult age ($p < .01$). MRDD version: People with Prader-Willi syndrome scored very high ($p < .05$).
Family	.79	.92	✓✓✓	Positively correlated with religiosity ($p < .01$). Positively correlated with Purpose in Life Scale ($p < .01$). Positively correlated with satisfaction in relationships ($p < .05$). Positively correlated with participation in varsity sports ($p < .001$).
Honor	.77	.82	✓✓✓	Positively correlated to Big 5 Conscientiousness scale ($p < .01$). Positively correlated with Purpose in Life Scale ($p < .01$). ROTC military officers scored above average ($p < .01$). Low-achieving high school students scored below average ($p < .01$). Positively correlated with religiosity ($p < .001$).

(continued)

Motive[a]	r[b]	a[c]	Factor validity[d]	Concurrent and criterion validity[e]
Idealism	.69	.84	✓✓✓	Positively correlated to Big 5 Agreeableness scale ($p < .01$) and Conscientiousness scale ($p < .01$). Positively correlated with Purpose in Life Scale ($p < .01$). Community volunteers scored above average ($p < .001$). Protestant seminary students scored above average ($p < .001$). Positively correlated with registration as potential organ donor ($p < .03$). Low-achieving high school students scored below average ($p < .01$). Positively correlated with relationship variables "intimacy," "passion," and "commitment" ($p < .05$).
Independence	.72	.71	✓✓✓	Negatively correlated with Relationship Satisfaction Scale ($p < .05$). Protestant seminary students scored below average ($p < .001$). Community volunteers scored below average ($p < .001$).
Order	.81	.87	✓✓✓	Positively correlated with Order scale on Personality Research Form ($p < .001$). Negatively correlated with Big 5 Openness to Experience scale ($p < .05$). Positively correlated with Judging on Myers-Briggs ($p < .001$). Negatively correlated with registration as potential organ donor ($p < .001$). MRDD[f] version: People with autism, Prader-Willi, and Williams syndrome showed above average scores ($p < .05$).
Physical Activity	.82	.89	✓✓✓	Positively correlated with participation in varsity sports ($p < .001$). ROTC military officers scored above average ($p < .001$). Positively correlated with Positive Affect scale ($p < .01$). Negatively correlated with adult age ($p < .01$). MRDD version: Positively correlated with quality of life ($p < .05$).
Power	.84	.86	✓✓✓✓	Positively correlated with Dominance scale on Personality Research Form ($p < .001$). Positively correlated to Big 5 Extraversion scale ($p < .01$). ROTC military officers scored above average ($p < .001$). Positively correlated with participation in varsity sports

Table 2.2 (*continued*)

Motive[a]	r[b]	a[c]	Factor validity[d]	Concurrent and criterion validity[e]
				(*p* < .05; *p* < .001). Positively correlated with participation in college fraternities/sororities (*p* < .001). Positively correlated with relationship variables "intimacy," "passion," and "commitment" (*p* < .001). Low-achieving high school students scored below average (*p* < .001).
Romance	.87	.89	✓✓✓	Negatively correlated with religiosity (*p* < .01). Positively correlated with watching reality TV (*p* < .01). Negatively correlated with adult age (*p* < .01).
Saving	.80	.76	✓	Positively correlated with Big 5 Neuroticism scale (*p* < .01). Negatively correlated with Big 5 Openness to Experience scale (*p* < .05). Positively correlated with extrinsic motivation scale (*p* < .01). Negatively correlated with registration as potential organ donor (*p* < .01).
Social Contact	.81	.86	✓✓✓	Positively correlated to Big 5 Extraversion scale (*p* < .01). Positively correlated with Myers-Briggs Extraversion (*p* < .01). Positively correlated with participation in college fraternities/sororities (*p* < .001). Positively correlated with participation in varsity sports (*p* < .01). MRDD version: People with autism scored very low for social contact (*p* < .001).
Status	.88	.88	✓✓✓	Positively correlated with participation in college fraternities/sororities (*p* < .001). College varsity athletes scored above average (*p* < .01). Protestant seminary students scored below average (*p* < .001). Negatively correlated with religiosity (*p* < .01). Community volunteers scored below average (*p* < .001). Positively correlated with watching reality TV (*p* < .001).
Tranquility	.74	.82	✓✓✓	Positively correlated with Big 5 Neuroticism scale (*p* < .001). Positively correlated with Anxiety Sensitivity Index (*p* < .001). *Note:* Includes items from ASI, validated in more than 900 peer reviewed studies as an indicator and predictor of panic attacks.

(continued)

Motive[a]	r[b]	a[c]	Factor validity[d]	Concurrent and criterion validity[e]
			Table 2.2 (*continued*)	
Vengeance	.86	.92	✓✓✓	Negatively correlated with Big 5 Agreeableness scale ($p < .05$). Positively correlated with Big 5 Neuroticism scale ($p < .01$). Positively correlated with Negative Affect Scale ($p < .01$). Negatively correlated with grades in high school ($p < .01$). Positively correlated with high school student referral for discipline problems ($p < .01$). ROTC military officers scored above average ($p < .001$). Protestant seminary students scored below average ($p < .002$). Negatively correlated with religiosity ($p < .01$). Negatively correlated with registration as potential organ donor ($p < .01$). Positively correlated with participation in varsity sports ($p < .06$). Negatively correlated with adult age ($p < .01$). MRDD version: Negatively correlated with relationship compatibility ($p < .001$).

[a] Scale name.
[b] Four-week test–retest reliability.
[c] Cronbach alpha.
[d] Each ✓ indicates a successful *confirmatory* factor study (exploratory factor studies not shown).
[e] Based on: Dykens & Rosner (1999); Engel, Olson, & Patrick, (2002); Havercamp (1998); Havercamp & Reiss (2003); Kavanaugh & Reiss (2003); Lecavalier & Tasse (2002); Olson & Chapin (in press); Olson & Weber (2004); Reiss (2000a); Reiss & Crouch (2004); Reiss & Havercamp (1998, 2005); Reiss & Reiss (2004); Reiss & Wiltz (2004); Reiss, Wiltz, & Sherman (2001); Takakuwa & Wakabayashi, (1999); and Wiltz & Reiss (2003).
[f] Mental retardation and developmental disabilities version.

much like the player who actually scored the goal. The vicarious experience of self-efficacy (which falls under the basic desire for power) is so apparent at sporting events that some fans thrust clenched fists into open air almost immediately upon viewing the achievement. The power experienced by the player is of higher quality than that experienced by the fan because it is more enduring and more readily re-experienced by recalling the achievement.

Prior Taxonomies

Four generations of Harvard University psychology professors – William James (1918/1890), William McDougall (2003/1908), Henry A. Murray (1938), and David McClelland (1961) – sought to identify the principal motives that drive

Table 2.3. Positive and negative emotions associated with sixteen basic desires

Basic Desire	Goal	Positive Emotion	Negative Emotion	Intrinsic Value
Acceptance	Avoid criticism	Self-confidence	Insecure	Self
Curiosity	Cognition (thinking)	Wonderment	Bored, confused	Ideas
Eating	Food	Satiation	Hunger	Sustenance
Family	Parenting	Feels needed	Burdened	Children
Honor	Character	Loyalty	Guilt	Duty
Idealism	Social justice	Compassion	Outrage	Fairness
Independence	Autonomy	Personal freedom	Dependent	Self-reliance
Order	Structure	Comfort	Discomfort	Stability
Physical Activity	Muscle exercise	Vitality	Restless	Fitness
Power	Influence	Self-efficacy, elation	Regret, embarrassment, humiliation	Achievement, Leadership
Romance	Sex	Ecstasy	Lust	Sensuality
Saving	Collection	Prudent	Wasteful	Frugality
Social Contact	Friendship	Fun	Lonely	Belonging
Status	Standing	Superiority	Inferiority	Reputation
Tranquility	Safety	Relaxation	Anxious	Caution
Vengeance	Self-defense	Vindication	Anger	Winning

human behavior and personality development. They based their initial tax-onomies on observations of people, ethological studies, and on anthropological research.

To what extent do Reiss's basic desires, which were validated scientifically, overlap with previous taxonomies of psychological needs and instincts, which were not validated scientifically? (In the remainder of this chapter, I will refer to the sixteen basic desires as Reiss's basic desires in order to be clear on which taxonomy I am discussing.) Using different methods, did James, McDougall, Murray, and Reiss end up with significantly different taxonomies, or were they substantially similar?

Table 2.4 shows that the sixteen basic desires have substantial similarity to previous taxonomies. In his epic work, *The Principles of Psychology*, William James (1918/1890) identified the following seventeen "instincts" based largely on

Table 2.4. Comparison of Reiss's sixteen basic desires with previous taxonomies of psychological needs

Reiss	James	McDougall	Murray
Acceptance			Infavoidance
Curiosity			Understanding
Eating		Eating	
Family		Parenting	
Honor			Counteraction
Idealism	Sympathy		
Independence			Autonomy
Order	Cleanliness		Order
Physical Activity			
Power (strong)		Self-assertion, Construction	Achievement, Dominance
Power (weak)		Self-abasement	
Romance	Love	Reproduction	Sex
Saving	Acquisition	Acquisition	Acquisition
Social Contact	Gregariousness, Play	Gregariousness	
Status			
Tranquility	Fear	Flight	
Vengeance	Pugnacity	Pugnacity	Aggression

observations of animals, children, or adults in natural contexts and on the observations of Preyer (1995/1880):

- Emulation, the impetus to imitate
- Pugnacity, the impetus to fight
- Gregariousness, the impetus to socialize
- Sympathy, the impetus to help others
- Hunting, the impetus to seek and kill prey
- Fear, the impetus for flight
- Acquisitiveness, the impetus to collect and save
- Constructiveness, the impetus to build
- Play, the impetus for leisure
- Curiosity, the impetus to explore novel stimuli
- Sociability, the impetus for social contact
- Secretiveness, the impetus to hide one's interests

- Cleanliness, the impetus to remove dirt
- Modesty, the impetus to cover certain parts of the body
- Love, the impetus for sex
- Jealousy, undefined impetus
- Parental love, the impetus to raise our children

Reiss scientifically validated eight of James's seventeen instincts. This indicates significant agreement between James's and Reiss's taxonomies, but also significant differences.

Reiss's sixteen basic desires and James's taxonomy of instincts differ in several ways. Some of Reiss's sixteen basic desires combine two or three of James's instincts into a single motive. James's instincts for gregariousness, sociability, and play all fall under Reiss's basic desire for social contact. People motivated to experience playful fun also tend to be motivated to socialize, and vice versa, so that only one basic desire is needed to encompass all three. The association between socializing and play is as simple as the idea of a party. Further, there are survival advantages to playing in groups rather than alone. Animals playing in groups have safety in numbers at a time of lessened vigilance for predators.

Some of James's instincts are not included in Reiss's sixteen basic desires either because they may not be universal or because they can be reduced to other basic desires. I do not regard secretiveness as a universal motivator. Emulation is reducible to other motives: The desire to emulate wealthy people, for example, may be motivated by a need for status, whereas the desire to emulate a parent may be motivated by a need for acceptance. James's instinct for cleanliness falls under Reiss's basic desire for order.

In 1908 William McDougall reinterpreted the construct of instinct to give emotion a central motivating role. He also made a greater effort than James had to construct a theory of universal motivation. He described the following twelve "principal instincts of man" (McDougall, 2003/1908):

- Flight, the instinct to flee danger
- Repulsion, the instinct to avoid disgust
- Curiosity, the instinct to explore
- Pugnacity, the instinct to oppose people frustrating goal attainment
- Self-display, the instinct for attention
- Self-abasement, the instinct to submit
- Parenting, the instinct to raise our children
- Reproduction, the instinct for sex
- Eating, the instinct for food
- Gregarious instinct, the desire for social contact
- Acquisition, the instinct to collect
- Construction, the instinct to build

As shown in Table 2.4, Reiss's sixteen basic desires include ten of McDougall's principal instincts. This indicates significant similarity, but there also are a number of important differences. One of the differences concerns McDougall's instinct of repulsion. I had considered including repulsion as a basic desire because avoidance of disgust is universally motivating and intrinsically valued. My preliminary psychometric results, moreover, had suggested that disgust does not fall under the basic desire for tranquility. I had considered recognizing disgust as a seventeenth basic desire, but I eventually decided that disgust falls short on the criterion of psychological significance. Disgust seems to play no significant role in personality development. I decided it was not worth the effort to include it.

McDougall's instinct of curiosity is not the same motive as Reiss's basic desire for curiosity. McDougall defined curiosity as exploratory motivation, whereas Reiss is concerned with intellectual curiosity (need for cognition). As discussed in Chapter 6, I suspect that exploratory curiosity and intellectual curiosity are unrelated motives. This represents a change in viewpoint from some of my earlier comments on curiosity. Explorers are not necessarily thinkers, and thinkers are not necessarily explorers.

Reiss's basic desire for vengeance is similar to McDougall's instinct for pugnacity. Both McDougall and Reiss consider aggressiveness part of a broader motive to confront others. Although some psychologists might say that pugnacity and vengeance are symptomatic of deeper personality problems such as anger, feeling unloved, or psychological pain, Reiss agrees with McDougall that pugnacity and vengeance are normal desires. Reiss regards vindictiveness as normal because it is intrinsically motivating (winning is its own reward) and universally desired (everybody is motivated to remove frustrations preventing goal attainment). Both competitiveness and vindictiveness are normal when they arise from universal motivation and seem unrelated to the genetic, biochemical, or unusual life events suspected as causes of mental illness.

Thorndike (1913) rejected McDougall's selection of emotion as the core of the instinct and urged classification of instincts based on the type of unlearned behavior that is manifested. Woodworth (1918) recognized instinct but argued that abilities also play a significant role in determining behavior.

Dunlap (1919) began a period of antiinstinct writings. Various theorists criticized the construct of instinct for everything from overlooking the "gestalt" or totality to placing undue emphasis on genetics and too little emphasis on experience (Murphy, 1929). The debate was influenced by many attitudes, including the belief that instinctual behavior is more descriptive of animal behavior than human behavior. McDougall and his allies did not deal effectively with the many criticisms on the construct of instinct. Even though McDougall's analysis of motivation was a significant advance, the critics won the day, and McDougall's work faded in influence.

Henry A. Murray (1938) substituted the construct of psychological need for that of instinct. He recognized the multifaceted nature of motivation and argued against efforts to reduce human motives to just a few kinds. His taxonomy of twenty-seven psychological needs was influential with psychodynamic theorists. He acknowledged that his "classification of needs is not very different from lists constructed by McDougall, Garnett, and a number of other writers" (Murray, 1938, p. 84). Here is Murray's taxonomy:

- Abasement, the need to surrender and accept punishment
- Achievement, the need to overcome obstacles and succeed
- Acquisition, the need for possessions
- Affiliation, the need for friendships
- Aggression, the need to injure others
- Autonomy, the need to resist others and stand strong
- Blameavoidance, the need to avoid blame and obey rules
- Construction, the need to build or create
- Contrariance, the need to be unique
- Counteraction, the need to defend honor
- Defendance, the need to justify actions
- Deference, the need to follow a superior
- Dominance, the need to control and lead others
- Exhibition, the need for attention
- Exposition, the need to educate and inform
- Harmavoidance, the need to avoid pain
- Infavoidance, the need to avoid failure/shame, or to conceal weakness
- Nurturance, the need to protect the helpless
- Order, the need to arrange, organize, and be precise
- Play, the need to relieve tension, have fun, or relax
- Recognition, the need to gain approval and social status
- Rejection, the need to exclude another
- Sentience, the need for sensuality
- Sex, the need for erotic relationships
- Similance, the need to empathize
- Succorance, the need for support
- Understanding, the need to analyze and know

As shown in Table 2.4, Reiss's sixteen basic desires include ten of Murray's needs. This indicates significant similarity, but there also are a number of important differences. Reiss's sixteen basic desires combine some of Murray's needs into a single motive, thereby shortening his list. Abasement and infavoidance, for example, are different intensities of Reiss's basic desire for acceptance and, thus, can be combined into a single need. Abasement is motivated by a very strong basic desire for acceptance, whereas infavoidance is motivated by a very weak basic desire for acceptance.

Murray's needs for achievement and dominance can be viewed as different manifestations of a single basic desire for will, which Reiss calls the basic desire for power. The same people who value achievement tend to value dominance, and vice versa. The correlation may be imperfect, but it is sufficiently high to be apparent in everyday life. My own boss, for example, is always talking about both achievement and leadership.

Murray's needs for autonomy, contrariance, and succorance can be combined into Reiss's basic desire for independence. Contrariance is a strong-intensity expression of independence; autonomy is a moderate-intensity expression; and succorance is a weak-intensity expression of the basic desire for independence.

Murray's needs for sentinence and sex can be combined into Reiss's basic desire for romance. Although some have criticized Reiss for suggesting that the desires for beauty and sex are strongly connected, the critics could not be more wrong. The connection is proven by the fact that everybody on the planet wants to appear beautiful to his or her lover prior to sex. If the critics were right in asserting that beauty and sex are not strongly connected, we would not prefer to have sex with someone who is beautiful to us as opposed to ugly.

Murray's definition of play is an invalid combination of Reiss's basic desires for social contact and tranquility. The basic desire for tranquility is about safety, whereas the basic desire for social contact is about friendship. How much a person values safety does not predict how much the person values friendship, and vice versa. Thus, Reiss's basic desires for tranquility and social contact cannot be combined into a single need.

Projective Assessment

The Harvard psychologists did not construct scientifically valid measures of psychological needs. Murray based his research almost entirely on a motivation assessment technique called the Thematic Apperception Test (TAT; Murray, 1943). The TAT is a storytelling assessment in which the examiner presents drawings of ambiguous scenes and asks the research participant to make up stories with a beginning, middle, and an end. The examiner subjectively interprets the stories, looking for common psychological themes based on psychodynamic principles. If several of the stories have angry characters, for example, the examiner concludes that the individual is motivated to express anger.

In the 1960s and 1970s the TAT became increasingly controversial because of concerns about its subjectivity (e.g., Zubin, Eron, & Schumer, 1965). Scientifically minded psychologists had conducted hundreds of studies without producing convincing evidence for the validity of the TAT. Today some experts believe that the stories people tell reveal absolutely nothing about their motives or personality. As research use of the TAT declined significantly, so did interest in the study of psychological needs. Scientists cannot study that which they cannot measure.

David McClelland was a brilliant Harvard psychologist who studied achievement motivation (McClelland, 1961). The vast majority of his studies were based on the TAT. When interest in the TAT declined among researchers, McClelland's work lost some of its initial influence.

One of the greatest mistakes of psychodynamic theorists was to embrace projective assessments while criticizing standardized self-report questionnaires. The research community has concluded the opposite. In the last twenty years, the use of standardized measures in psychological research studies has increased significantly, while the use of projective assessments in psychological research studies has declined significantly.

Douglas N. Jackson (1984) constructed a questionnaire measure of Murray's psychological needs, called the Personality Research Form. Jackson may have been ahead of his time in seeking comprehensive, objective measures of motivation. His measure deserves wider use than it has gained thus far.

Before a scientist evaluates a theory, he or she needs valid measures. In the 1980s, I spent years developing the Anxiety Sensitivity Index (ASI) as a valid assessment before we conducted studies on anxiety disorders (Reiss et al., 1986). The ASI has outperformed every anxiety scale to which it has been compared. In the 1990s I spent years developing the RMP as a comprehensive measure of motivation prior to conducting studies. This wasn't what I had wanted to do – I wanted to test my theory – but without good measures, we cannot have good science.

Conclusions

Basic desires are those motives that are universal, intrinsically motivated, intrinsically valued, psychologically significant, and can be only temporarily satiated before they reassert themselves and motivate behavior anew. We do not choose basic desires – they occur automatically. Since both animals and people show similar basic desires, I assume that basic desires have a genetic and evolutionary origin.

A series of scientific studies have repeatedly demonstrated sixteen basic desires of human nature. This conclusion initially was based on the results of exploratory and confirmatory factor studies. The sixteen basic desires are empirically derived factors, or clusters of correlated motives.

Research on the sixteen basic desires has gone significantly beyond the initial demonstrations of factor validity to include evidence of concurrent validity with other psychological measures and predictive validity of behavior in real-life situations. In total, the work on the sixteen basic desires encompasses more than 25,000 people on three continents. The scientific validity coefficients are high (see Havercamp & Reiss, 2004). Anecdotal evidence suggests that the sixteen basic desires may have significant validity in predicting behavior in many real-world situations, some of which are discussed in the remainder of this book.

The taxonomy of sixteen basic desires shows significant similarities and dissimilarities with previous taxonomies of principal motives and psychological needs. Critics of theories of psychological needs have exaggerated the extent to which individual theorists have put forth different taxonomies. Despite the use of widely different methods – observations of animals, anecdotal observations, projective assessments, philosophical inquiry, and empirical derivation using psychometric methods – there is significant similarity among the various taxonomies of universal motives.

3 Intensity of Basic Motivation

The same basic desire (or psychological need) at varying intensities produces different personality traits. Aristotle's (1953/330 B.C.E., Book III) brilliant analysis of vices, virtues, and moderation made this point centuries ago. According to Aristotle, deficient, moderate, and excessive intensities of the same life motive can yield different, and even opposite, personality traits. Insufficient, moderate, and excessive predispositions to become fearful, respectively, cause the personality traits of foolhardiness, courage, and cowardice. Insufficient, moderate, and excessive desires for wealth, respectively, cause the personality traits of shabbiness, magnificence, and vulgarity. Insufficient, moderate, and excessive desires for social contact, respectively, cause the personality traits of boorishness, friendliness, and buffoonery.

Table 3.1 shows the theoretical connections between the sixteen basic desires and personality traits. The table is intended to show how certain personality traits might be caused by the same motive but at different intensities.

Here is how to read Table 3.1. The need for acceptance is one of the sixteen universal desires of humankind. Everybody is motivated to be accepted, but to different extents. People who have an insufficient (very weak) basic desire for acceptance appear to others as overconfident. Those with a low-intensity (or weak) basic desire for acceptance impress others as self-confident. People who have an average-intensity basic desire for acceptance make no distinctive impression on other people with regard to how confident they are. They may have confidence in some situations and lack confidence in others. People who have a high-intensity (or strong) basic desire for acceptance impress others as insecure and lacking in self-confidence. People who have an excessive (or very strong) basic desire for acceptance impress others as self-abasing.

Curiosity, the need for intellectual activity, is one of the sixteen universal desires of humankind. Everybody experiences curiosity, but to different extents. People who have insufficient curiosity impress others as mindless, whereas those

Basic desire	Insufficient motivation	Low-Intensity motivation	Average motivation	High-Intensity motivation	Excessive motivation
Acceptance	Overconfident	Self-confident	No trait	Insecure	Self-abasing
Curiosity	Mindless	Practical	No trait	Intellectual	Overly analytical
Eating	Malnourished	Thin	No trait	Overweight	Obese
Family[a]	Abusive	Noninvolved	No trait	Responsible	Doting
Honor	Unethical	Expedient	No trait	Trustworthy	Righteous
Idealism	Unjust, unfair	Uninvolved	No trait	Humanitarian	True believer
Independence	Dependent	Interdependent	No trait	Self-reliant	Stubborn
Order	Chaotic	Disorganized	No trait	Organized	Perfectionist
Physical Activity	Inactive	Lazy	No trait	Energetic	Exhausting
Power	Submissive	Laid-back	No trait	Ambitious	Controlling
Romance	Abstinent	Undersexed	No trait	Romantic	Oversexed
Saving	Wasteful	Spender	No trait	Frugal	Miserly
Social Contact	Boorishness	Private	No trait	Friendly	Buffoonery
Status	Shabby	Informal	No trait	Formal	Snob
Tranquility	Fearless	Risktaker	No trait	Cautious	Coward
Vengeance	Keeps peace	Gentle, kind	No trait	Warrior	Mean, brutal

Table 3.1. Personality traits and intensity of motivation

[a] Parenting style

with a low-intensity basic desire for curiosity impress others as practical. People who have an average-intensity basic desire for curiosity make no distinctive impression on other people with regard to how curious they are. They may be curious about some, but not many, topics. People who have a high-intensity basic desire for curiosity impress others as being intellectual, whereas those with excessive curiosity impress others as being overly analytical and living in an ivory tower.

The remainder of Table 3.1 is read in a similar manner. Each of the sixteen basic desires is a psychological need. Insufficient (very weak), low (weak), high (strong), and excessive (very strong) intensities of each need theoretically produce the personality traits shown in the table. Average-intensity desires, however, create no distinctive impressions because the individual shows mixed traits from both the strong- and weak-intensity categories.

Intensity of motivation is central to understanding personality from a motivational standpoint, but it is virtually ignored in mainstream psychology and counseling. Your counselor or therapist, for example, tends to overlook intensity of motivation when teaching you self-understanding. Motivation analysis is one of the few theories of personality to recognize the importance of intensity of motivation.

Reiss Motivation Profile

Everybody embraces all sixteen basic desires, but at different intensities. The intensities with which an individual habitually experiences each of the sixteen basic desires are called a Reiss Motivation Profile.[1] The RMP shows the individual's rank ordering, or prioritization, of the sixteen basic desires. Many personality traits can be understood in terms of the individual's RMP.

Intensity of motivation is central for understanding personality functioning. For the sake of simplicity, three intensities of motivation will be called *Strong, Average, and Weak.*

> ***Strong-Intensity Desires*** – indicate a stronger-than-average need (upper 20 percent when compared with the general population). People develop habits, or personality traits, to satiate these desires repeatedly. Example: A person with a high-intensity need to think is motivated to spend so much time engaged in intellectual activities that he or she shows traits of an intellectual.

> ***Weak-Intensity Desires*** – indicate a weaker-than-average need (lower 20 percent when compared with the general population). People develop habits, called personality traits, to satiate these desires repeatedly. Example: A person with a low-intensity need to think is motivated to spend such little time engaged in intellectual activities that he or she will show traits of a practical, action-oriented person.

> ***Average-Intensity Desires*** – indicate an average need (includes 60 percent of the general population). These needs are satisfied by everyday life experiences and do not require distinctive habits or personality traits to gratify them. People with average-intensity desires sometimes show traits associated with strong-intensity desires and sometimes show traits associated with weak-intensity desires.

The following comments show the theoretical connections between strong and weak basic desires and personality traits. The order of presentation is alphabetical. These descriptions are backed generally by peer-reviewed scientific studies showing the validity of the RMP (see Table 2.2); many specific details, however, are still theoretical in nature and require empirical evaluations. The system as a whole has been used professionally in counseling and coaching with thousands of people; the feedback is uncommonly positive. All of the suggested connections between basic desires and personality traits are fully testable scientifically using the RMP standardized instrument.

Acceptance

Acceptance is the universal desire not to be criticized and rejected. This desire motivates you to avoid situations where you might be criticized or rejected and to stay away from people who dislike you. Acceptance is the reason you sometimes get nervous when you are evaluated, tested, or interviewed for a job.

You need the acceptance of some people much more than others. When you were a child, you especially needed the acceptance of your parents. As an adult, you may seek acceptance from your partner, peers, colleagues, or community. Perhaps the simplest way to know whose acceptance you need the most is to ask yourself whose criticism hurts (or would hurt) the most.

Acceptance strengthens your desire to live. When you feel accepted, you may have a zest for life and be ready to take on the world. When you feel rejected, you may have self-doubts and a tendency to be down in the dumps. Some people who experience devastating rejection have suicidal thoughts.

Acceptance is intrinsically desired. Adolescents and adults want to be accepted by people they care about apart from any extrinsic benefits acceptance may bring, such as favoritism for inheritance or advancement at work. Acceptance is not about something else – it is not about self-love(narcissism), guilt reduction, or dealing with childhood trauma. Acceptance is about being valued for who you are.

> People with a **Strong Basic Desire for Acceptance** lack self-confidence. They are insecure and have a tendency to be hurt by criticism, rejection, and failure. They see themselves in negative terms and are quick to blame themselves when something goes wrong. They may worry they will be judged inferior. As described by Karen Horney (1939), when insecure people catch a cold, they blame themselves for not dressing warmly. When a friend does not call for a while, they wonder if the friend no longer likes them. Insecure people often require significant encouragement from others to try new things. Personality traits that may describe them include lacking self-confidence, downbeat, inconsistent effort, insecure, self-doubting, and perhaps indecisive or pessimistic.

> People with a **Weak Basic Desire for Acceptance** are self-confident. They have the basic optimism required to go after what they want in life and to expect success. They usually deal constructively with criticism, rejection, or failure. They have a positive view of themselves and expect to make favorable impressions. They may not need others to tell them they are beautiful or smart or athletic because deep down they already believe this themselves. Expectations of success can be a self-fulfilling prophecy. Personality traits that may describe them include confident, game (willing to try things), optimistic, and self-assured.

Curiosity

Curiosity is the universal desire for intellectual activity (need for cognition). Satisfaction of this desire produces a feeling of wonder, whereas frustration produces boredom or confusion.

Your curiosity determines your potential to enjoy the intellectual aspects of life. Curious children ask adults many questions to stimulate thinking (Maw & Maw, 1964). Curious adults like to engage others in intellectual conversations. Incurious people ask few questions and avoid intellectual conversations because they dislike thinking for more than a minute or two at a time.

The results of our research suggest that many (but not all) adults experience a decline in curiosity as they grow older. I know many professors who became significantly less curious in their forties and fifties, but some remained highly curious their entire lives. Ben Franklin, for example, remained intellectually active right up to his death. I do not know anybody whose curiosity at age 50 was greater than it was at age 30.

Curiosity has survival value. As human knowledge has expanded, so has our ability to find and produce food, defend ourselves, and avoid and treat diseases.

People with a **Strong Basic Desire for Curiosity** love intellectual pursuits such as thinking, reading, writing, and conversing. Their ideas and theories mean a great deal to them. No matter what the circumstances – whether they live at a time of poverty, war, or pestilence – these people manage to keep their intellects engaged and pursue scholarship. They embrace the values of theoretical knowledge, ideas, and truth. They are easily bored and need frequent intellectual stimulation to be happy. They show a wide range of interests, even though they may focus on a particular area of expertise. They may think about an issue over and over again until they feel they understand it. They may have the potential to become absorbed in their thoughts. They may be oriented toward logical reasoning or creative, imaginative ideas. Personality traits that may describe them include contemplative, deep thinking, inquisitive, intellectual, reflective, and thoughtful.

People with a **Weak Basic Desire for Curiosity** like to keep their intellectual activity to a minimum. They become easily frustrated when they try to think. They rarely read books, watch documentaries on television, debate ideas, or enjoy intellectual conversations. They may have little patience with intellectual matters and even may see intellectuals in a negative light. They may like to speak with actions rather than words. As former football great Johnny Unitas put it, "Talk is cheap – let's do our talking on the field." Personality traits that may describe them include action-oriented, nonintellectual, and practical.

Eating

Eating is the universal desire to consume food. Satisfaction of this desire produces feelings of satiation, whereas frustration produces feelings of hunger. The desire to eat motivates you to value good cooking.

Since eating is biologically essential for life, many psychologists believe it is an especially strong desire. Abraham Maslow (1954) wrote that eating takes primacy over psychological motives, as in the example of hunger pains interrupting someone who is reading a book. Maslow believed that hunger and other biological survival needs must be gratified before other basic needs can motivate us.

> People with a **Strong Basic Desire for Eating** have hearty appetites. Food is among their greatest joys in life. They may enjoy many different kinds of food. In adulthood they may become overweight. Personality traits that may describe them include gluttonous, overeating, voracious, and possibly hedonistic.

> People with a **Weak Basic Desire for Eating** have little appetite for food. They may think about eating only rarely and may be fussy about what they eat. Personality traits that may describe them include eats like a bird, eats sparingly, fussy eater, light eater, and possibly thin.

Family

Family is the universal desire to raise one's children. It encompasses what has been called the maternal and paternal instincts. The desire for family motivates people to spend time with their children and to place their children's needs before their own. This desire, which binds parent to child, is unrelated to the basic desire for honor that binds child to parent.

This universal desire motivates people to value their family – including children, brothers, and sisters – and to be attentive to their family's needs. It may prod people to support education, coach Little League, or serve as a Boy/Girl Scout leader. When people satisfy their desire for family, they feel needed and loved.

Although raising children is essential for the survival of the species, it is not a universally strong desire. Some adults do not want to be tied down by children; some do not want to have children. Weak desires for family motivate parents to abandon their children. Historically, some parents have sacrificed children to gods, while others left infants to die from exposure to the elements.

> People with a **Strong Basic Desire for Family** want to have children and spend significant time raising them. Their children may be everything to them. Raising a family is essential for their happiness. They strongly value parenthood and family life. Personality traits that may describe them include family person, family values, loving person, motherly (or fatherly), and perhaps nurturing.

People with a **Weak Basic Desire for Family** consider the duties of parenthood to be burdensome. They may not want to become a parent. If they have children, they may not spend much time raising them. Personality traits that may describe them are wants to be childless, noninvolved parent, and absentee parent.

Honor

Honor is the desire to behave morally. Satisfaction of this desire produces feelings of loyalty, whereas dissatisfaction produces feelings of guilt and shame. Honor is primarily about embracing traditional codes of conduct.

Honor motivates your loyalty to your parents and clan. It makes you proud of your ethnic heritage. It motivates you to be honest, loyal, trustworthy, and responsible. By embracing the moral code of your parents, you honor them. You also honor your parents by embracing their religious denomination and making it your own.

Honor motivates you to make whatever personal sacrifices may be required to do your duty. Mark Twain was a good example of someone who endured personal sacrifice to fulfill his duty. In 1898 when the United States was suffering from an economic depression, Mark Twain was 58 years old and became overwhelmed with debts. He could have bypassed his debts by declaring bankruptcy but instead he hit the lecture circuit, wrote more books, and paid every penny he owed.

Honor has survival benefits because it motivates people to live in small family units or in clans. When people live in small groups, they gain benefits from the presence and cooperation of others. In primitive societies, clans or families provide safety in numbers and permit division of labor. When one family member is taking care of the children, others may be out finding food, building shelter, or looking out for predators.

Military honor codes help bind soldiers together into cohesive units. When the members of a military unit embrace the same code of honor, the shared values create a common sense of purpose. The American combat principle of "no American soldier left behind," moreover, is an excellent example of how a code of honor leads to group protection for loyal individuals.

People with a **Strong Basic Desire for Honor** are righteous. They may be focused on issues of character, morality, and principle. They may be loyal to their ethnic group and parents. Personality traits that may describe them include dependable, genuine, honest, loyal, principled, sanctimonious, scrupulous, sincere, steadfast, trustworthy, truthful, and upright.

People with a **Weak Basic Desire for Honor** are expedient. They are inclined to do whatever it takes to get an important job done. They may believe that everybody is more or less out for themselves. They may think there is nothing wrong in changing one's mind and breaking one's word should circumstances change. Personality traits that describe them include expedient, opportunistic, and perhaps breaks promises.

Idealism

Idealism is the desire to improve society. Satisfaction of this desire produces feelings of compassion, whereas frustration produces feelings of outrage over social injustices. The desire for idealism motivates people to become involved in social causes, pay attention to current affairs, or give to charities.

Idealism motivates you to value mankind and to have compassion for unfortunate people you do not know. It also motivates your attitude toward becoming involved in efforts to eradicate disease, poverty, and racism. Idealism has survival benefits because humanitarian efforts have significantly improved world health and reduced destructive war.

Bono's idealism motivated his efforts to help the sick and poor of Africa. As a well-known singer of a rock band, Bono has lobbied governments on behalf of the world's poor, and in 2005 he organized the World Aid rock concerts to support debt relief for African nations. He persuaded U.S. President George W. Bush to give HIV medicines to hundreds of thousands of Africans.

According to the theory of sixteen basic desires, there are two types of morality, herein called *traditional and humane values.* Traditional values bind you to your clan or ethnic group and fall under the basic desire for honor; humane values bind you to your species (humanity as a whole) and fall under the basic desire for idealism. The two types of morality are only moderately correlated with each other. Some humanitarians I know, for example, lie and cheat when they think it will benefit their cause. I also know people who never lie and cheat but care very little about the downtrodden.

People with a **Strong Basic Desire for Idealism** are impressed with humanitarianism and volunteerism. Social justice and fairness may be very important to them. They may care deeply about social causes such as world peace, uplifting the downtrodden, or world health. They may pay attention to current events. Personality traits that may apply to them include altruistic, compassionate, do-gooder, dreamer, fair, humanitarian, idealistic, involved, volunteer, philanthropic, volunteer, and perhaps martyr.

People with a **Weak Basic Desire for Idealism** are focused on the events in their life rather than the great issues facing society. They may think that injustice is part of life and there is little one should do about it unless it directly affects oneself or loved ones. They may show little interest in current events or world peace. Personality traits that may apply to them include hard-nosed, pragmatic, man (woman) of the world, realistic, and possibly looks the other way.

Independence

Independence is the universal desire for self-reliance. This desire motivates you to take care of yourself and not ask others for favors or money. Independence motivates people to make their own decisions. Satisfaction of this desire produces the joy of personal freedom, whereas frustration produces feelings of dependency.

Your desire for independence motivates your attitude toward individuality, or how much you want to stand out as an individual. This desire is especially strong during adolescence. Many teenagers who are strongly motivated by independence find ways to call attention to their individuality, such as sporting a goatee or wearing unusual clothes.

Many experts have overestimated the correlations between independence and power, as in the stereotype of a strong-willed, independent leader. I distinguish between two basic desires. Power determines how much you want to lead, but independence determines your leadership style. An independent leader makes decisions on his own, whereas an interdependent individual leads by consensus. It also is possible to be very independent but dislike leadership, as in the example of a relative of mine who shuns giving advice (which falls under a weak basic desire for power) and never asks for favors (which falls under a strong desire for independence).

Independence has survival benefits because it motivates the young to leave home and strike out on their own. In animals independence spreads the search for food over a larger geographical area, increasing the chances that sufficient food will be found for survival.

People with a **Strong Basic Desire for Independence** are self-reliant. Their personal freedom may be everything to them; they may dislike being in need of others. It may be very important to them that things be done their way ("my way, or the highway"). They may not "go along, to get along." They may prefer logic, science, and rationality – as opposed to intuition – when evaluating situations or others. Personality traits that may describe them include autonomous, independent, self-reliant, and perhaps proud, stubborn, and uncomfortable with touchy-feely experiences.

People with a **Weak Basic Desire for Independence** trust others to meet their needs. They value psychological support, especially when making decisions. They may devalue displays of individuality. They may rely on their intuition when evaluating situations and other people. They may seek mystical experiences such as "unity of consciousness," nirvana, "being in the zone," "peak experience," and "flow." Personality traits that may describe them include humble, interdependent, and perhaps mystic or likes touchy-feely experiences.

Order

Order is the desire for structured and stable environments. Satisfaction of this desire produces a sense of comfort, whereas dissatisfaction produces feelings of discomfort. Order is about form, stability, and purity; disorder is about formlessness, change, and impurity. The desire for order motivates you to plan, schedule, and organize.

Order has survival benefits partially because it motivates cleanliness. According to psychiatrist Judith L. Rapoport (1990), dirt, wounds, and other potential contaminants create the impression of being "out of place" on the skin. Animal licking instincts and other rituals remove "out of place" dirt and contaminants. In humans we see a desire for things to be "in their place," and a preference for cleanliness versus dirtiness. All human societies value cleanliness more than being dirty.

> People with a **Strong Basic Desire for Order** are organized. Tidiness, organization, and punctuality are very important to them. They may pay attention to details, rules, and schedules, and they may be comfortable with predictable and relatively unchanging situations. They may embrace ritual. They may think there is only one way to do things; they may have difficulty adapting to change; and they may dislike doing things on impulse. Personality traits that may describe them include careful, inflexible, methodical, neat, organized, orderly, precise, prepared, punctual, thorough, and tidy.

> People with a **Weak Basic Desire for Order** are flexible. They have a high tolerance for ambiguity. They may dislike structure and hate following rules and schedules. They often change their plans or mind. They focus on the "big picture" to the extent of perhaps missing key details. Personality traits that may describe them include changes mind frequently, disorganized, flexible, follows nose, hates planning, keeps options open as long as possible, spontaneous, tardy, and untidy.

Physical Activity

Physical activity is the universal desire for muscle exercise. Satisfaction of this desire produces the joy of vitality, whereas frustration produces restlessness. This desire motivates people toward physically vigorous activity, such as sports. The RMP provides a standardized assessment of your need for physical exercise. It shows how much you enjoy vigorous physical exertion compared with the average person.

According to the results of the RMP with various college teams (Reiss, Wiltz, & Sherman (2001), five motivational traits define the "Athletic Personality": strong basic desires for physical exercise, family, power (achievement), vengeance (competition), and social contact. The main trait, of course, is a very strong basic desire for physical exercise.

We intrinsically desire physical activity apart from any health benefits it may have. This basic desire motivates us to value fitness and possibly muscle strength. The basic desire for physical activity may have evolutionary significance. In primitive societies, for example, strong people push others away from food and have their first pick of a mate. Strength also helps individuals defend themselves in fights against foe or predator.

The sixteen basic desires provide a new, powerful basis for sports psychology. A highly curious athlete, for example, is predicted to have difficulty with split-second timing; an athlete with a strong need for acceptance is predicted to be inconsistent; and an athlete with a strong need for status is predicted to be vulnerable to letdowns against a low- status opponent. Sports consultant Peter Boltersdorf has used this method successfully with a number of professional teams in Germany.

People with a **Strong Basic Desire for Physical Activity** seek an active lifestyle. Workouts or sports are an important part of their lives. Many physically active people embrace amateur athletics to stay fit. They may value fitness, vitality, strength, and stamina. Personality traits that may apply to them are active, athletic, energetic, fit, outdoorsy, perky, and physical.

People with a **Weak Basic Desire for Physical Activity** prefer a sedentary lifestyle. They need encouragement and extrinsic reasons – such as health – to exercise regularly. Personality traits that apply to them are lackadaisical, listless, inactive, lethargic, and sedentary lifestyle.

Power

Power is the universal desire for self-assertion (influence of will). Power drives achievement motivation, willpower, determination, and leadership. Satisfaction of this desire produces the joy of self-efficacy and feelings of competence, whereas frustration produces regret or possibly embarrassment or humiliation.

Power motivates your willpower, desire for achievement, and how hard you are willing to work to get ahead. Examples of achievement include writing a book, winning a championship in sports, or creating a work of art. The primal association between achievement and power is apparent at athletic contests. When a team scores a goal, for example, their fans thrust clenched fists into the air. In other words, when the team goal is achieved, the fans react by displaying power.

Your desire for power determines the extent to which you seek to influence people, events, or environment. Power motivates your feelings about being a leader and giving others direction or advice. It has been said of some powerful personalities that they cannot stand to see somebody go in one direction without urging him or her to go in a different direction.

I tentatively classify the desire to build things as self-assertion. According to William James (1918/1890) and William McDougall (2003/1908), the need for constructiveness is as genuine and irresistible an instinct in man as it is in the bee or beaver. The satisfaction of building something is very real, quite apart from the value or usefulness of the object made. Young children like to break things apart and put them back together. They build with blocks and with their Legos.

Please notice that winning and achievement fall under different basic desires. The need to win is motivated by the basic desire for vengeance, whereas the need to achieve is motivated by the basic desire for power. We need different motives for winning and achievement because it is possible to want to win without achieving or to want to achieve without winning. Writing a book and building a house, for example, are achievements motivated by power but not vengeance.

Power has survival benefits for animals in the wild because the dominant animal pushes others away from food and eats first. Dominant animals also have their choice of mates. Another survival benefit is that power motivates people to build shelter and tools.

People with a **Strong Basic Desire for Power** like to take charge of situations and assume leadership roles. They may seek out challenges and work hard to accomplish their goals. They may enjoy giving others advice. Personality traits that may describe them include ambitious, assertive, bold, hardworking, determined, focused, single-minded, and willful.

People with a **Weak Basic Desire for Power** dislike self-assertion. They tend to let events unfold without trying to influence them. They may be nondirective and lacking in ambition. They may dislike leadership roles or giving advice or guidance to others. They may keep their work and career in perspective by giving at least equal weight for personal and family life. They may avoid challenging achievement goals. They are not lazy or unconcerned; they are motivated instead by an intrinsic dislike of controlling and influencing others. Personality traits that may describe them include easygoing, laid-back, onlookers, nonassertive, nondirective, and unambitious.

Romance

Romance is the universal desire for sex. Satisfaction of this desire produces feelings of ecstasy, whereas frustration produces feelings of lust. Your desire for romance motivates you to care about your appearance and to pursue potential sex partners. The striving for romance is moderately correlated with the desire to experience beauty, which explains why in every society people prepare themselves for sex by aiming to look beautiful to their partner.

When people are in romantic love, their feelings for each other are experienced as boundless and eternal. They perceive each other to be beautiful, graceful, grand, handsome, or adorable. Their minds are filled with thoughts of each other. They want to tell each other their most intimate thoughts. They may feel as if they would rather die than be without the other. They may behave childishly when together. They may say or write each other's name over and over again. They may feel miserable when separated for more than a few days at a time. They may risk all to be with each other.

Romance is not part of a larger desire for sensual pleasure. The goal of romance is sex, not sensual pleasure ; the goal of eating is food, not sensual pleasure. If human beings were motivated by sensual pleasure rather than by separate and unrelated desires for romance and eating, it would be possible to satiate hunger by having sex. Sensual pleasure is a signal that you have experienced your goal; it is not the goal itself.

The desire for romance declines in intensity throughout adulthood. Even Casanova experienced a drop in libido after the age of 40. Yet a person's need for romance may be relatively stable when the need is compared to other people of similar ages. A person who is more sexually active than his or her brother at age 30, for example, likely will remain more active as years pass even though both may become less active as they grow older.

> People with a **Strong Basic Desire for Romance** seek active sex lives. They may value sexual skills or passion. They may often think about sex. They may be attracted to many potential partners. Personality traits that may apply to them are amorous, flirtatious, lover, oversexed, passionate, romantic, and perhaps promiscuous.

> People with a **Weak Basic Desire for Romance** may spend little time thinking about, and pursuing, sex. Personality traits that may apply to them include celibate, chaste, Platonic, puritanical, and undersexed.

Saving

Saving is the desire to collect things. People collect many different objects including antiques, art, autographs, automobiles, books, clothes, coins, firearms, furniture, jewelry, magazines, military memorabilia, music, photographs, religious relics, sports memorabilia, stamps, tools, and toys.

Saving influences how well you take care of the things you own and your attitude toward spending. Saving motivates you to value frugality and devalue wastefulness. Saving has survival benefits because it motivates stockpiling/hoarding essential supplies.

As previously noted, saving was added as the sixteenth basic desire based on suggestions from colleagues studying hoarding. It was the only basic desire that was added to my taxonomy based on expert observations rather than on the results of our surveys.

> People with a **Strong Basic Desire for Saving** are collectors. They may hate throwing things away and may be tight with money. Personality traits that may describe them include accumulator, collector, hoarder, saver, pack rat, and possibly frugal and thrifty.

> People with a **Weak Basic Desire For Saving** tend to use things and then dispose of them. Personality traits that may describe them include spendthrift, profligate, wasteful, and possibly extravagant.

Social Contact

Social contact is the universal desire for companionship with peers. Satisfaction of this desire produces feelings of fun and belonging, whereas frustration produces feelings of loneliness.

William McDougall (2003/1903) suggested what he called a "gregarious instinct," or an inborn tendency to live in small groups such as herds or tribes. The South African ox, for example, display no affection for their peers so long as they are among them; but, after being separated from the herd, an individual displays extreme distress that does not let him rest until he has rejoined the herd. "There we see the working of the gregarious instinct in all its simplicity," wrote McDougall (2003/1908), "a mere uneasiness in isolation and satisfaction in being one of the herds" (p. 72).

The gregarious instinct has apparent survival advantages for animals and for people living in primitive societies. Small groups provide safety in numbers. When one person plays, another may look out for possible danger. When a hunt is needed to find food, the group can divide the tasks based on the abilities of each individual member. While some members of the group raise the young, others can protect them, and still others can hunt for food.

The basic desire for social contact creates a psychological need for friends. People who want many friends learn social graces and skills to attract and keep friends. The desire to socialize is so highly valued that withholding opportunities to socialize – as in ostracism – is a form of punishment.

Dale Carnegie (1981/1936) was a popular author who gave advice on how to win friends and influence people. He advised people to smile; to listen carefully to what the other person has to say; to remember the other person's name and use it often in speech; to avoid criticizing other people; to give deserved praise at every opportunity; and to be concerned with one's appearance. He also advised against being selfish or snobbish.

The universal desire for social contact is about companionship from peers and does not include companionship from lovers, parents, and children. How much time you want to spend with your parents or your children does not predict how much time you want to spend with peers. The strivings for romance, honor, and family, respectively, motivate interest in lovers, parents, and children. Only the striving for social contact motivates interest in peers.

> People with a **High Basic Desire for Social Contact** are friendly. They may show mannerisms and habits that attract and ingratiate themselves to others. They may be fun loving and upbeat. Personality traits that may describe them include affable, charming, cheerful, engaging, extroverted, friendly, fun-loving, gracious, gregarious, outgoing, playful, prankster, sociable, vivacious, and warm.

> People with a **Weak Basic Desire for Social Contact** enjoy solitude. They dislike parties, small talk, and socializing, and they may show little interest in most people they meet. They may have few friends. They often seem to be in a serious mood. Personality traits that may describe them include aloof, avoidant, brusque, detached, distant, hermit, introvert, private, serious, and withdrawn.

Status

Status is the desire for social standing based on wealth, title, social class, or high birth. Satisfaction of this desire produces feelings of self-importance and superiority, whereas frustration produces feelings of insignificance or inferiority. Although psychoanalyst Alfred Adler (1971/1927) suggested that people seek status to compensate for unconscious feelings of inferiority, I assume that people seek status because they intrinsically value respect. Generally, the attention other people pay us is a primal indicator of our status. People pay attention to important people and ignore unimportant people.

Gratification of the basic desire for status can motivate pride in one's social position. "A proud man," wrote Charles Darwin (1965/1872), "exhibits his sense of superiority over others by holding his head and body erect. He is haughty (*haut*), or high, and makes himself appear as large as possible; so that metaphorically he is said to be swollen or puffed up with pride" (p. 263). He looks "down" on others, and with lowered eyelids, condescends to see them. In contrast, the emotion of humility is expressed with a lowered head and an averted gaze.

Status is something other people must give you; you cannot give it to yourself. Your status is an indicator of how much respect and deference is your due. People feel slighted when they receive less deference than is their due, and they feel flattered when they receive more deference than is their due. Status motivates people to pay attention to and value their reputation.

Status motivates materialistic values including living in prestigious residential neighborhoods, owning expensive cars, and wearing designer clothes. How do people who are poor satisfy their need for status? After all, few of us can afford to live in prestigious homes or drive a Mercedes Benz. One family made it a point to wear stylish clothes, which they made themselves because they could not afford to buy nice garments. Another family put all their available cash into buying a Hummer – although they lived in an economically disadvantaged neighborhood, they drove around in a prestigious car. A third family bought a house they could not really afford. They lived house poor but still impressed anyone who knew the prestige of the suburb in which they lived.

Status motivates people to consider social class when choosing a potential spouse. People with a strong desire for status may aim to marry "up" in class, marry someone who is wealthy, or marry someone who is beautiful or handsome (a so-called trophy spouse). People with a weak desire for status, however, may disregard money or social class when choosing a spouse.

Status motivates interest in clothes. "White-collar" workers, for example, have higher status than do "blue-collar" workers. Lawyers dress in three-piece suits to project the image of success; physicians dress in lab coats to project an image of scientific expertise; and priests dress plainly to show their status before God.

The striving for status motivates people to imitate the hairstyles, fashions, and mannerisms of celebrities. Elvis made sideburns popular, the Beatles brought back long hair, and Michael Jackson had American teens wearing white gloves. Marilyn Monroe had American women dressing with glamour, Jackie Kennedy had them dressing elegantly, and Madonna had them dressing sexy.

Since nobody likes vain people, some high-status people find ways of calling attention to their status without appearing to be braggarts. A well-known rock singer, for example, hangs awards in his bathroom. He figures everybody who visits him would see them there, and yet think he is humble for relegating the display to a bathroom.

Status has survival benefits. Wealthy people eat well and receive the best medical care. In 1906 when the luxury liner *Titanic* sank, the first- class passengers rowed away from the sinking ship in lifeboats while the lower-class passengers were locked in their compartments because the ship carried too few lifeboats for all.[2,3]

People with a **Strong Basic Desire for Status** value wealth, material things, and social class. They may associate themselves with anything that is popular and dissociate themselves from anything that is unpopular. They may admire high society and may be impressed with marks of social distinction such as social titles and privileges. They are motivated to embrace the mannerisms, dress, and habits of prestigious or wealthy people. They like to be associated with the "right" people, and they are impressed by membership in prestigious social clubs. Personality traits that may apply to these people are formal, materialistic, patrician, proud, lofty, and dignified.

People with a **Weak Basic Desire for Status** are unimpressed with high society, wealth, and fame. They believe it is wrong to admire someone just because he or she happened to be born into a certain family or is wealthy. They may not care what others think of them. They may identify with the middle or lower class. Personality traits that describe them are casual, down-to-earth, egalitarian, informal, and unceremonious.

Tranquility

Tranquility is the desire to avoid experiencing anxiety or pain. Satisfaction of this desire produces feelings of relaxation, whereas frustration produces fear, anxiety, or worry. This desire influences your attitudes toward safety, danger, adventure, and possibly financial risk. The desire for tranquility has survival benefits because it motivates avoidance of danger. When the choice is "fight or flight," tranquility motivates flight.

Tranquility motivates your attitudes toward danger. Danger is diabolical – it threatens yet excites us. We seek a balance between safety and excitement. Maggi's late grandfather provided a humorous example of how intolerable life can be without any excitement. At age 93, he moved so slowly he seemed to need an eternity just to get from his upstairs bedroom to the first-floor living room. During one Christmas afternoon he sat in his living room chair for hours, looked down the entire time, said nothing, and barely moved a muscle. I thought he was semicomatose because he seemed to have no idea of what was going on around him. When it was time to go, one of his grandsons said, "Goodbye Grandpa. Take it easy." Grandfather became animated and exclaimed, "Are you kidding? I can't possibly take it any easier than this!"

Psychodynamic theorists have assumed that anxiety is a negative experience everybody wants to avoid. Yet many individuals approach stressful and anxiety-evoking situations everyday. *I disagree that everybody seeks to avoid anxiety: I think people regulate how much danger versus safety they want to experience, but they differ in terms of preferred equilibrium points.* The results of hundreds of recent research studies show that individuals vary significantly in preferred equilibrium points, which I call sensitivity to anxiety (Reiss & McNally, 1985). High anxiety sensitivity individuals avoid minimally dangerous or stressful situations, but low anxiety sensitivity individuals often approach all but the most dangerous or stressful situations. It is invalid to assume that everybody is equally motivated to defend against anxiety or minimize anxiety experiences (McNally, 2002).

Anxiety sensitivity (which falls under the basic desire for tranquility) has changed the way we think about panic attacks. Psychiatrists used to believe that people who have panic attacks develop a secondary fear of having them again. This fear of panic attacks was regarded as relatively insignificant. In 1985 Richard McNally, now Harvard University professor of psychology, and I put forth a theory of sensitivity to anxiety that implied that the fear of fear may precede and predict panic attacks. Many studies have confirmed our idea of anxiety sensitivity (e.g., Reiss et al., 1986; Schmidt, Lerew, & Jackson, 1997). Scores of studies have shown that strong desires for tranquility predict future panic attacks.

> People with a **Strong Basic Desire for Tranquility** place a high value on their personal safety. They may have many fears and may be highly sensitive to physical pain. They may worry about money, romance, job, health, or the future (Horney, 1939). They may be risk avoidant. Personality traits that describe them include fearful, anxious, apprehensive, cautious, timid, and possibly worrier.

> People with a **Weak Basic Desire for Tranquility** are risktakers and perhaps thrill seekers. They may be fearless. They may have a high capacity for handling stress. They may expose themselves to danger. Dare-devil Philippe Petit, for example, walked seven times across a 138-foot cable strung 1,350 feet above lower Manhattan at the World Trade Tower prior to 9-11 (Keyes, 1985). Personality traits that may describe people with a weak basic desire for tranquility are brave, calm, courageous, explorer, fearless, risktaker, relaxed, and venturesome.

Vengeance

Vengeance is the desire to get even with people who frustrate or offend us. Satisfaction of this desire produces the joy of vindication, whereas frustration stimulates the fighting spirit and possibly anger.

The primal provocations are threats to your status, your territory, and your children; competition for resources; access to potential mates; strange or unfamiliar people; and aggressive or unfriendly displays by other people (see Aureli & de Waal, 2000).

We have the potential to use peacekeeping and reconciliation behavior to manage aggressive impulses. These behaviors include submissive displays, sharing, cooperative play, apologies, holding hands, and kissing. Reconciliation behavior signals the end of a conflict and serves to reduce future conflict (see Aureli & de Waal, 2000).

The desire for vengeance motivates the competitive spirit. Competitive people are not necessarily physically aggressive, but they are quick to confront others. Competitive people value winning.

The primal connection between aggressiveness and competitiveness is why rivalry athletic games hold the potential for after-game violence. Rivalry games are opportunities to express vengeance in a socially appropriate manner. The games are not about the release of pent-up aggressive energy, as psychodynamic theorists have said, but about asserting the intrinsic value of winning. It is a fun or positive experience to assert one's values. For one week every year, for example, society tolerates many Ohio State University and University of Michigan football fans wishing each other the agony of defeat. A person with aggressive personality traits can misinterpret the permissible bounds (especially when inebriated) and has the potential to behave violently after the game is over.

The inclination toward aggressiveness is stable over much of the lifespan. Relative to the people your age, you are predicted to be about as aggressive ten or twenty years from now as you are in the current phase of your life. Researchers have shown, for example, that disproportionate numbers of schoolyard bullies grow up to become criminals. Aggressive behavior in third grade predicts aggressive behavior at age 30 (Eron & Huesmann, 1990).

> People with a **Strong Basic Desire for Vengeance** are quick to confront others. They value competitors and winners. Personality traits that may describe them include competitor, fighter, pugnacious, and perhaps aggressive, angry, argumentative, combative, or mean.

> People with a **Weak Basic Desire for Vengeance** avoid confrontation, fights, and violence. Often their first impulse is to cooperate rather than to compete. They may search for ways to settle problems amicably. They may value peace, cooperation, compromise, and nonviolence; they may devalue conflict, competing, winning, fighting, and arguing. Personality traits that may apply to them include cooperative, kind, merciful, nonaggressive, and peacemaker.

4 Normal Personality Types

Very strong, as well as very weak, basic desires can dominate a person's life to the point of defining the individual's personality. When this happens, some experts speak of a "personality type." In this chapter, we will consider seven personality types: workaholic, competitor, humanitarian, thinker, romantic, loner, and ascetic. I will show how the sixteen basic desires might explain each of these types. I also will comment on the normality of these types, even though some experts have suggested otherwise.

Workaholic

> *Conventional wisdom:* Unconsciously motivated to escape from personal troubles.
> *Motivation analysis:* Consciously motivated by a strong need for achievement.

Tom is a professor of sociology, teaching at a Texas university. I have known him personally for more than twenty years. Tom is friendly, likeable, and pleasant. He played football in high school and still works out every day. Yet Tom's two most outstanding qualities are his intellect and his capacity for work. Tom always seems to be reading, thinking, writing, teaching, or lecturing.

When it comes to working, Tom takes the cake. He seems to read everything published in his field. His knowledge of sociology is voluminous. When I visit him, I am interrupting his work. When I leave him, he immediately goes back to work. When I call him, I am interrupting his work; when he calls me, he is almost always calling from work.

I recall one year when a group of friends were attending a conference. In the evening we all watched a movie on television, but Tom went off into another room to read some academic journal articles.

Tom's marriage ended in divorce after about fifteen years. Tom worked so much his wife must have felt lonely many days, evenings, and even weekends. Tom

Table 4.1. Tom (Type: Workaholic)		
Strong	**Average**	**Weak**
Curiosity	Eating	Acceptance
Power	Family	
	Honor	
	Idealism	
	Independence	
	Order	
	Physical Activity	
	Romance	
	Saving	
	Social Contact	
	Status	
	Tranquility	
	Vengeance	

is a great guy, but it can be a challenge to be married to someone who is always working.

Although Tom is successful and happy, some psychologists would question his mental health. In particular, they would suspect that Tom is a "workaholic." This term is derived from *alcoholic* and means "addicted to work." According to Frank J. Bruno (1993), workaholism is a psychological "symptom" because of its substantial costs. Bruno suggests that workaholism can be diagnosed when an individual works at least 60 hours per week, works even when ill, and obtains nearly all psychological gratification from work. He further suggests that workaholics are avoiding problems at home, especially with their partners.

Based on Bruno's criteria, Tom is a workaholic. Yet Tom is one of the most mentally healthy people I know. He says he is happy working so hard, and I believe him. He is almost always in a good mood. His divorce was handled maturely and with far less contentiousness than is typical in such affairs. When asked why he works so much, he says he enjoys it. Tom is happy and successful, so why diagnose him?

Table 4.1 shows how I think Tom prioritizes the sixteen basic desires. I think his personality is characterized by very strong desires for work (which falls under the basic desire for power) and knowledge (which falls under the basic desire for curiosity), which in combination motivate him to spend his waking hours reading, thinking, and writing.

Understanding the normal personality helps us avoid overdiagnosing abnormality. Hard work is a normal manifestation of the basic desire for power (self-assertion). Maybe Bruno would not be happy working as hard as Tom – at least 99 percent of the population would not – but this only shows that we are individuals. Diagnosing Tom as a workaholic confuses individuality with abnormality.

I realize that Bruno could produce examples of people who have clear psychological problems and escape into work. I agree that some people escape from life by burying themselves in work. What I am saying is that simply working nearly all the time is insufficient to diagnose a psychological symptom or disorder. There must be other, independent evidence of a disorder before a diagnosis can be justified. If we applied strict psychiatric diagnostic criteria to workaholics, we might find some who have a significant psychological disorder, but we also would find many like Tom who are normal and happy people with a passion for work.

Competitor

> *Psychodynamics:* Unconsciously motivated by sibling rivalry or insecurity about a parent's love.
>
> *Motivation analysis:* Consciously motivated by a strong intrinsic need to win.

Bobby Knight, whose nickname is "the General," has more wins as a college basketball coach than anyone in history. He grew up in a small town in rural Ohio. Although his relationship with his father seemed emotionally distant to some, Knight himself says he respected his father as "the most disciplined man I ever saw" (Berger, 2000, p. 51). He admired his father for doing his duty and giving great effort all the time.

Knight admires competitors but disrespects quitters. In his senior year in high school, he complained that his basketball coach did not have sufficient "fire in his belly." His criticism of his coach nearly got Knight booted off the team, but his father persuaded the coach to keep him.

Knight played basketball for The Ohio State University Buckeyes from 1958 to 1962. The Buckeyes won the NCAA national championship in 1960. Not good enough to be a starter on such a talented team, Knight played sparingly. Teammates from that era remember Knight as someone who told tall tales, liked to make people laugh, but could be verbally abusive toward other players.

Knight started his basketball coaching career at Cuyahoga Falls (Ohio) High School, where he was described as a "fire-breathing, demanding" coach who displayed an "intense competitiveness" (Berger, 2000, p. 72). He moved on to coach at the U.S. Military Academy at West Point. After seven winning seasons as Army head coach, Knight began a 29-year tenure as head basketball coach at Indiana University. At IU, Knight's basketball teams won NCAA national championships

Table 4.2. Bobby Knight (Type: Competitor)*		
Strong	**Average**	**Weak**
Power	Acceptance	
Vengeance	Eating	
	Family	
	Honor	
	Idealism	
	Independence	
	Order	
	Physical Activity	
	Romance	
	Saving	
	Social Contact	
	Status	
	Tranquility	
	Vengeance	

* Based on Berger's (2000) biography.

in 1976, 1981, and 1987. He also coached the 1984 U.S. basketball team to a gold medal at the Olympic Games.

At IU, Knight ran a squeaky-clean basketball program that never had a recruiting scandal. At times he acted like a father to his players, helping them get jobs after they graduated and sending them gifts (not just cards) every Christmas. He promised parents that their sons would be educated, and he made good on his promises. If a player did not take academics seriously and attend classes, Knight would not let him play. Knight's teams had a combined graduation record of over 90 percent, one of the highest in the history of college sports.

Throughout much of the 1980s and 1990s, Knight was a hero to IU alumni and a popular figure throughout the state of Indiana. Yet Knight damaged his status by a series of boorish outbursts and by his openly critical attitude toward people he disliked. In 2000 Indiana University President Myles Brand fired Bobby Knight as IU's basketball coach.

Knight sometimes makes fun of people who rub him the wrong way. At the 1979 Pan American games, he reportedly referred to a Brazilian basketball women's team as a "bunch of whores" and then pushed the policeman assigned to the practice gym. While eating dinner, a fan taunted him, "Knight is an asshole! Knight is an asshole!" Knight stuffed the fan into a garbage can. In 1985 he threw a chair across a basketball court to protest a referee's call. During a 1987 game, he banged his fist on a scorer's table and was fined $10,000. In 1993 he kicked his son, who was a player on the team. In 2000 he was fired shortly after reports became public that he allegedly grabbed a player around the neck. "When my time on Earth is gone and my activities here are past," Knight once said, "I want them to bury me upside down and my critics can kiss my ass."

Freudians explain competitiveness in terms of real or imagined rivalry for a parent's love. The young boy, for example, desires his mother's love and regards his father as a rival. Afraid of the father's retaliation, the boy represses his anger, which is eventually vented as a competitive spirit in sports or business arenas. Freudians also might say that Knight valued achievement as an unconscious means of gaining the love of a distant father.

Table 4.2 shows how I would explain the main themes of Knight's adult life. Knight wants to win because he intrinsically loves it (which falls under the basic desire for vengeance). I believe it is a mistake to explain the competitor's need for winning as instrumental to other ends; I think the competitor is best understood as intrinsically valuing winning for its own sake.

Since Knight has paid a heavy price for not learning to control his boorish outbursts, some psychodynamic experts might say that Knight has a "death wish." These experts might further speculate that Knight has a deep-rooted feeling of inferiority and seeks to compensate with extraordinary achievements as a coach. I disagree with these psychodynamic ideas. I suspect that Knight underestimated the full personal consequences of boorishness (see Chapter 7 on personal blind spots). In the heat of battle, he may have forgotten how much outbursts can cost him. Maybe he thought he could get away with them, or perhaps he underestimated the degree to which boorishness can overshadow a person's reputation and achievements.

Many experts believe that "something must be wrong" with people who have trouble controlling their competitive instincts. I disagree: I think Knight's competitive drive motivated boorish outbursts that caused him significant problems, but it also motivated him to win basketball games and inspired many young players. I am not making excuses for Knight; I am just refusing to judge his very real personality problems as a disorder or abnormality.

Humanitarian

Psychodynamics: Unconsciously motivated by self-destructiveness and guilt.
Motivation analysis: Consciously motivated by an intrinsic valuation of social justice.

John Brown was born in 1800 to an intensely religious family. He devoted his life to the abolitionist cause and the rights of African Americans. In 1825, Brown

Table 4.3. John Brown (Type: Humanitarian)*

Strong	Average	Weak
Idealism	Acceptance	Family
Vengeance	Curiosity	Tranquility
	Eating	
	Honor	
	Independence	
	Order	
	Physical Activity	
	Power	
	Romance	
	Saving	
	Social Contact	
	Status	

* Based on Hinton's (1968) biography.

escorted an African American couple to sit with him in a pew, rather than at the back of the church. "The whole church was down on him then," wrote John Brown's daughter Ruth. "My brothers were so disgusted to see such a mockery of religion [in the reaction of the congregation] that they left the church and have never belonged to another" (Hinton, 1968, p. 37).

Hoping that Kansas would become a free state and tip the congressional balance of power in favor of abolition, John Brown left his family and moved to Kansas. He tirelessly traveled throughout that state giving speeches calling for abolition. Brown is best remembered, however, for having organized a raid on a federal arsenal at Harper's Ferry, Virginia. When the United States hanged him, he became a martyr to the antislavery movement.

Karl Menninger (1938), the famed psychoanalyst, wrote that John Brown's martyrdom was motivated by self-destructive tendencies with an "aggressive component." Menninger complained that while Brown "wandered about the country, pursuing his vision, his patient wife struggled with cold, hunger, and wretched poverty on a bleak Adirondack farm" (p. 112). Even worse, suggested Menninger, Brown exposed his family to violent danger and attack by those who supported slavery. "One son had gone mad. Another had been shot. But still their father held them grimly to his [antislavery] purpose."

Menninger did not have a kind word to say about John Brown. The implication of his analysis was that a mentally healthy John Brown would have looked the other way and tolerated slavery out of fear of retaliation for himself and his family. According to Menninger, John Brown should have spent more time with his wife and family and less time pursuing his dream of abolition.

Were John Brown's efforts to fight slavery really a manifestation of unconscious self-destructive tendencies, as Karl Menninger claimed? Table 4.3 shows how the sixteen basic desires might explain Brown's personality. My analysis suggests that Brown was responding to a higher calling when he devoted his life to fighting against the injustices of slavery. Brown was not trying to destroy himself; he was trying to bring justice to America. He did not seek justice to reduce guilt; he sought justice because human beings intrinsically value fairness. Brown was not a neurotic; he was a sane person living under the racial policy of slavery. Remaining quiet about slavery is cowardice, not prudence. Brown did not want to die because he was unhappy or harbored guilty or aggressive feelings; he wanted to be executed because he correctly calculated that the sacrifice would contribute to his just cause.

Why was John Brown more sensitive to the need for justice for African Americans than he was to the suffering of his own family? According to the implications of our research on the sixteen basic desires, the striving for idealism is largely unrelated to the striving for family. Justice and children are two different values; humanitarians are not necessarily family-oriented, and family-oriented people are not necessarily supportive of humanitarian causes.

Thinker

Psychodynamics: Unconsciously motivated by sublimated sexual energy.
Motivation analysis: Consciously motivated by a strong intrinsic valuation of knowledge and ideas.

Isaac Newton (1643–1727) was one of history's most influential scholars. In the seventeenth century, he put forth revolutionary concepts of inertia and gravity to explain the mechanical universe. He also invented calculus and is credited with having merged mathematics and physical science.

Newton had a difficult childhood. His father died before he was born, and for six years he lived with his grandparents, who treated him like an orphan. As a young man, he did not date and spent much of his time in a room at Cambridge University. He had few friends, and with little money, he lived very frugally. He eventually left the university to become the King's Master of the Mint. He died a painful death from kidney disease at age 84.

Newton was strongly motivated by curiosity. His pursuit of knowledge was relentless. He reflected deeply on everyday observations most people disregard as trifles. When he looked at a pond, he wondered why the water formed the pattern

Table 4.4. Isaac Newton (Type: Thinker)*

Strong	Average	Weak
Acceptance	Eating	Family
Curiosity	Honor	Romance
	Idealism	Social Contact
	Independence	
	Order	
	Physical Activity	
	Power	
	Saving	
	Status	
	Tranquility	
	Vengeance	

* Based on biography by Gleick (2003).

it did as it passed stones. When he saw a tennis game, he wondered why the ball curved when it was "sliced" by the racket – why not a straight trajectory? He kept track of his ideas by writing them in notebooks.

Newton would become lost in his thoughts even when he was supposed to be paying attention to the matter at hand. On one occasion, for example, he was thinking about a mathematical problem when the sheep he was supposed to be watching ran into the neighbor's farm. When it became obvious he was not suited to be a farmer, he enrolled at Cambridge University. Newton achieved the rank of full professor at the young age of 24.

Newton published very little. When he solved a problem, he usually kept it to himself rather than share it with others. He withheld the publication of his greatest discoveries for decades. When asked why, he said he wanted to avoid disputations. He knew his ideas about the universe were valid, but he could not stand to watch others criticize them.

Newton spent much of his life by himself. He lived alone at Cambridge, worked alone, had no close friends, and did not date women. He never married and had little fun in his life.

Freudians believe that intellectualism is motivated by "sublimated" sexual energy. (*Sublimation* is an unconscious process that supposedly converts sexual impulses into creative energy.) In favor of the sublimation hypothesis, Freudians might note that Newton was interested in science to the exclusion of romance.

Table 4.4 shows how I would explain Newton's personality. I think Newton's strong need for cognition (which falls under the basic desire for curiosity) motivated his intellectual nature. Thinking was its own reward; he intrinsically

loved intellectual activity. Newton organized his life to satisfy his need to think –
for example, he became a professor and lived alone with few distractions.

Curiosity motivates people to care about their ideas. Newton valued his
ideas so strongly he wrote them down in his notebook so as not to forget them. He
thought so deeply about science that he often paid little attention to the mundane
events going on around him.

The fact that Newton accepted a life alone with little romance can be explained
by weak-intensity basic desires for both romance and social contact. If he had had
average intensity basic desires for romance or social contact, he would not have
tolerated such a lifestyle. The fact that he published little suggests an above-average
fear of criticism (which falls under the need for acceptance). His above-average
need for acceptance may have been traceable to his having been abandoned as a
child, or perhaps he was just born that way.

Romantic

Psychodynamics: Unconsciously uses sex to compensate for the love parents had
withheld during childhood.
Motivation analysis: Consciously motivated by an intrinsic valuation of sex.

People with very strong strivings for sex show a Romantic Personality Type. They
are always thinking about sex and romance, which is their reason for being. They
are attracted to many potential partners and are not inclined to resist temptation.
They are vigilant to sexual cues given off by others. As Katherine Hepburn once
said of the great actor John Barrymore, he was utterly incapable of letting a girl
walk by without grabbing some part of her anatomy (Gill, 2002, p. 90).

Peggy Guggenheim, the wealthy benefactor and collector of modern art,
prided herself on her sexual "vitality" and her "passion." She thought better of
people who showed romantic passion than those who showed less "life." She valued
romance above nearly everything else. Her strong striving for romance motivated
her to have many sexual partners throughout much of her life. When asked, "How
many husbands have you had?" she replied, "Do you mean my own, or other
people's?" (Gill, 2002, p. 80). According to her autobiography, where she recorded
and probably exaggerated her sexual exploits, she had two real husbands, innu-
merable lovers, and one great love. She experienced between three and seventeen
abortions; her biographers differ on the exact number.

Guggenheim had an unhappy childhood: Her parents spent long periods
apart. Her mother hired nannies to raise her after her father died in the sinking of
the luxury liner *Titanic*. She inherited wealth and moved to Europe but was forced

Table 4.5. Peggy Guggenheim (Type: Romantic)*		
Strong	**Average**	**Weak**
Romance	Acceptance	Family
Saving	Curiosity	Honor
Status	Eating	Idealism
	Independence	
	Order	
	Physical Activity	
	Power	
	Social Contact	
	Tranquility	
	Vengeance	

* Based on a biography by Gill (2002).

to return to New York when World War II broke out. While living in New York, she started an influential gallery for modern art and created an important forum for young artists. She "supported three of the most important art movements of the last hundred years: cubism, surrealism, and abstract expressionism" (Gill, 2002, p. xv).

Table 4.5 shows how the sixteen basic desires might explain Peggy Guggenheim's personality. She had a very strong desire for romance: Sex played a significant role in her self-concept. She spent considerable time pursing romance and used her position as a benefactor of art to gain access to artists as potential lovers.

Some experts say that promiscuity shows a lack of self-respect and, therefore, is a neurotic trait. Promiscuous people may be trying to compensate for the love their parents never gave them when they were children. Biographer Anton Gill wrote that Guggenheim used sex to fulfill a need to be loved and to bolster her self-esteem. He suggested further that Guggenheim sought sex with many artists because it gave her an unconscious psychological sense of acquiring their creativity, which she lacked.

In contrast, I suspect that Guggenheim's promiscuity was driven by an unusually strong passion for sex. When people have a strong appetite, they eat many different foods; when they have a strong sex drive, they have many different partners. Such was the case with Peggy Guggenheim. Further, she did not value the traditional morals that might have inhibited promiscuity.

Some experts think there must be more to understanding promiscuity than a strong sex drive and weak traditional morals. Existential psychologist Rollo May (1969), for example, suggested that promiscuity reflects an inability to relate to people except superficially. In his book *Love and Will*, May (1969) distinguished Eros from libido. *Eros* is the desire to unite, create, and love a partner, whereas *libido* is a desire for release. Relationships based on Eros are fulfilling and spiritually satisfying, whereas those based only on sex are purely physical and unfulfilling. May believed that in a purely sexual relationship, it is only a matter of time before the partners experience feelings of emptiness.

I don't think Guggenheim considered her promiscuity a venture into emptiness – on the contrary, sex was one of the few things that was meaningful to her. She didn't write a diary of her sexual exploits to reveal existential angst but to brag about her passionate nature; she was asserting the meaning in her life, not lamenting the absence of meaning.

Some experts think it simplistic or circular reasoning to say that Guggenheim was promiscuous because of a strong sex drive. They assume that "something must be wrong" with people who go from lover to lover without a deeper commitment. They know they would experience promiscuous relationships as meaningless, so they are baffled as to why anybody would embrace such a lifestyle.

Yet I am suggesting the opposite of what experts such as Rollo May say. People like May need a monogamous relationship to experience life as meaningful, but people like Guggenheim find meaning in sexual passion. Rollo May confused individuality with abnormality.

Loner

> *Behaviorism:* Lacks social skills.
> *Psychodynamics:* Multiple causes: abnormal development, schizoid personality traits, distrust of others, unconscious hostility, fear of rejection.
> *Motivation analysis:* Consciously motivated by an intrinsic valuation of solitude.

Loners (also called private people) intrinsically value solitude. Solitude can be peaceful, quiet, and may facilitate harmony with the environment. It provides an opportunity to experience life at a relaxed pace with few distractions. In solitude some people can derive pleasure from simple things such as admiring the beauty of nature, singing to oneself, reading a good book, or observing animals carefully.

Solitude provides opportunities to take stock of our experiences and lives. Naturalist Henry David Thoreau and pole explorer Richard E. Byrd kept diaries to help them reflect and digest their experiences. Religious retreats, such as monasteries, use solitude as a place for meditation and spiritual experiences. Some people view life in a retreat as a positive opportunity to live spiritually.

Many loners show traits that discourage other people from getting to know them (Tressler, 1937). They may be abrupt, contemptuous, critical of others, slow to praise or flatter people, self-centered, grouchy, or show little interest in what others have to say. They may make light of other people's problems. They may not get to know people very well or may rarely smile or monopolize conversations.

We can distinguish privacy from insecurity. Whereas the private person or loner intrinsically dislikes socializing, perhaps finding it burdensome, the insecure person would like to socialize more but is afraid of rejection. Motivation analysis holds that a weak basic desire for social contact motivates privacy but that a strong basic desire for acceptance motivates insecurity.

Henry David Thoreau (1817–1862), the American writer and naturalist, organized his life around his needs for solitude and tranquility. He once said that the order of things should be reversed – the seventh day should be man's day of toil, and the other six days his Sabbath for taking care of the soul.

Thoreau was an independent and curious person. As a young man, he taught schoolchildren, but he quit to establish his own school rather than comply with the school board's requirement that he use corporal punishment. He later quit teaching to become a naturalist and a writer. He loved to study nature, and he liked to read.

In 1845 Thoreau built a small-framed house on the shores of Walden Pond, where he lived for two years as a hermit, studying nature. He found he could live so simply that in six weeks of manual labor he could earn the money he needed for a year. He was a vegetarian and ate plainly. He did not drink wine or smoke or use tobacco. He dressed plainly.

Thoreau was loyal to his parents, even choosing to live with them after he moved from Walden Pond. He was patriotic, responsible, honest, and fair. He supported abolitionists and wrote the essay, "Civil Disobedience," regarding his opposition to slavery.

Table 4.6 shows how the sixteen basic desires might explain Thoreau's personality. His very weak-intensity basic desire for social contact motivated him to place a high value on solitude. He refused invitations to dinner parties, saying they are a waste of time. He had few friends. He also did not marry (possibly motivated by a weak basic desire for romance compounded with his weak basic desire for social contact).

Psychodynamic theorists have regarded the desire to socialize as a natural part of normal development. They have suggested that loners fear rejection, are victims of overprotective parents, harbor unconscious hostility, distrust people, or may lack social skills. White & Watt (1973, p. 178) suggested that social isolation is caused by abnormal development. Cameron (1963, pp. 647–8) suggested that

Table 4.6. Henry David Thoreau (Type: Loner)*

Strong	Average	Weak
Honor	Acceptance	Romance
Independence	Curiosity	Social Contact
Idealism	Eating	Status
	Family	Tranquility
	Order	
	Physical Activity	
	Power	
	Saving	
	Vengeance	

* Based on biography by Harding (1965).

loners have a "schizoid personality" disorder characterized by abnormal distrust-fulness of others.

In contrast, motivation analysis implies that many loners are normal people who happen to value solitude. Everybody regulates the amount of social contact they experience based on how strongly they intrinsically value social experiences versus solitude. Sometimes we need to be with others, but sometimes we need to be alone. Sociable people, who need to be with others much more often than the average person, acquire habits that attract people. Loners, who need to be alone much more often than the average person, acquire habits that repel people. Some loners may be mentally ill, of course, but the same can be said of some gregarious people (such as gregarious con men). The point is that the personality trait of being a loner is caused by individual variations in normal motives and values, not by schizophrenia or schizophrenic-like processes.

Ascetic

Psychodynamics: Unconsciously motivated by self-destructiveness.
Motivation analysis: Consciously motivated by extreme valuation of personal honor.

The word *asceticism* originated in reference to the arduous physical training under-taken by Greek athletes and warriors. Today the word means the endurance of bodily deprivations for spiritual purposes. In order to make a statement that spirit is more important than body, ascetics reject worldly comforts. They may live, for example, within a restricted area such as a cell, cave, or monastery. They may never have sex, not even once in their lives. They may carry weights, cut their bodies, and endure discomforts such as sitting on hard chairs without cushions or dispensing with fire when it is cold outside. They eat simple foods, such as barley and water, and they dress plainly. They deny themselves all amusements such as dancing, art, games, and parties. They do not socialize. Some ascetics break family ties and live alone. They renounce all ambitions. Acts of self-debasement include self-flogging, inflicting pain on their bodies, and living in filth.

Christian asceticism is well known in America. Monks and nuns live separate from society, wear simple clothes, and take vows of celibacy. Many of the Christian saints were ascetics.

Saint Benedict (480–547) was one of the Catholic Church's most influential figures regarding monastic life. Disgusted by Rome's vices, Benedict left the city to live as a hermit alone in a cave. His gift for prophecy, performance of miracles, and reputation for piety attracted disciples eager to become monks. He assumed leadership of a monastery at Subiaco, and he subsequently founded the monastery at Monte Cassino. The latter monastery became one of the most influential retreats in the history of Christendom.

Saint Benedict wrote the *Rules*, which is a manual spelling out the duties of monks and the organization of monastic life. When the Lombards sacked Monte Cassino, the monks had advance warning and fled to Rome with a copy of Benedict's *Rules*. Saint Benedict's *Rules* became an influential guide for life within Christian monasteries throughout the world.

Psychologists have generally regarded loners as possibly disturbed. Yet when Benedict left Rome to live in a cave, some people were so inspired by his idea of retreat they just had to join him in his cave. These people didn't think, "Poor Benedict can't make it in the big city and has crawled into a cave to lick his wounds. Wonder what his diagnosis is?" Instead they thought, "Wow! What a great idea Benedict has. Live in a cave where you can pursue spirituality and not be distracted by the superficiality of the big city." Most people couldn't stand living in a cave, but for some who value their spirituality very highly, it is the only way to live.

Psychiatrist Karl Menninger (1938) wrote that asceticism is a form of self-destruction. Menninger's theory implies that Saint Benedict lived in a cave because he was guilt ridden and unconsciously thought he was unworthy of pleasure.

Table 4.7 shows how the sixteen basic desires might explain Saint Benedict's personality. Benedict's very strong desire for honor may have motivated him to value moral discipline. Benedict sought to deny himself the pleasures of the flesh in order to make a value statement that spirit is more important than body. Saint Benedict's strong need for honor also motivated his honesty and moral behavior.

Whereas people with a high need for status proudly seek wealth and fame, those with a weak need for status humbly reject wealth and fame. Saint Benedict's

Table 4.7. Saint Benedict (Type: Ascetic)*		
Strong	Average	Weak
Honor	Acceptance	Family
	Curiosity	Romance
	Eating	Social Contact
	Idealism	Status
	Independence	
	Order	
	Physical Activity	
	Power	
	Saving	
	Tranquility	
	Vengeance	

* Based on the biography by McCann (1958).

weak desire for status motivated him to dress and live plainly, reject worldly wealth, and ignore what others thought of him for living like a hermit.

Conclusions

The sixteen basic desires potentially explain personality types as repeated efforts to gratify very strong and very weak basic desires. Very strong basic desires for power, vengeance, idealism, curiosity, romance, and honor, respectively, motivate people to develop the personality types called workaholic, competitor, humanitarian, thinker, romantic, and ascetic. Very weak basic desires for social contact motivate people to become loners. The sixteen basic desires potentially explain personality type without consideration of unconscious psychodynamics.

These seven personality types are normal even though some experts have thought them abnormal. Psychodynamic experts have argued that many of these personality traits are caused by unconscious and often irrational mental forces. They have claimed that all or most of these traits are motivated by anxiety reduction. I consider these views erroneous. The seven personality types are affirmations of the individual's values (such as achievement, winning, social justice, knowledge, sensuality, privacy, and spirituality). The values are not unconscious, and individuals are not defensive about acknowledging them. Since the values alone explain personality in greater detail than do efforts at "deeper" psychodynamic analysis, I explain personality types as value assertion rather than as an expression of unconscious psychodynamics.

The case for considering these personality types to be normal is substantial. The personality types help people fulfill their individual nature. People experience their personality types as a meaningful part of their life. These individuals exhibit normal psychological functions such as normal information processing, rational thinking, memory, and perception. The individuals are not depressed, anxious, hyperactive, irrational, delusional, or hallucinatory. The case for abnormality is based on the idea that many people would be unhappy living such lifestyles, or that everyone would be happier living some other lifestyle. These ideas are invalid value judgments that confuse individuality for abnormality. Maybe you or I would be unhappy living some of these lifestyles, but that does not mean that most individuals with these personality types are particularly unhappy relative to the average person.

Although this chapter demonstrates the conceptual significance of the sixteen basic desires for understanding personality types, none of the people discussed actually had been assessed on the sixteen basic desires. This chapter is a statement of the conceptual relevance of the sixteen basic desires for potentially explaining personality. The chapter does not provide scientific evidence for the validity of motivation analysis. Such evidence was summarized in Chapter 2. Since the case examples in subsequent chapters are about people who completed the RMP, those chapters provide empirical evidence of the utility of the applications of motivation analysis.

5 Overcoming Personal Troubles

We will consider the implications of the sixteen basic desires for coaching/ counseling people to overcome personal troubles. These problems can cause significant unhappiness for months or even years, but are they mild mental illnesses? Do personal troubles have anything to do with "real" mental illnesses such as Schizophrenia or Mania? Freud (1951/1901) thought so, but I disagree.

Freud believed that personal troubles are mild mental illness. He supported this belief with three assertions, each of which I challenge. Freud held that the need to manage anxiety causes both mental illnesses and personal troubles and speculated that both personal troubles and mental illnesses are expressions of unconscious childhood experiences. He suggested that both personal troubles and mental illnesses are best resolved by coming to grip with unconscious childhood feelings.

In contrast, I reject Freud's hypothesis that personal troubles are the results of efforts to manage anxiety. I think any of the sixteen basic desires may be implicated as motivators of various personal troubles in different people. A child with failing grades in school may be motivated by a weak need for curiosity, not anxiety. A businessman passed over because his superiors do not trust him may be motivated by a weak need for honor, not anxiety. Although Freud may have correctly noticed that anxiety management is prominent in certain mental illnesses, he erred in assuming that anxiety management is the primary motive underlying personal troubles.

I question the Freudian strategy of trying to resolve the personal troubles of adults by better understanding how they felt when they were children. Analysis of childhood are time-consuming, expensive, often invalid, and rarely necessary for resolving personal troubles. We need to study childhood so we can help children and parents, not to help adults solve problems.

The best strategy for resolving personal troubles is to understand how individuals are mismatched to their current careers or mates. Partners with different sex drives, for example, may quarrel repeatedly over how often they should have sex. After they analyze their childhoods and conclude that their different sex drives originated from different parental attitudes, they still have to come to terms with their incompatible sex drives. It might help them a little to think they understand the origin of their differences, but this understanding often is insufficient to solve their current problems.

In motivation analysis, we analyze the conflicts as they exist today, and we search for compromises and solutions consistent with people's principal values. We spend little time worrying about how childhood experiences might have determined adult values or conflicts. *Instead of asking clients about their childhoods, counselors should ask them about their motives and values.* Instead of assuming that anxiety from unresolved childhood conflicts is motivating their client's troubles, counselors should evaluate their client's sixteen basic desires. Instead of helping clients clarify childhood feelings toward parents, counselors should help them clarify how their sixteen basic desires are frustrated by their current life experiences. Often personal problems are caused by a conflict of values between the individual and current work and home situations, or when an individual's needs are frustrated and unfulfilled.

Joe is a good example of a person whose stress at work was motivated by a conflict of values. Joe supervised a blue-collar worker who had a child with complex disabilities needing chronic medical care. Joe's boss wanted him to fire the blue-collar worker to cut the company's health insurance costs, but Joe considered it wrong to punish an employee for parenting a child with complex medical needs. The stress Joe experienced at work arose from a conflict of values (Joe's honor versus his boss's expedience). Since Joe has a strong basic desire for honor, he needs to work for a company that rewards people with high ethical standards. Joe's solution is to change jobs or supervisors, not to analyze his childhood.

Sam provides another example of how conflicts of values can motivate personal problems. Sam was a corporate manager who spent little time with his people and was not given to small talk. In Sam's mind, he was doing a good job because he was focused on his company's objectives and did not waste time at the water cooler or holding the hands of the people he supervised. Some of Sam's employees, however, interpreted Sam's abruptness as meaning he did not care about them; others thought he was arrogant and regarded the workers as beneath him. Sam had a weak basic desire for social contact that motivated him to be impatient with small talk and to spend a lot of time alone in his office. His strong privacy needs were in conflict with his role as a supervisor. Sam needed to make a conscious effort to spend more time with his workers, or perhaps he should have found work in a nonsupervisory capacity.

Since many personal problems arise from conflicts of values between an individual and his or her work or home situation, counselors should teach people how to make smart choices so they can fulfill their natures and avoid future problems. Choose the right career or job, and you will not need a counselor to teach you to blame problems at work on your childhood.

If you want to understand how your motives and values might be causing your current personal troubles, you can take the RMP. Your strongest and weakest basic desires are the ones most likely to motivate any personal problems you might have. Average-intensity desires are easily gratified and rarely motivate personal troubles. A person with an average-intensity need for curiosity, for example, can get along with many supervisors, but a highly curious person will get along best with supervisors who appreciate intellectuals. Similarly, a person with an average need for tranquility can get along with many supervisors, but a constant worrier will get along best with a supervisor who avoids risk (which falls under a high need for tranquility).

Job coaching is a short-term method of helping people resolve personal problems or lessen negative consequences. Here are some examples of how job coaches have used the RMP to help people with personal troubles.

What Makes Judy a Lady Boxer?

Judy, age 36, wanted to understand what motivated her to become a champion lady boxer. The results of her RMP are presented in Table 5.1. According to these results, Judy's boxing gratified her strong basic desires for physical activity and vengeance acting in combination. She told me that she really enjoys hitting other women, which falls under a strong basic desire for vengeance, and the boxing ring was the only socially appropriate place where she could do this.

Since some people regard lady boxing in a negative light, I asked Judy what she thought of this attitude. She said she likes the negative attention because it makes her feel like a rebel. Her remarks were consistent with her weak basic desire for status, which can motivate people to thumb their nose at propriety. Since boxing is a sport associated with the lower social classes, Judy chose boxing in part to assert her identification with the ordinary fellow and in part to thumb her nose at how society thinks a lady should behave.

I asked Judy if she worried about getting hurt in the ring. She replied, "I have zero fear and a high tolerance for pain." If she were otherwise, I suppose, she probably could not have enjoyed boxing to anywhere near the degree that she did. On the RMP, fearlessness and pain insensitivity both fall under a weak basic desire for tranquility.

Table 5.1. The RMP for Judy

Strong	Average	Weak
Physical Activity	Acceptance	Status
Vengeance	Curiosity	Tranquility
Eating	Family	
Romance	Honor	
	Idealism	
	Independence	
	Order	
	Power	
	Saving	
	Social Contact	

By participating in a physically demanding sport like boxing, Judy can eat well without putting on much weight. She said she did not want to gain weight because she enjoyed romance, had an active sex life, and wanted to stay maximally attractive to potential partners.

Judy's parents did not like her being a boxer: Judy admitted that part of her motivation was to get back at them for things they did to her when she was younger. Conventional wisdom would say that Judy's anger toward her parents is at the root of her choice to be a boxer. Traditional counselors might hope that by helping Judy better resolve her anger toward her parents, she would embrace a less competitive and aggressive lifestyle going forward. In contrast, motivation analysis implies that Judy intrinsically values vengeance. A strong basic desire for vengeance is not about bottled-up childhood anger, as Freudians say, but rather a genetically initiated desire to experience confrontation at a higher-than-average rate. *Judy isn't vengeful because she is angry at her parents; she is angry at her parents because she is vengeful.* Judy may be confrontational her entire life because she loves and experiences winning as meaningful.

Why Kenneth Can't Sell

Ken was a 40 year-old married businessman living in India. He sought job coaching from Mike Jay because he was not attracting enough customers to his business of spirituality training for corporate executives. He wanted to know what he could do to be a better salesperson and build his business.

The results of Ken's RMP, which are shown in Table 5.2, revealed three motives that limited his effectiveness as a salesperson: A weak basic desire for social contact, a strong basic desire for acceptance, and a weak basic desire for status.

Table 5.2. The RMP for Kenneth*		
Strong	**Average**	**Weak**
Acceptance	Curiosity	Eating
Saving	Family	Honor
Tranquility	Idealism	Independence
	Power	Order
	Vengeance	Physical Activity
		Social Contact
		Status

* Need for Beauty (not shown) is substituted for Romance on the business applications of the RMP.

Effective salespeople are extroverts – friendly, likeable, and good at small talk. Ken, however, was an introvert (which falls under a weak basic desire for social contact). He was abrupt with potential customers because he was hoping to terminate the interaction as quickly as possible. It is difficult to sell to people when they sense that you are uncomfortable being with them.

Behaviorists might teach Ken social skills in order to improve his interactions with potential customers. Although Ken would quickly learn such skills, it would be only a matter of time before he would revert back to being an introvert. *Ken wasn't an introvert because he lacked skills; Ken lacked social skills because he was an introvert. Ken intrinsically valued solitude.*

Effective salespeople have the self-confidence needed to shrug off the rejection of one customer and move on to the next. Ken, however, tended to dwell on rejection (which falls under a strong need for acceptance). He was insecure and lacked self-confidence. People who fear rejection hold back effort because failure hurts less when they do not try. Ken, for example, did not ask people directly for their business because he was afraid they would turn him down.

Effective salespeople give potential customers the right amount of deference based on the customer's status. Ken, however, was inattentive to status (which falls under a weak basic desire for status). Some customers felt offended when he did not give them the special attention they thought was their due. Others felt uncomfortable because he gave them more deference than they thought they deserved.

Ken's weak basic desire for independence may have motivated his interest in spirituality. He valued oneness and mystical experience and was interested in metaphysics and touchy-feely experiences. Although he did not enjoy ordinary social intercourse (because of his weak basic desire for social contact), he highly valued close relationships in which he felt a spiritual connection (because of his weak basic desire for independence).

Table 5.3. The RMP for Tom*		
Strong	**Average**	**Weak**
Honor	Curiosity	Acceptance
Physical Activity	Idealism	Eating
	Power	Family
	Independence	Saving
	Order	Tranquility
	Social Contact	Vengeance
	Status	

* Need for Beauty (not shown) is substituted for Romance on the business applications of the RMP.

Since the results of Ken's RMP showed that he was motivated to be a spiritual trainer but not a salesperson, Coach Mike Jay advised Ken to build a business team to complement his interests. Ken hired a salesperson and a good administrative assistant. Ken was advised to concentrate on what he loves to do, training business executives in spirituality.

Trapped by Success

Tom was a 58-year-old man who owned a successful real estate business. Although he had a significant income, Tom sought coaching because he felt unfulfilled. Work that used to be challenging and exciting had become boring. Tom was thinking of starting a new business, but he worried about the risk — at age 58, an unsuccessful business venture could consume his nest egg and ruin his retirement years. Should he play it safe and retire now, with all the money he needs, or should he risk his nest egg on a new business adventure?

Tom sought the advice of master coach Mike Jay, who administered the RMP to help Tom make smart decisions on how to proceed with the rest of his life. As shown in Table 5.3, Tom had an unusually high number of basic desires that departed from the benchmark. Tom had a zest for life because he cared about more things more deeply than most people do.

Tom had an adventurous spirit. His weak basic desire for tranquility motivated him to need risk and excitement in order to feel alive. His weak need for acceptance motivated the self-confidence necessary to try new ventures. Tom's safe and successful real estate business frustrated his adventurous nature, and this conflict was at the root of the existential angst that had led him to seek coaching.

When people have jobs that do not satisfy their basic desires, they begin to wonder about the meaningfulness of their work. They may experience a vague

Table 5.4. The RMP for Rolf		
Strong	**Average**	**Weak**
Family	Acceptance	Social Contact
Power	Curiosity	
Physical Activity	Eating	
Saving	Honor	
	Idealism	
	Independence	
	Order	
	Romance	
	Status	
	Tranquility	
	Vengeance	

sense that something is missing without being able to put their finger on just what the problem is. Tom sought coaching because he wanted to start a new business, but at age 58 he could not afford to lose any money. He was trapped by his own past success. He anticipated the excitement of starting a new business venture, but he also realized that if he lost his money he might not have enough left for retirement. The results of the RMP helped Tom understand his existential angst.

Weak Leader

Rolf is the CEO of a medium-sized manufacturing company. His executives saw him as a "weak" leader, which bothered him. He sought coaching from Peter Boltersdorf to better understand his leadership style. The results of his RMP are shown in Table 5.4.

The basic desires most important for understanding leadership style are power, vengeance, and independence. People with a strong basic desire for power enjoy leadership roles and tend to be hard working, whereas those with a weak basic desire for power dislike leadership roles and tend to balance work with other areas of life. Since Rolf had a strong basic desire for power, he enjoyed being a CEO. At first he was happy working long hours, but when his children were growing up he wanted to spend more time with them. Rolf's strong basic desire for family was a "greater motive" than was his need for power. Rolf was usually fine when work dominated his life, but not when it interfered with his parenting role. (If Rolf had had a weak basic desire for power, he would have shunned working long hours at nearly all times in his life and would have resented whenever work interfered with leisure activities. Since he had a strong basic desire for power and an even stronger basic desire for family, he embraced hard work except for the one period in his life when it interfered with parenting.) Coach Boltersdorf suggested that Rolf hire an assistant to reduce his workload and give him time to spend with his children.

A strong basic desire for power motivates advice giving. When Rolf gave employees personal advice, many resented the intrusion. Rolf was slow to realize the resentment because he thought he was helping people. (See Chapter 7 for a discussion on how strong basic desires motivate personal "blind spots.") Since Rolf saw nearly everything as a problem that needs a solution, he expected his employees would appreciate his advice on solving their personal problems.

Rolf was perceived as a "weak" leader because he was conflict avoidant (which falls under a weak basic desire for vengeance). Rolf's RMP score for vengeance was at the very bottom of the average range, just above the cut-off score for weak. His below-average desire for vengeance motivated him to avoid confrontation.

Rolf's case reminded me of a friend, Jane, who became a university dean. Like Rolf, Jane was very ambitious but conflict avoidant. Her ambition drove her to move up the chain of command in university governance by making friends and avoiding confrontation, competition, and rivalries. When she got to the level of dean, her job required her to mediate conflicts. She had to confront people over poor spending habits or ineffective performances or ethical lapses. Jane experienced her job as stressful; she quit after only one year as university dean. She was perceived as a likeable but weak leader.

Slow to Make Decisions

Some experts distinguish between task-oriented versus process-oriented managers. Task-oriented managers favor quick decisions and getting the job done, whereas process-oriented managers lead by consensus. Process-oriented managers take the time necessary to consult with stakeholders, discuss diverse opinions, and build common ground before proceeding. Thus process-oriented managers tend to make decisions more slowly than do task-oriented managers.

Roland was the head of a sales team of 30 people working for a German grocer. His superiors complained that he took too much time making decisions. The company hired Peter Boltersdorf to coach Roland to make quicker decisions.

Table 5.5 shows the results of Roland's RMP. Roland liked to influence people (strong need for power), but he wanted the people reporting to him to buy into his agenda (weak basic desire for independence). Since it takes time to bring about a consensus, Roland was slow to make final decisions. Coach Boltersdorf

Table 5.5. The RMP for Roland*		
Strong	**Average**	**Weak**
Power	Family	Independence
Curiosity	Honor	Acceptance
Social Contact	Idealism	Eating
	Order	
	Physical Activity	
	Saving	
	Status	
	Tranquility	
	Vengeance	

* Need for Beauty (not shown) is substituted for Romance on the business applications of the RMP.

advised Roland that he needed to be more of a task-oriented manager to please his superiors.

According to Roland's RMP, he was motivationally well suited to head a sales team. His strong-intensity basic desire for social contact meant he knew how to ingratiate himself to customers so they would like him. His weak-intensity basic desire for acceptance motivated self-confidence so he could shrug off rejections and move on to the next customer. His average-intensity desire for status was sufficient for him to know that many high-status customers expected special attention.

Manager Can't Say No

Frank is a 37-year-old executive in charge of union negotiations at a German company. He sought coaching from Peter Boltersdorf because he had a strong tendency to please people. Frank was such a pleaser that he gave his union workers concessions he could not afford. He even approved his assistant's request to take a week off even though he needed her during that week.

Table 5.6 presents the results of Frank's RMP. Frank's strong basic desire for acceptance motivated him to seek approval from others and to be sensitive to criticism. He was afraid to say "no" to people because he feared they might dislike him.

Since Frank's tendency to please people was greatest when someone first approached him, coach Boltersdorf advised Frank to always respond, "I'll get back to you in 15 minutes." This gave Frank time to reflect on the merits of the request rather than to respond on impulse. Frank reported that the technique successfully

Table 5.6. The RMP for Frank*		
Strong	**Average**	**Weak**
Acceptance	Curiosity	Social Contact
Power	Eating	
Order	Family	
Status	Honor	
Tranquility	Idealism	
Vengeance	Independence	
	Physical Activity	
	Saving	

* Need for Beauty (not shown) is substituted for Romance
   on the business applications of the RMP.

lessened the adverse business consequences of his personality tendency to want to please people.

Unmet Intellectual Needs

Too much of the behavior shown by people with mental retardation is attributed to their having subaverage intelligence and not enough to their other human qualities (Reiss & Reiss, 2004). People with mental retardation sometimes have unmet needs because others tend to see only their mental retardation. In order to help assess these needs, I developed a special version of the RMP for people with mental retardation and developmental disabilities. The RMP/MRDD is completed by teachers and parents, who rate the motives and needs of individual adolescents or adults.

Martin was a 13 year-old boy who had mild mental retardation. His teacher completed the RMP/MRDD as one part of a school evaluation for special education services. As shown in Table 5.7, Martin had an above-average score for curiosity. This finding was consistent with the inquiring behavior Martin showed in the classroom and during psychological testing sessions. Martin asked a lot of questions in class, and he asked an unusual number of questions during the testing sessions. When the school psychologist showed Martin a picture of a hand with one fingernail missing, for example, Martin asked if this could really happen to people. When asked to define the word "alphabet," he answered correctly and then asked who invented the alphabet. When he could not identify the important part missing in a picture in a supermarket shelf, he was still puzzling about this missing part two days later.

Martin demonstrated significant intellectual curiosity in the context of mental retardation. He was a slow learner, but he had a thirst for knowledge. Yet people

Table 5.7. The RMP/MRDD for Martin*		
Strong	**Average**	**Weak**
Curiosity	Independence	Order
	Honor	Idealism
	Physical Activity	Social Contact
	Status	
	Vengeance	
	Acceptance	
	Tranquility	

* Because of "method variance" (differences in the information
obtained from self-report versus ratings made by others), some
of the basic desires assessed by the MR/DD version differ from
those assessed in the self-report RMP.

tended to ignore his intellectual needs because of his subaverage intelligence. If this were to continue, Martin might experience significant unhappiness.

In an effort to meet the intellectual needs of people with MRDD, Tom Fish at The Ohio State University Nisonger Center has created a national chain of book clubs called, "The Next Chapter Book Club" (Fish et al., 2006). People with MRDD meet at local coffee shops or bookstores to read a book and to socialize. Since many book club members cannot read, volunteers read for them while they repeat the words. The book clubs provide an uncommon opportunity for people like Martin to experience the joy of intellectual stimulation. They are extremely popular with individuals and parents.

Hospice Counseling

Dr. Mary Ellen Milos demonstrated an innovative application of the RMP to counseling John, a 61-year-old man dying of cancer. Based on the construct of value-based happiness (Reiss, 2000a), Dr. Milos helped John have meaningful experiences in his last days. Here are some of the highlights of Dr. Milos's case consultation.

- Since John's RMP showed a strong-intensity basic desire for honor, Dr. Milos arranged for twenty-four people to write him a letter commenting on their observations of his honor and then had the letters bound in a scrapbook.
- Since John had a strong-intensity need for family, arrangements were made for John to spend quality time with his family.
- Since John had a strong-intensity desire for romance, a romantic dinner with his wife was arranged.

- Since John was religious and had a strong-intensity need for social contact, his close friends were invited to pray with him.

Both John and his family rated the experience very positively.

Conclusions

Motivation analysis can be helpful when analyzing the personal problems of men-tally healthy people. Generally, the most common causes of personal problems are unfulfilled basic desires or a conflict of values at home or work. The following three-step method is used when coaching people who have personal problems.

> **Step 1. Describe the nature of the individual's personal problem for which counseling/coaching is sought.** Examples: Judy wanted to know why she had chosen to become a lady boxer. Kenneth had poor results as a salesperson. At age 58 Tom had become bored by his work and was wondering if he should start new businesses. Rolf was perceived as a weak leader. Roland's superi-ors thought he was too slow when making decisions. Frank was a pleaser with an unwanted reputation for being an easy touch. Martin was unhappy at school.

> **Step 2. Using the RMP, analyze how the stated personal problem is motivated by one or more of the individual's strong- or weak-intensity basic desires.** Examples: Since Judy intrinsically enjoyed hitting people, boxing offered her a rare, socially appropriate opportunity to do so. Ken couldn't sell because he had a weak basic desire for social contact and, thus, did not enjoy small talk. Tom had a need for adventure (weak basic desires for acceptance and tranquility) and, thus, was bored operating a successful business that was no longer risky. Rolf was conflict-avoidant (motivated by a below average desire for vengeance). Roland's strong basic desire for power motivated him to make decisions before he consulted with other people, but his weak basic desire for independence motivated him to consult with other people even though he already had made his decision. Frank's strong basic desires for acceptance and vengeance moti-vated him to please everybody and then become angry for being such an easy touch. Martin was intellectually curious and yet had mental retardation.

> **Step 3. Develop a practical plan for resolving the personal problem, taking into account the individual's RMP.** Examples: Judy was advised that she finds meaning in being a champion lady boxer because this activity satisfied her strong basic desire for vengeance. Kenneth was advised to build a business team and sales force that complemented his interests. Tom was advised that he faced an existential choice in which he would be happier starting a new business but not if the business failed. Rolf was advised that he is perceived as a "weak"

leader because he is conflict-avoidant, not because he wanted to take time off to be with his family. Roland was advised that his need for interdependence is annoying his bosses by causing him to make decisions more slowly than they want. Frank was advised to delay making decisions so he does not act on his impulse to please people. Martin's parents were advised to gratify Martin's strong basic desire for curiosity despite his mental retardation.

6 Six Reasons for Adolescent Underachievement

When students do poorly in middle or high school, their parents wonder what went wrong. They search for explanations, but sometimes none is apparent. Their child may have been an average or model student when he or she unexpectedly brought home failing grades, stopped turning in homework, started talking back to teachers, ran away, or befriended the wrong crowd. Some parents reach wits' end trying to figure out what happened to cause such behavior.

Harvey P. Mandel and Sander I. Marcus (1995) presented a compelling analysis of adolescent underachievement. Based on work with thousands of underachievers, they concluded that "Underachievers are, in fact, highly motivated – in directions other than getting good grades. And finding out precisely where their motivation lies is the key to helping them turn around and become achievers at school"(p. 3).

I will discuss six common motivational reasons for underachievement, each of which can be identified based on standardized test scores on the Reiss School Motivation Profile. Four of the six reasons are normal; only two are possible symptoms of a psychological disorder. In saying that underachievement is often the result of normal motivational forces, I am not saying that it is permissible for adolescents to get failing grades in school; rather, I am saying that the solution is not therapy for misdiagnosed or nonexistent disorders.

By definition, underachievement refers to a chronic discrepancy between one's overall performance and one's potential to perform. Adolescent underachievers obtain grades far below their potential.

Psychodynamics of Underachievement

Adolescence is a time when the teenager's desire for independence is frustrated. Adolescents want to be independent adults, but they still need their parents for economic support. Teenagers sometimes express frustration by engaging in activities to spite their parents such as running away, talking disrespectfully, trashing the parents' values, getting poor grades, or dating people of whom the parents disapprove.

Psychodynamic experts have suggested a number of factors in scholastic underachievement (Rimm, 1986; White & Watt, 1973). These include overprotective parents who frustrate the child's natural desire for independence; sibling rivalry, which supposedly contributes to the teen's underlying rebelliousness; and parents who fight with each other or divorce. Other possible psychodynamic factors include poor self-concept, unrealistic aspiration levels, and unconscious guilt(feeling unworthy of success).

Learning Disorders

What was called "underachievement" in the 1950s was called "learning disabilities" in the 1960s. The idea was that anytime a student performs below his or her potential, the student must have some kind of learning disability to account for the discrepancy. In the 1990s, Attention-Deficit Hyperactivity Disorder (ADHD) became a common diagnosis for students with learning problems. ADHD is considered to be a disorder of inattentiveness and sloppiness and is treated with stimulant medications such as Ritalin. Although Ritalin works (e.g., Gimpel et al., 2005), some experts think it is overprescribed (e.g., Rafalovich, 2005).

I believe that learning disabilities and ADHD are real disorders that explain underachievement for some children. I also believe they are overdiagnosed. Many children are inattentive in school simply because they are bored, so that a normal lack of intellectual curiosity is sometimes misdiagnosed as ADHD. Some children are diagnosed because they are sloppy and forgetful, which are normal signs of a weak basic desire for order. Many professionals tend to diagnose/label everybody who is having a problem in school, which results in significant overdiagnosis of learning disorders and ADHD. Often the causes of underachievement in school are motivational and unrelated to any "disorder" or disability.

Intrinsic and Extrinsic Motivation

Stanford University social psychologist Mark Lepper has blamed the schools for the many students who underachieve (Lepper, Corpus, & Lyengar, 2005). Lepper believes that students are born with the potential to become lifelong learners, but our educational system turns learning into a rat race for gold stars, grades, and other extrinsic rewards. In schools the natural joy of learning is replaced with the drudgery of working for grades and diplomas. If schools would educate students without tests, grades, and deadlines, the students' natural curiosity would flourish, and they would learn much more than they do now.

Author Alfie Kohn (1993) asserted:

All of us start out in life intensely fascinated by the world around us and inclined to explore it without any extrinsic inducement. . . . Most American schools marinate students in behaviorism, so the result, unsurprisingly, is that children's intrinsic motivation drains away. They typically become more and more extrinsically oriented as they get older and progress through elementary school. (p. 91)

When they first get to school, they are endlessly fascinated by the world. They are filled with delight by their newfound ability to write their names in huge shaky letters, to count everything in sight. . . . By the time the last bell has been rung, the spell has been broken. . . . They count the minutes before the end of the period, the days left before the weekend. . . . "Do we have to know this?," they ask. (p. 142)

The Lepper–Kohn thesis that human beings are born with the potential to enjoy high school is based on misunderstandings of human motivation. The fact that babies explore their environment does not suggest that adolescents are born with the potential to enjoy high school. We need to distinguish between exploratory and intellectual curiosity. *Exploratory curiosity (the attraction of novel stimuli) motivates both babies and adults to scan and roam their environments except when novelty arouses fear or a sense of strangeness. In contrast, the basic desire for intellectual curiosity (the need for cognition) motivates people to sustain thinking in the pursuit of knowledge and truth.* Intellectual curiosity is about abstraction, thinking, and problem solving. The results of our research on the sixteen basic desires found little connection between exploratory and intellectual curiosity.

The simplest way to appreciate the error in Kohn's analysis is to consider people you know who are explorers or thinkers. Notice that explorers are not necessarily thinkers, and thinkers are not necessarily explorers. From his assumption that babies are natural explorers, Kohn erroneously expected high school students to be thinkers and then asked, "What went wrong?" Kohn concluded that because many high school students are not thinkers, the problem must be that our schools are "marinated" in behaviorism.

Are students born intellectually curious? Is thinking fun? According to the theory of sixteen basic desires, thinking can be fun *up to a point*, after which continued thinking is frustrating. Individuals are born with different proclivities in how much they want to think (Cacioppo et al.,1996). *The key question for educators is how long most students can sustain thinking before they scream in frustration.* Although some students can sustain thinking for hours, others can sustain thinking for only a few minutes. Yet the school day is six to eight hours, for everyone. This suggests that school learning is naturally frustrating for many students. Teachers cannot stimulate the natural intellectual curiosity of their students because many of them naturally dislike thinking for more than a few minutes at a time. *The educational system is based on an invalid model of human nature, one that assumes all students have the potential to be intellectually curious for six to eight hours a day.*

Lepper and Kohn made the common error of overlooking intensity of motivation. Babies roam their environments for only a few minutes at a time. High school students are supposed to spend at least six hours a day in intellectual pursuits. It is a leap of logic to claim that because babies explore their environments for a few minutes at a time, high school students were born with the potential to enjoy intellectual pursuits for six hours or more each day.

Lepper and Kohn overlooked the question of the *amount* of curiosity that might be present at birth. If high school were only thirty minutes long each day, for example, many fewer students would complain about it. The problem isn't that our schools are marinated in behaviorism, but that the school day is too long for most students. Schools must provide many nonintellectual activities or their students would become even more bored and frustrated than they are today.[1]

Six Reasons for Underachievement

The Reiss School Motivation Profile (RSMP) is an application of the RMP to adolescents. The RSMP is used by guidance counselors and school psychologists to help assess scholastic underachievement, career interests, and other motivational issues. The RSMP can help schools identify normal reasons for underachievement and, thus, reduce the number of unnecessary diagnoses of learning disorders.

Paula Kavanaugh is a former guidance counselor at Hinsdale Central High School in Illinois. She administered the RSMP to forty-nine (33 boys and 16 girls) ninth-, tenth-, and eleventh-grade students (Kavanaugh & Reiss, 2003). The students had a grade point average in the bottom 10 percent of their class, exclusive of students in special education, and they had scored below average on the ACT standardized achievement tests.

Each student participated in the study in individual sessions of about forty-five minutes. Following a general conversation designed to relax the student and obtain background information, the student completed the RSMP self-report instrument. The results were mailed to the students along with an interpretive report. Interested parents called Paula Kavanaugh to discuss their child's test results.

The results of these assessments suggested six common motivational reasons for academic underachievement. Using standardized scores, the RSMP can evaluate which of these reasons applies to any particular student. Some students showed more than one reason. In total, forty-three of the forty-nine low-achieving students in the Kavanaugh sample had one or more of the following six motivational outcomes on the RSMP.

REASON NO. 1: LACK OF CURIOSITY. As previously noted, motivation analysis distinguishes between intelligence and intellectual curiosity. Intelligence is an indicator of one's ability to solve problems, whereas intellectual curiosity is an indicator of one's motivation (or need) to think. The two traits are only moderately correlated (Cacioppo et al., 1996). Some people are more intelligent than they are curious, and others are more curious than they are intelligent.

On the RSMP, the students with low grades in high school showed levels of intellectual curiosity significantly below the norm. These students disliked thinking. They had a general lack of intellectual curiosity, as opposed to a lack of curiosity in particular subjects. These students did poorly in science, for example, because they quickly became frustrated when asked to concentrate and sustain their thoughts on anything.

Incurious people dislike having to think. As one middle school student wondered, "Why can't they invent a pill I could take when I need to know something?" This student wanted to bypass frustrating learning processes and get right to the valuable result. He wanted to be knowledgeable, but he did not want to think.

Incurious people have the potential to value knowledge they can put to use. I recall a radio talk show host who criticized a president for lacking intellectual curiosity. The radio host was baffled by the president's detailed knowledge of politics. How can a president lacking in intellectual curiosity spend many hours studying the precinct-by-precinct results of the last several elections? Apparently, the radio host did not know that a person can lack intellectual curiosity but still show interest in practical knowledge. A weak need for intellectual curiosity predicts only that the president will not apply himself to the study of theoretical, impractical ideas. Ambition (which falls under a strong need for power) can motivate a president running for reelection to study precinct results for many long days.

Incurious students may be interested in relevant knowledge but not theoretical ideas. They might be interested in learning how to fix cars, for example, but not about the "big bang" that gave birth to the universe. They might be interested in learning how to shoot a basketball or make furniture, but not about the inauguration of President James Madison in 1809. They may complain the school curriculum is boring or irrelevant, but this is because they naturally dislike intellectual activities that require them to learn about anything they cannot put to use in their current life.

Although a weak basic desire for curiosity is an explanation for poor grades, it is not an excuse. These students lack natural motivation for school learning, but they can be motivated to learn with self-discipline, rewards, incentives, and good parenting. Parents should expect intellectually incurious students to complete their homework assignments on time, pass their tests, and graduate from high school.

Students who lack intellectual curiosity will struggle in school, but they may have the potential to excel in other areas of life such as business, industrial arts, performing arts, athletics, construction, and agriculture. They may do best in practical courses with hands-on instruction. They may need discipline and extrinsic incentives to earn decent grades.

REASON NO. 2: LACK OF AMBITION. On the RSMP, low scores for power indicate sub-average ambition. Unambitious students lack will and initiative and are viewed by others as laid-back or nondirective. They resist trying to influence other people; they may be onlookers who watch events unfold without trying to influence what happens.

A lack of ambition is unrelated to a lack of self-confidence. Unambitious students do not lack ambition because they are insecure; they lack ambition because they dislike expressions of will. Some are secure in the knowledge that they should not let their schooling or career interfere with their enjoyment of life.

These students underachieve because they do not apply themselves. They set modest goals and avoid challenging courses because they do not want to work hard. Unambitious students who are smart still may earn average or even above average grades, but only when they can do so without working hard.

Unambitious students may be willing to work at a moderate pace but no harder. Some teachers dismiss them as "unmotivated" or "lazy," but actually they are strongly motivated to avoid hard work and the influence of will. Compared to the average student, unambitious students place higher value on leisure and lower value on achieving.

When an unambitious student is pushed to work hard, the individual quits. Teachers and parents need to be careful in how much pressure they place on an unambitious student. Many unambitious students are willing to work at a moderate pace but rebel when pushed to work harder to achieve their full potential.

Since achievement is not one of their priorities, students who lack ambition may have a tendency to underachieve throughout life. Parents and counselors need to work with these children to set mutually agreed standards for study hours and for grades. These students may want to avoid the most challenging courses, but they may do fine in moderately challenging courses. What is "challenging" or "moderately challenging," of course, depends on the student's potential. Parents and teachers need to be careful not to think something must be wrong with students who lack drive. Nothing is wrong with unambitious students; they just have values different from those of high achievers.

REASON NO. 3: LOOKING FOR TROUBLE. Some students with high RSMP scores for vengeance are looking for trouble. They are out to prove themselves by fighting peers who challenge or frustrate them. They can get themselves into so much trouble it distracts them from their school work, leading to grades significantly below their capability.

Combativeness is an important cause of underachievement throughout life. Combative schoolchildren get into fights on the playground, school cafeteria, school hallways, or even in the classroom itself (Mandel, 1997). Combative adults fight so many battles with others they become distracted from what they need to do to get ahead. They have a tendency to make enemies of potential friends. Boys are more likely to be combative than are girls.

Students with a high need for vengeance are attentive to issues of insult, competition, and conflict. They are quick to take offense and to fight back. They are impressed with peers who win fights. In the Kavanaugh study, the students with a strong basic desire for vengeance were twice as likely as the average student to be referred to the principal's office for discipline violations.

Often combativeness is a personality trait resulting from normal variations in the basic desire for vengeance. Combativeness is normal when it is expressed as a burning desire for competition and winning or when it motivates self-defense. Combativeness may be abnormal, however, when it is expressed as persistent violence, brutality, or poorly managed anger, or when it is one part of a specific pattern of symptoms recognized as a mental disorder.

Parents and counselors should help combative students find socially appropriate outlets for their competitive nature. Many careers including sports, military life, and business reward competitiveness. Competive students may need to learn the difference between socially appropriate competition versus inappropriate or excessive confrontation or aggression. They may need to be taught the potentially severe damage to reputation or status that can result from inappropriate confrontations and outbursts. Some highly competitive students may benefit from anger management training.

REASON NO. 4: FEAR OF FAILURE. A number of scholarly papers have linked the fear of failure to underachievement (e.g., Atkinson & Feather, 1966; Hill, 1972). On the RSMP, high scores on the basic desire for acceptance indicate an above-average fear of failure and a lack of self-confidence. These students worry about not doing well on tests and may show test anxiety or give inconsistent effort. They may try hard on easy tasks but not on challenging tasks. They may become known for poor effort or for inconsistent effort.

Students who fear failure respond poorly to criticism. When teachers or parents criticize them, they may not hear what the teacher or parent is saying. Criticism may cause them to quit or at least perform poorly. Some underachieving students would improve their grades if their teachers or parents became less critical of them.

These students are at their best when parents and teachers stand behind and encourage them. They may respond to teachers who are nonjudgmental, and they work best in supportive, noncritical environments. They may need self-confidence. They should be encouraged to concentrate on their strengths, not their weaknesses. They need encouragement to give maximum effort.

Psychological feelings of insecurity are very common and, in that sense, are normal. Almost everybody feels insecure in one situation or another. A strong basic desire for acceptance (insecurity in the upper 20 percent of the population), however, is *sometimes* an indicator of a psychological disorder and need for counseling. School psychologists using the RSMP have noticed that many students referred to them score high on need for acceptance, indicating a possible lack of self-esteem.

REASON NO. 5: EXPEDIENCE. In the Kavanaugh study, twenty-one of forty-nine (42.9 percent) low-achieving students had significantly below-average RSMP scores for honor. These students placed lower-than-average value on morality and character. Low RSMP scores for honor are associated with expediency.

Expedient students see nothing wrong in breaking promises when better opportunities come along. Opportunism can lead to personal gains in the short run, but in the long run expedient people can pay a heavy price when others realize their opportunism. Expedient individuals may be loyal to others only to the extent that others are loyal to them. Their lack of loyalty to their superiors is perhaps the most important reason expedient adults have a tendency to "fall from grace" and, thus, underachieve.

Expedient students can be disloyal, irresponsible, and untrustworthy. They underachieve when they shirk their homework and other school responsibilities. Some teachers mark them down for being irresponsible or lacking in character.

These students need to learn that their teachers and parents are not going to let them get away with anything. They need to be taught that people who cheat are very likely to get caught eventually. They may need strict ethical limits. They will play by the rules when it is to their advantage to do so.

Expedience can result from normal variations in valuations of honor and character. Being out for Number 1 is common and is not indicative of a psychological disorder. In the context of a person who is aggressive, however, expedience can mean the absence of moral inhibition for aggression.

REASON NO. 6: SPONTANEITY. In the Kavanaugh study of low-achieving students, fourteen of forty-nine (28.6 percent) students had significantly below-average RSMP scores for order. A weak need for order motivates students to be spontaneous and disorganized.

Spontaneous people underachieve primarily because they have too many balls in the air. They do not complete what they begin: They tend to start a new task before they finish work on the old task. Their lack of attention to detail and general lack of planning and organization skills may hold them back, too. Some teachers mark them down for being careless. Teaching them organization or planning skills is largely unhelpful because they are disorganized by choice, not by a lack of skills. Since they value their ability to adjust to events as they arise, they have little use for plans.

Students with a low need for order can be creative. Although some teachers appreciate creativity, sometimes schools punish creativity. Further, many teachers tend to have a high need for order and tend to dismiss creative new ideas as strange or confused.

These students need to be taught to stay focused on a single course of action at a time. They need to learn to complete one task before moving on to the next. They also may need to learn how others perceive them. Some spontaneous students think they are impressing teachers by working on multiple projects, when in reality the teachers are thinking they are too scattered to do any one job well.

Popular Student

Tom Peters, age 12, was a seventh-grade student who was referred for evaluation because he was struggling in his Indiana public middle school. His mother blamed a lack of self-confidence, saying that Tom wants to do well in school but thinks he is "dumb." His mother said that Tom compares himself unfavorably to his older brother, who is a good student.

The school psychologist administered the RSMP and assessments of intelligence, achievement, and social and emotional functioning. The results suggested that Tom has average intelligence, average scores on standardized achievement tests, and no apparent social or emotional problems. His poor grades were not caused by a lack of intelligence, but rather by his not fulfilling his potential.

Tom is well liked, polite, and athletic. When asked about his personal strengths, he reported being a good athlete in a variety of sports. He said he

Table 6.1. RSMP for Tom Peters*		
Strong	**Average**	**Weak**
Family	Acceptance	Curiosity
Physical Activity	Honor	Independence
Social Contact	Idealism	
Status	Order	
	Power	
	Tranquility	
	Vengeance	

* Tom was not administered scales for Eating, Romance, and Saving.

has many friends and gets good grades when he tries hard. When asked about his personal weaknesses, Tom said that he gets too many Cs on his report card because he doesn't try hard enough. He said that some classes make his "brain hurt."

Table 6.1 shows the results of Tom's RSMP. These results suggested that Tom's participation in athletics satisfied his needs for physical activity and social contact.

The results of the RSMP did not support the mother's concern that Tom lacked self-confidence. Tom showed an average-intensity basic desire for acceptance, implying that his fear of failure was within normative ranges. The average scores for both acceptance and tranquility, moreover, ruled out test anxiety as a significant factor in his underachievement.

On the RSMP, Tom's score for curiosity fell in the bottom 2 percent of the population, which is very low and indicates that he hates thinking. Tom's grades were below his potential because he is not an intellectual, which was the real problem.

The school psychologist recommended that Tom continue in regular classes. His parents were encouraged to remind Tom often that he needed to maintain minimal grade point averages to maintain his eligibility for athletics.

Misdiagnosed Student

Kevin Smith, age 14, was an eighth-grade student who had recently moved to a new middle school in New York. The previous psychological report stated that he often failed to complete his school work and sometimes sat with his head down. The school psychologist attributed these behaviors to depression, which is a serious mental illness. He diagnosed Kevin as "emotionally disturbed" and recommended him for special education. The new school asked its own psychologist to review Kevin's case.

Table 6.2. RSMP for Kevin Smith*		
Strong	**Average**	**Weak**
Family	Acceptance	Curiosity
Physical Activity	Honor	Independence
Social Contact	Idealism	Power
Status	Order	
	Tranquility	
	Vengeance	

* Kevin was not administered scales for Eating, Romance, and
Saving.

The new school psychologist interviewed Kevin and his mother, asked Kevin's teachers to rate his social and emotional behavior, and administered the RSMP. The mother reported that Kevin had a good relationship with his parents and that he showed some sibling rivalry but still managed to play ball and games with his two older brothers. She viewed him as a basically happy student, a good athlete, but someone who never liked school. His career plan was to work in the family construction business.

As shown in Table 6.2, Kevin had average RSMP scores for the basic desires of acceptance, tranquility, and vengeance. He had a high score for social contact and for family. This pattern of results is inconsistent with a diagnosis of emotional disturbance. Further, his mother reported no significant symptoms of mental illness, and the teachers' ratings of social and emotional behavior were inconsistent with emotional problems. He appeared to be happy, and happy people are rarely mentally ill.

Kevin's poor achievement can be attributed to his lack of effort in school. He had weak basic desires for both curiosity and power, suggesting that he disliked intellectual activities and lacked ambition. Of the six common causes of underachievement assessed by the RSMP, Kevin showed two.

Kevin's eligibility for special education was revoked. The diagnosis of "emotionally disturbed" was found to be an error. Kevin was placed in regular classes where he belonged.

Violent Student

Although Gregory Izza's grades in school were barely passing, he was referred for evaluation because the police had found drawings and notes suggesting he was planning to explode a bomb in his middle school. Gregory was 13 at the time of referral.

Table 6.3. RSMP for Gregory Izza*		
Strong	**Average**	**Weak**
Acceptance	Family	Curiosity
Status	Independence	Honor
Tranquility	Power	Idealism
Vengeance	Physical Activity	Order
	Social Contact	

* Gregory was not administered scales for Eating, Romance, and Saving.

Table 6.3 shows the results of Gregory's RSMP. His score for vengeance fell in the upper 2 percent of the population, indicating potential for aggression. His score for status fell in the upper 10 percent of the population, suggesting that Gregory was seeking to feel important (perhaps by gaining attention). His very low scores for honor and idealism, both in the bottom 2 percent of the population, suggested that he lacked moral inhibition for his aggressive tendencies.

Gregory was a dangerous student – he was angry, looking for attention, and did not care at all about morals, fairness, or community. The primary factor limiting his potential for violence may have been a fear of hurting himself, which was suggested by his high score for tranquility. By building a bomb and leaving it in his school, however, Gregory may have figured he would be in a safe place when the bomb exploded. Had Gregory tested with a weak basic desire for tranquility, he would have been angry, seeking attention, immoral, not giving a hoot about fairness or community, and fearless. In other words, he would have been even more dangerous than he already was.

Gregory's underachievement was motivated by weak basic desires for curiosity, honor, and order. The overriding problem in his case, however, was his strong basic desire for vengeance that dominated his school life and interfered with his learning. The potential for violence was real. In total, Gregory showed four of the six common reasons for underachievement.

Gregory most likely had a conduct disorder, which was not a condition suitable for special education in the school district where he lived. He was expelled from the school for the remainder of the year. Gregory's high score for acceptance suggested a fear of failure. As previously noted, high scores for acceptance sometimes indicate self-esteem problems and other psychological issues. Gregory's underachievement was not the result of normal causes.

How to Motivate Adolescents

How can parents and teachers motivate underachieving students to improve their grades? This depends on the individual. The RSMP shows not only the possible motivational causes for underachievement, but also how to motivate students for better school performance.

Consider the example of the student who has a weak basic desire for curiosity and a strong basic desire for honor. The student dislikes thinking and intellectual pursuits but values character and self-discipline. The solution may be to make school performance a test of character and self-discipline. The parents, for example, may ask the student to pledge to meet a certain standard of performance. The student would still intrinsically dislike intellectual learning but would be duty-bound to keep his or her grades up to potential.

Counselors working with low-achieving students need to find specific goals that resonate with each adolescent – such as specific ambitions, specific financial goals, and motivating competitions. Parents and teachers should link better school grades to the students' cherished goals. A student who is motivated by vengeance, power, and status, for example, might dream of a successful military or athletic career. Perhaps counselors can motivate this student by showing connections between school grades and admission to military academies or with maintaining athletic eligibility.

As was shown in Tables 6.1 and 6.2, both Tom Peters and Kevin Smith were strongly motivated by athletics and being popular but not by academics. Their parents should limit their participation in social or athletic activities unless they keep their grades to some mutually agreed level. Tom and Kevin were able to understand and accept such external discipline. If their parents do not use extrinsic incentives, however, Tom and Kevin might fail courses and get themselves into serious academic trouble.

Gregory Izza, however, is too dangerous to be in school. He needs to be referred to mental health experts who specialize in potentially violent adolescents. The best way to reach him may be through material rewards because of his need for status. He needs a supportive environment that minimizes criticism.

Conclusion

Underachievement is often not symptomatic of a psychological disorder. Underachievers are not unmotivated – they can be highly motivated but in directions other than school. Six motives that compete with achievement are avoidance of thinking, avoidance of expressions of will, looking for trouble, fear of failure, looking out for Number 1, and spontaneity. Based on standardized scores, the RSMP assesses these competing motives for any student. The RSMP also can indicate ways to reach the student. Parents and teachers need to relate academics to the student's intrinsic goals, not to what counselors or parents think the student's goals should be.

When underachievement is a result of a disorder or mental illness, some likely possibilities are anxiety disorder including test anxiety (e.g.,Gordon & Sarason, 1955, Speilberger et al., 1978), learning disability, and Attention-Deficit Hyperactivity Disorder. Now that motivation analysis has given us a better idea of what is normal, hopefully it will help us diagnose what is truly abnormal. Perhaps motivation analysis can partially correct the overdiagnosis of adolescent disorders.

Five of the six common reasons for adolescent underachievement (all except a lack of curiosity) also apply to adult underachievement. Adults who lack ambition tend to underachieve because they avoid challenges, rarely work hard, and even may tolerate long periods of unemployment. Adults who are combative tend to underachieve because they make many enemies. Adults who are insecure tend to underachieve because they hold back effort and have difficulty coping with being evaluated. Adults who are expedient tend to underachieve because others conclude they are just out for themselves. Adults who are spontaneous tend to underachieve because they have too many balls in the air at the same time.

7 Self Hugging and Personal Blind Spots

came across George Ramsay's 1843 book on the nature of happiness when I was working on a research project in the library stacks at Ohio State University. The pages were discolored and brittle from more than 150 years of exposure to the elements, but I did my best to read as much as I could. The following passage caught my attention:

> The same difference of feeling and dullness of imagination in men explain what often has been observed, that one half of mankind pass their lives in wondering at the pursuits of the other. Not being able either to feel or to fancy the pleasure derived from the other sources than their own, they consider the rest of the world as little better than fools, who follow empty baubles. They hug themselves as the only wise, while in truth they are only narrow-minded.

I have pondered the meaning of these words for years. I now suspect that George Ramsay – an obscure, nineteenth-century professor of philosophy at Oxford University in England – had unlocked the psychological secrets of long-term relationships. His idea of "self-hugging," I now believe, explains why people with opposite pursuits tend to misunderstand each other and quarrel repeatedly.

Self-hugging is a natural tendency to think that our values are best, not just for us, but potentially for everyone. When people learn that a particular lifestyle makes them happy, they think they have learned something about human nature, when in reality they have only learned something about themselves. Sociable people think, "Socializing is fun," when they should think, "Socializing is fun for me." Intellectuals assume, "It is human nature to enjoy learning," when they should conclude, "I enjoy learning." Self-reliant psychologists assert, "Autonomy is a sign of human growth," when they should assert, "Autonomy is important for my growth."

Self-hugging explains why couples tend to have the same quarrels over and over again. Consider the example of a saver married to a spender. The frugal spouse complains to the free-spending partner, "You are wasting our hard-earned money." The free-spending spouse responds, "What is the point of having money if you can't spend it?" The quarrel recurs repeatedly because deep down each partner believes that his or her values are valid.

Savers and spenders lack experiences that might cause them to appreciate each other's values. Savers have few or no experiences of having spent money and enjoyed doing so. Consequently, they react with disbelief when spenders tell them how much fun shopping can be. On the other hand, spenders have few or no enjoyable experiences of having felt good about deferring purchases. Consequently, they react with astonishment when savers tell them how responsible they feel deferring purchases of a new car or big-screen television. Since people tend to trust their feelings above all else, savers are confident that frugality produces the greatest happiness over the long haul, and spenders feel the same way about buying.

We are baffled when others reject that which makes us happy or when they embrace that which makes us unhappy. As Ramsay put it, half the world goes through life wondering about the pursuits of the other half. We cannot feel or imagine how other people can enjoy that which we can't stand. We cannot feel or imagine how other people can dislike that which we enjoy. We presume that since our pleasures and discomforts are real, *something must be wrong* with others who can't experience the same pleasures or discomforts.

Because of self-hugging, many not-so-happy people never doubt what leads to happiness. They think, "If only I were more successful or wealthy or better looking, I would be truly happy." Many not-so-happy people are so confident they know what leads to happiness that they give advice to people who are happier than they are. A miserable intellectual can tell a happy nonintellectual, "You can't be really happy. To be really happy, you must acquire great knowledge and understanding." A not-so-happy puritan looks at a happy playboy and thinks, "His happiness is shallow. How can anybody relate to people in such a superficial manner? He would be happier if he could find deep, enduring relationships."

Self-hugging occurs with regard to our strongest and weakest basic desires. Strong basic desires motivate us to embrace strong values, which makes it more difficult for us to understand people who hold opposite values. Weak basic desires have similar effects, but they motivate opposite values. Consider the example of an ambitious parent and a laid-back child. The ambitious parent asks the unambitious child, "Why don't you get a job and work harder and make something of your life?" The unambitious child responds, "Why don't you do something other than work, work, and work?" In this example, the parent has a high need for power, whereas the child has a low need for power. The quarrel is motivated by self-hugging – that is, the parent invokes his or her values in judging what is best for the child. Conflict resolution requires that ambitious and unambitious people understand that they are individuals so that one intrinsically enjoys what the other intrinsically dislikes and vice versa. Tolerance of individuality is often the only possible solution.

Self-hugging occurs between formal (strong basic desire for status) and informal (weak basic desire for status) people. Formal people may think informal people are unimportant and can be ignored because of their lack of significance. On the other hand, informal people may wonder, "Are formal people snobs?"

No matter how much formal and informal people explain themselves to each other, they remain baffled at each other's values. In the case of a long-term relationship – such as boss/employee, parent/child, or husband/wife – they may quarrel over and over again. The formal spouse complains to the informal partner, "Your car looks shabby parked in front of the house. What will the neighbors think? You must learn to keep up appearances!" The informal spouse responds, "I don't care what the neighbors think. I don't have to own an expensive car just to impress the neighbors."

The Apprentice

Self-hugging often occurs between curious and practical people. Intellectuals think everybody should become lifelong learners, whereas practical people think everybody should focus on the task at hand and just do it. Let's consider, for example, the viewpoints of two titans of industry, William "Bill" Gates III and Donald Trump.

On an episode of the television show *The Apprentice*, Donald Trump fired a young man because he used too many words and asked too many questions. The Donald aimed to teach the young man a lesson about success in business, namely, that actions speak louder than words. At first blush, the example appears to be one in which a young man has not performed as well on his job as he might have. If we examine the firing more closely, however, we can see that the real reason the young man was fired is that his intellectual values conflicted with the practical values of his boss.

People who "talk too much" and ask many questions likely have a high need for cognition, which falls under a strong basic desire for curiosity. Intellectuals tend to be highly verbal and inquisitive people who expect their supervisors to be impressed with their intellectual skills. Intellectuals are slow to realize when their analytical nature annoys their supervisors.

People who think actions speak louder than words tend to have a weak basic desire for curiosity. Practical people tend to lose patience with intellectuals, thinking that intellectuals are too focused on "ivory tower" or irrelevant issues. They may value ideas with immediate practical relevance but not theoretical ideas without any obvious practical implications.

I suspect that Donald Trump is a practical person with a weak need for curiosity and that the young man he fired for asking too many questions is an intellectual with a strong need for curiosity. The Donald fires intellectuals because he has discovered that *he* is a practical person, and through self-hugging, he has concluded that he does not need to employ intellectuals.

Although many business executives would agree with Donald Trump that business is not a place for intellectuals, William "Bill" Gates III, the cofounder of Microsoft, is a notable exception. Gates was born in 1955 and showed a high degree of intellectual curiosity even as a young child. He planned to become a scientist when he was in fourth grade, and he read widely and developed an early interest in bridge. By age 9, he had read the *World Book* encyclopedia. One time as a boy his parents asked him why he did not respond to their call to dinner, and he explained that he was "thinking."

As a child, Gates chastised his parents for not thinking about things more deeply. He repeatedly asked them, "Don't you ever think?" He attended the private Lakeside School, where he wrote his first computer program at age 13. He attended Harvard University under the National Scholar program but dropped out in his junior year to cofound Microsoft with Paul Allen.

In building Microsoft, Gates hired the brightest and most curious people he could find – he gave preference to intelligent employees over experienced ones. Saying the work at Microsoft was "to sit and think," Gates wanted employees who were sufficiently curious to stay current with their fields and to use their intelligence to develop new products. The hiring process he supported at Microsoft confronted potential employees with intellectually challenging questions in order to assess their curiosity and ability to think.

Trump hires doers, whereas Gates hires thinkers. Trump is a doer, whereas Gates is a thinker. The differing opinions on whom to hire, I suggest, are the result of self-hugging. Trump thinks his practical values lead to business success, not just for him, but generally. Gates thinks his intellectual values lead to business success, not just for him, but generally. I suspect that each is right about himself and wrong about the general case.

The Saver

In addition to influencing business judgment, self-hugging influences our political opinions. A case in point is a letter published in the *Wall Street Journal*. The letter writer, Sam, commented on the plight of the unionized workers in the automobile supply industry. The workers at bankrupt companies have lost significant health and pension benefits that have set them back financially.

After shedding some crocodile tears for unionized workers, Sam blamed the workers for their spendthrift ways. Sam thinks that throughout Detroit's boom years the union workers should have put aside money and saved for their retirement. He wrote, "I grew up in Detroit, and one thing I have learned by the time I left in 1972 was that you must depend on yourself, you must save, and if it seems too good to be true, it probably is." He added that people should "worry less about what you buy, and start worrying more about what you save."

Sam's letter touts the values of saving. He argues that if the workers had had his values, they would not be in the predicament in which they now find themselves. When auto parts manufacturer Delphi says, "Sorry, workers, your pension will be cut in half, and half of what you get you will need for health insurance," Sam thinks workers should have responded, "No problem. I never trusted you from the get-go. When I started to work here at age 19, I knew your promises were too good to be true. My wife and I have been living like misers all these years, and now we have a cache of funds and don't need your lousy pension and benefits."

Notice that Sam did not write a letter saying, "Boy, I am lucky to have saved my money rather than having spent it on my family or my happiness." Instead Sam wrote a letter saying, "You guys should have been more like me. Now you will get what you deserve for having been different from me." Sam blames the workers for not having realized that his own values are superior to theirs. Sam believes that when it comes to saving, what is best for him is best for everybody.

Like Sam, the financial press has blamed the unions for the plight of the American automobile industry. Why have editorial writers blamed the unions for being greedy even more than they blamed the CEOs? At first blush, this seems incredible since the CEOs have pay-and-benefit packages worth many millions of dollars per year while the workers earn a tiny fraction of that amount. If a worker is greedy making $75,000, isn't a CEO making $300 million in stock options even greedier? Counting stock options, some CEOs were paid more for a few hours' work than the average unionized worker earned in a year. Yet the financial press thinks the workers are greedier than the CEOs!

The financial press may be guilty of self-hugging the basic desire for status. Status-oriented people value wealth and identify with the upper class, whereas egalitarians are less impressed with wealth and identify with the common man. Since status-oriented people think CEOs are more important contributors to the success of a company than are the workers, it seems right to them that CEOs would earn higher compensation. Although many status-oriented people might agree that CEOs are overpaid, the difference of opinion is more about proportions than values. The greed of the worker is a more significant violation of status values than is the greed of the CEOs.

The Coach

My colleagues and I have assessed the RMP of a number of college and professional athletic teams. Additionally, James Wiltz, Michael Sherman, and I compared the RMPs of 415 college students who had participated in zero, one, or two varsity sports at the high school or college level (Reiss, Wiltz, & Sherman, 2001). Our results showed that physical activity was the most important basic desire associated with athleticism. The students who had participated in two or more varsity sports showed significantly greater intrinsic enjoyment of physical activity than did students who had participated in only one varsity sport, and those who had participated in only one varsity sport showed significantly greater intrinsic enjoyment of physical activity than did those who had not participated in any varsity sport.

We also showed, apparently for the first time in a scientific study, that athletes are family oriented. The connection between sports and family life is apparent. In youth leagues and even at the high school level, the audience for athletic contests consists largely of parents. Sports are a frequent topic of family conversation. During the baseball season, my father and I often talked about the ineptitude of the 1960s New York Mets. My children, Michael and Ben, love to talk with their parents about sports. They call before, during, and after important Ohio State University football games.

Peter Boltersdorf, the man who pioneered the application of the sixteen basic desires to sports, believes that coaches have a tendency to give motivational talks that address their own values, which are sometimes significantly different from those of their team. Many individual athletes, for example, value expedience (which falls under a weak basic desire for honor). Expedient athletes see nothing wrong in breaking rules or committing a penalty when they think the referees aren't watching. The only reason expedient athletes usually follow the rules is because they are afraid of getting called for a penalty.

Some teams with expedient players happen to have honorable coaches. Honorable coaches value character, rules of conduct, and respecting tradition. When they engage in self-hugging, they may try to motivate their team by appealing to their players' honor. They tell their team that the game will be a test of their character. They say things like, "Go out and show what you are made of!" They remind their team of the importance of tradition. They may enforce strict codes of conduct for on- and-off-the-field behavior.

It makes no sense for a coach to try to motivate his or her players by appealing to values they do not have. Speeches on character motivate honorable coaches but do not motivate expedient players. The honorable coach may believe that outstanding character helps teams win, but actually there are many rogues who have helped teams win, too. O. J. Simpson, for example, was instrumental in winning many football games. Yet Simpson was found civilly liable for the murder of his wife and Ron Goldman. Don't get me wrong: I am not saying that many athletes share Simpson's character. I am simply saying that, on average, athletes tend to be more expedient than is the typical person in our society.

Coaches have a better chance of firing up their team by appealing to family values than to honor. Coaches might talk about how much children look up to the team and want them to win.

Personal Blind Spots

Motives and values create personal blind spots that cause people to misjudge what others think of them. You may think you are creating a favorable impression when the opposite is true. You may be irritating or annoying someone and be slow to realize it. These misjudgments can happen when you value a behavior very differently than most people do. Because of self-hugging, you overestimate how much other people share your values and underestimate the extent to which you are different from other people. You think your behavior is impressing people, when actually it is turning them off because they do not share your values.

John Kerry's 2004 bid for the U.S. presidency was a good case in point. Kerry had a tendency to answer questions with long, nuanced sentences. Initially he thought he was showing the 2004 American voting public that he is more thoughtful than his rival, President George W. Bush. Kerry's thoughtfulness, however, created a much less favorable impression than he had hoped it would. The public did not say, "Kerry is just the kind of thoughtful person we need in the White House." Instead the public said, "I don't like him. He's too hard to understand." The Bush campaign played on this public reaction by suggesting that Kerry's U.S. Senate colleagues disliked him, too.

When Kerry suggested that thoughtfulness is an important quality for a president to have, he expressed his intellectual values. Since he has a strong basic desire for curiosity, he is impressed with thoughtful people. If President Bush had thought more deeply before he went to war in Iraq, Kerry argued, postwar Iraq would not have become such a mess. When asked how he would do things differently, Kerry said he would have thought more deeply before he acted. When reporters protested there wasn't much difference between what he would do and Bush's policy, Kerry explained that his greater thoughtfulness would reduce the chances of future, additional error. This argument appealed to people who thought Bush was simple and lacking in thoughtfulness. Although intellectuals cheered Kerry, the general public concluded that Kerry offered nothing new on Iraq.

President Bush countered with the message that decisive action is important. Bush expressed the values of practicality (motivated by a weak basic desire for curiosity) and leadership (motivated by a strong basic desire for power). Bush suggested that America needs leaders who can get the job done, not leaders who think up nuanced plans. Bush's spinners suggested to the public that the election offered them a choice between a thinker and a doer. Bush won the election partially because he expressed the values of the public better than did his opponent.

Kerry tried to sell the American public a message that went against their values. The American public does not place a high value on intellectuals and thoughtfulness. The American public values decisiveness, straightforwardness, and action in their leaders. In a sense, Kerry presented himself as being above the public, the thoughtful leader they need whether they know it or not. Kerry's values did not match the public's values as well as Bush's, and thus Bush was reelected to a second term as president of the United States.

Kerry misjudged how people would respond to his message of thoughtfulness because he failed to appreciate how much more intellectual he is than is the public at large. If we could have asked him, "Does the public want an intellectual in the White House," I bet he would have said, "No." Why then did he run for office expressing the value of thoughtfulness? Blind spot! Kerry did not make the connection between his touting the value of thoughtfulness and the public's possibly seeing him as an intellectual who is too involved in the world of ideas and not focused enough on the world of deeds. The public saw his nuance as indecisiveness.

Like Kerry, we all sometimes think we are creating a more favorable impression than we really are. Remember the boy who asked too many questions in class? He thought he was impressing people with how inquisitive he was; he did not realize that some people thought he was just seeking attention. What about the boss who calls people idiots when they disagree with him? He thinks he is just setting a high standard of performance for the company; he does not realize that many people interpret his ambition as egoism.

Another example is that of former President Jimmy Carter, a conflict avoidant individual. He has devoted his postpresidency to peacekeeping, for which he earned a Nobel Peace Prize. In 1979 Carter was slow to take action when Iranian militants took American hostages in Teheran. Carter may have hoped the American public would see him as mature and responsible for his handling of the Iranian hostage situation without provoking a wider conflict. Instead, Carter lost reelection partially because many people believed he was a "weak" leader. Carter underestimated the political demand for symbols of "toughness" and military bravado.

Blind Ambition

Some people with a strong basic desire for power develop what I call a "take-charge" personality. They may impress others as having a "strong" personality – they can be bold of thought, action, or tongue. They may be quick to offer advice and may seek leadership roles. They may aim high and can pursue their goals with single-minded determination. They may have an enormous capacity for work.

Take-charge people tend to overestimate how much they impress others with their determination, strength, and leadership. The late General Alexander Haig, for example, declared himself in control of the White House shortly after President Ronald Reagan was shot in 1982. Haig thought he was reassuring the public that the country was in strong hands when the president was down. Haig expected the public to appreciate his boldness in announcing he was ready to seize control of the government if needed, but many people thought he was a bit too eager to assume power. It was an embarrassment he never lived down. Like General Haig, individuals who strongly pursue power also tend to overestimate the extent to which other people are likely to appreciate their controlling ways or advice.

Under stress, we have a tendency to embrace our true values. General Haig knew his authoritarian, take-charge manner rubbed many people the wrong way. He had learned that he sometimes needed to hide or moderate his strong personality. With the president down, however, he instinctively presumed that the immediate issue on the public's mind was who is in charge of the White House, so he rose to reassure the public that he was ready to take over if needed. He may have thought it was an act of patriotism to come forward. Actually, he was satisfying his own need for power (influence of will) and his own values (need for authority).

Actor Tom Cruise provided another example of misjudging the public's reaction. Cruise is ambitious (which falls under a strong need for power), and like many ambitious people, he is quick to give others advice. Cruise publicly advised Brooke Shields not to use antidepressant medications. People with a strong basic desire for power expect to be appreciated for giving others what they consider to be helpful advice. They can be slow to realize when the advice is unwanted and unappreciated. Cruise has been criticized by the media and the medical community for overstepping his expertise.

Too Important to Fall

Leona Helmsley is an example of someone who found herself in significant trouble because she overestimated her importance. After a successful career in New York real estate, she married Harry Helmsley when she was 53 and he was 63 (Randsdell, 1989). He was one of the wealthiest and most powerful people in New York City, known as "Mr. Real Estate." She persuaded Harry, who at the time owned the prestigious Plaza Hotel in New York City, to let her run the hotel's daily operations.

Unfortunately, the excesses of Leona Helmsley's personality overshadowed her considerable achievements. She was pushy, controlling, and insulting to people. When her employees did not do what she wanted, she threw tantrums to intimidate and humiliate them into submission. On one occasion, for example, she spotted lint on the floor, a crease in the bedspread, and a crooked lampshade in one of her hotel rooms. "The maid's a slob," she shouted, "Get her out of here! Out! Out!" On another occasion she marched into the hotel kitchen and shouted to a waiter, "You with the dirty fingernails: You're fired!"

Helmsley was aware that people thought she mistreated the workers at her hotel. Rather than change, however, she told herself that she was hard on the staff because she was setting a high standard. She overestimated how much her high standards would impress others and never fully appreciated that yelling at people does not inspire loyalty and make them better workers. The blinders were caused by her strong basic desire for power; she did not realize that other people respected displays of willpower far less than she did. The bottom line is that she preferred to be powerful even if that meant not being liked.

Leona Helmsley disliked paying taxes. "Taxes are for little people," she supposedly once said. Federal and state prosecutors did not see it that way and indicted her. At the time of her indictment, she had few friends and many enemies. She was convicted and served time in prison.

Why would somebody as wealthy as Leona Helmsley not pay taxes? She certainly could have afforded to pay her full taxes. I suspect, however, that she thought she was too important to be caught and punished. She thought only the "little people" get caught. Her strong basic desire for status made her blind in falsely thinking that tax investigators and prosecutors would defer to her high position.

Conclusion

Because we trust our own experiences above all else, we have difficulty appreciating the full extent of individuality. We have difficulty understanding how anybody can choose values or pursuits with which we have had only unpleasant experiences. We are baffled when somebody rejects values and pursuits with which we have had mostly pleasant experiences.

We tend to confuse individuality with abnormality. When other people cannot enjoy that which we find pleasurable, we think something must be wrong with them. When other people freely choose that which we find unpleasant, we think something must be wrong with them. We are naturally suspicious of anyone who rejects our values or asserts values opposite to our own.

These patterns of thinking are inherent to the human condition. I call this thinking *self-hugging* in honor of philosopher George Ramsay. We all self-hug, and we do it often. Self-hugging motivates us to confuse our individual nature with human nature.

Motivation is the assertion of *our* values, not the values of someone else. Self-hugging convinces us that our values are best, not just for us, but potentially for everyone. We tend to use our values to judge other people. We quarrel with our children when they do not embrace our values. We repeatedly quarrel with our spouse to embrace our values more completely.

We are a naturally intolerant species. Advocates of tolerance are almost always talking about political or racial tolerance. Except for Myers-Briggs experts (see Chapter 9) and motivation analysts, there are almost no advocates for tolerating diverse personalities.

8 Relationships

David Buss (1994), an evolutionary psychologist, believes that romantic attraction is based on traits that have powerful sexual and reproductive advantages. In prehistoric times, women needed to be protected while bearing and raising children. They chose mates who had traits well-suited to these needs. Men who were strong and family-oriented were more likely to get a mate and pass their genes to children. Over generations males became stronger and presumably more likely to stay with their women.

Males show a number of characteristics that attract female interest. They display resources/wealth (which falls under the basic striving for status), commitment (which falls under the basic striving for family), physical prowess (which falls under the basic striving for physical activity), self-confidence (which falls under the basic striving for acceptance), bravado (which falls under the basic striving for tranquility), appearance (which falls under the basic striving for romance), and fidelity (which falls under the basic striving for honor). Males also show competitiveness. "In the ruthless pursuit of sexual goals," wrote Buss (1994, p. 5), "men and women derogate their rivals, deceive members of the opposite sex, and even subvert their own mates."

In contrast, psychoanalysts believe that the unconscious mind exerts a powerful influence over romantic attraction (Strean, 1985). Freud identified two ways in which people select their ideal romantic partner. When the choice is narcissistic, the person is unconsciously motivated to fall in love with someone similar to himself or herself, or with someone he or she would like to be, or with someone who is unconsciously reminiscent of a parent or a sibling. When the choice is anaclitic, the person is unconsciously motivated to fall in love with someone who feeds, nurtures, or protects.

Motivation analysis distinguishes between short-term and long-term attraction. Over the short term, attraction is significantly influenced by sexual interests, looks, and circumstances. Over the long term, values and pursuits determine attraction and relationship outcomes in accordance with the following two principles:

> **Principle 1.** We naturally bond to people whose values and pursuits are similar to ours.
> **Principle 2.** We naturally separate from people whose values and pursuits are very different from ours.

These principles are summarized with the saying, "Birds of a feather flock together." You are compatible with people who are similar to you in values and basic desires. You are incompatible with people who hold opposite values and basic desires. If you have a high-intensity basic desire for status, for example, you may appreciate people who have a similar high-intensity need for status; you may get along with people who have an average-intensity need for status; and you may find annoying people who have a weak-intensity need for status.

Some readers may dispute the idea that "birds of a feather flock together" in favor of the "opposites attract" principle. Take the example of a smart person who is all thumbs marrying a less smart person who is handy with tools. As a couple, the smart partner can make the financial decisions while the handy partner keeps the house in repair. This simple example would seem to support the idea that opposites attract.

The opposites-attract analysis is intuitively appealing, but it is invalid. Although complementary skills and abilities can be helpful to partnerships, opposite personality traits, values, or motives lead to conflict. Researchers have conducted many studies evaluating whether people are attracted to others who have similar versus opposite traits, and the results show that similarity is the basis for compatibility (e.g., Carey, Hamilton, & Shanklin, 1986; Carli, Ganley, & Pierce-Otay, 1991; Jones, McCaa, & Martecchini, 1980; Lapidus, Green, & Baruh, 1985; Wiltz & Reiss, 2003). Rarely has social science research resolved an issue so convincingly.

Troubled Relationships

Some marriage counselors believe that troubled relationships occur when one or both partners have personality shortcomings. As marriage expert George Thorman (1996) put it,

> those who had a happy, secure childhood and whose emotional needs were adequately met will be likely to have a secure and satisfactory relationship to their marriage partners, while those who have gone through an insecure and unhappy childhood will face serious problems in their marriage. (p. 33)

I hope to convince you that the problem in troubled marriages is with the match, not with the individuals. You can be mentally healthy and yet find yourself in a troubled relationship because you paired off with someone with significantly different values. Differences in values and pursuits hold the keys for understanding troubled relationships. Childhood experiences may play a role in forging those values and pursuits, but it is much easier to decode the confusion in relationships when one focuses on values and pursuits rather than on unconscious psychodynamics.

In order to understand how differences in values and pursuits motivate troubled marriages, I propose the following principles:

Principle 3. The problem in troubled marriages is with the match, not the individuals.
Principle 4. Conflicts of intrinsically held values are very difficult to resolve.

If you intrinsically value socializing but your partner intrinsically values privacy, nothing your partner can say or do is likely to persuade you to become a private person. Your partner may explain all of the pleasures he or she derives from quiet time away from the crowd, but you will not be persuaded because you often experience solitude and quiet evenings as boring. On the other hand, nothing you can say or do will persuade your partner to embrace your intrinsic value of socializing. You can pressure your partner to comply with your needs, of course, but compliance is not persuasion because the underlying differences remain below the surface.

Principle 5. Perpetual marriage quarrels are motivated by conflicts of intrinsically held values (which are caused by significant differences in the intensities of basic desires).

Differences in intrinsically held values motivate quarrels that rarely resolve. University of Washington psychologist John Gottman observed that 69 percent of marital conflicts are perpetual (Gottman & Silver, 1999). "Time and again, when we do four-year follow-ups of couples, we find that they are still arguing about precisely the same issue. It is as if four minutes have passed rather than four years" (Gottman & Silver, 1999, pp. 129–30). I believe that perpetual marriage quarrels are motivated by a mismatch on one or more of the sixteen basic strivings.

Incompatibility of Basic Desires

Some basic desires may be more important than others in determining the outcome of a relationship. Orderly and spontaneous people may quarrel over housekeeping matters, but these quarrels rarely spell significant trouble for a marriage. My wife Maggi and I, for example, are mismatched for order (see Chapter 1), but we have been married since 1971. We must have had scores of quarrels about orderliness, but we never thought of breaking up over them. I have my office, she has the rest of the house, and her house cleaners are instructed not to clean my office. On the other hand, couples who quarrel over children have a much more serious problem. The family-oriented partner, but not the non-family-oriented partner, wants children. No compromise is likely to resolve this difference.

Sexual compatibility is obviously very important for a successful marriage. When one partner wants to have sex much more frequently than the other, the stage is set for repeated frustration, quarrels, infidelity, and acts of revenge. The passionate partner may complain that the Platonic partner is only infrequently interested, and the Platonic partner may complain that the passionate partner has a one-track mind. The passionate partner will be tempted to satisfy his or her need elsewhere.

A strong sex drive significantly increases the likelihood of infidelity even when both partners are passionate people. Please don't misunderstand this point: I realize that many people with strong sex drives are faithful spouses. Yet a general rule of motivation is that strong intensity is correlated with multiple gratification objects. People with a strong-intensity basic desire for eating, for example, have a tendency to eat many different foods, whereas those with a weak appetite tend to be reluctant to try new foods. Highly curious people tend to be interested in learning about many things, whereas incurious people tend to be interested in learning about only a few subjects. Ambitious people aim for competence on many different tasks, whereas unambitious people are more content to gain competence on only a few tasks. I have little doubt that future researchers will correlate strength of sex drive to infidelity, although there will be many individual exceptions to this general rule.

Honor motivates valuation of marriage vows. Two conscientious partners have the potential to admire each other's character and may consider it their duty to stay together for the benefit of the children. Two expedient partners are both motivated by self-interest and have the potential to appreciate each other's opportunism. When a couple is mismatched on honor, however, the conscientious partner may grow to disrespect the expedient partner's situational ethics, and the expedient partner may come to resent the honorable partner's self-righteousness.

Some marriage counselors say that quarrels over money are the most damaging of all. When both partners are savers, they have the potential to enjoy building a nest egg. When both are spenders, they may splurge themselves into the poor house, but at least they do it together. Couples mismatched on the basic desire for saving have the potential for bitter quarrels over money. The saver may insist on living within a strict monthly budget focused on necessities. The spender may bust the budget almost every month wanting to buy now on credit and worry about paying later. Savers prefer to mend old things, whereas spenders prefer to buy new. The saver may come to think of the spender as irresponsible, and the spender may come to think of the saver as a tightwad.

The basic desire for vengeance is very important for relationships. Two competitive people may find themselves competing against each other, but at least they have the potential to admire each other's fighting spirit. Two peacekeepers have the potential to admire each other's gentle and kind nature. When a couple is mismatched on the need for vengeance, however, the competitive partner is tempted to take advantage of the gentle partner knowing that the gentle partner will not fight back. When one partner has a *very* strong basic desire for vengeance and the other has a weak basic desire, an abusive situation may occur.

The success of a relationship can depend more on how curious the partners are than on how smart they happen to be. Two curious partners have the potential to share intellectual conversations and values. Two incurious partners spend little time engaged in intellectual pursuits. If one partner is curious and the other is incurious, however, they are incompatible even if they are both very smart. The curious partner will want to have intellectual conversations much more often than will the incurious partner, who will tend to find such conversations boring.

Many people incorrectly assume that in a marriage of two "dominants" – that is, two people with a strong basic desire for power – the partners would quarrel endlessly over issues of control. Doesn't this show that dominant and submissive personalities match, not two dominants as Principles 1 and 2 imply? Actually, two willful people are both dominant compared with the average person, but they are not necessarily equally dominant. When compared to each other, one is usually more dominant than the other.

A willful person needs to marry a willful partner who can hold his or her own in the relationship and not become dominated. Real problems can occur when a dominant marries a "submissive" (very weak basic desire for power). The dominant may tend to humiliate and control the submissive individual in many areas of life, leading to much unhappiness. The dominant may expect to be appreciated for his or her leadership and may be blind to how resentful the submissive partner has become. When both partners are willful, each can take charge of different aspects of the marriage. One might take charge of the finances, for example, while the other takes charge of social life.

Independence is another basic desire that plays out in relationships. Two independent partners need less than average support from each other because they are self-reliant. Two interdependent partners seek a close relationship in which each provides significant support for the other. Problems arise, however, between an independent and interdependent partner. The interdependent partner needs the support that the independent partner is motivated to withhold. This can lead to significant dissatisfaction in the relationship.

Incompatibility of the Sexes

Thus far we have considered incompatibility arising from individuality, but now we examine potential incompatibility between the sexes. John Gray (1992) suggested that men and women are naturally incompatible regarding certain differences. The results of our research on the sixteen basic desires supported the possibility of gender differences, but we do not know if these are cultural or biological. Men and women tend to value differently some of the sixteen basic desires, and these differences play out in relationships. We have to keep in mind that there are many individual exceptions for general statements about gender. We do not want to stereotype people on the basis of gender.

We computed standard scores on the sixteen basic desires for 1,049 American women and 682 American men who had participated in one of three research studies (Reiss & Havercamp, 1998, Samples 3 and 4, plus Reiss, Wiltz, & Sherman, 2001). We also computed comparable scores for a German sample of 1,224 men and 826 women.

The American men scored significantly higher than the American women on the basic desire for vengeance. These men were more aggressive and more competitive than the women we studied. The German sample showed no gender differences in the desire for vengeance.

In both the United States and Germany, men scored significantly higher than women on the basic desire for romance. This means that on average men tend to have strong sex drives. This does not mean that women are uninterested, only that the average man may have more libido than the average woman. There were many individual exceptions to this general result.

In both the United States and Germany, men reported more interest than women in physical activity and in sports. This was the largest gender difference we have obtained thus far.

In both the United States and Germany, men and women showed equal interest in family. The maternal and paternal instincts appear to be about equally strong. This finding contradicts common beliefs that on, average, mothers are more interested in child care than fathers.

In the United States but not in Germany, men were more independent than women. This means that women may have a greater need for support and close relationships. Possibly, men are more likely to embrace displays of individuality.

Reiss Relationship Profile

Ever since the Reiss Motivation Profile was published in my 2001 book *Who Am I*, people have been seeking insight into their relationships by comparing the intensities of their sixteen basic desires with those of their partner. It seems that these comparisons quickly reveal the basis for attraction and the likely incompatibilities. In 2005 I developed a more formal method, the Reiss Relationship Profile (RRP), for comparing desire profiles. Dr. Stephan Judah (2006), a marriage counselor with more than twenty years of professional experience, evaluated the validity of the RRP with more than 100 couples seeking marital counseling and more than 25 not seeking counseling. The spouses tended to agree with the results, often commenting on how revealing they were or how much sense they made. Anecdotally, scores of couples have told me that the results were highly valid.

The RRP assesses the compatibility of basic desires between any two individuals. The results reveal those basic desires that are matched; those that are mismatched; and the Incompatibility Index score, which is the total degree of dissimilarity of basic desires.[1] The higher the Index score, the greater is the potential incompatibility of the couple.

Figure 8.1 compares the RRPs of a couple who are happily married with a couple who have a dysfunctional marriage. For the happily married couple, for example, the wife has a strong need for acceptance, and the husband has an average need. Notice how much more similar are the basic desires of the happy couple versus the dysfunctional couple.

I am often asked how many mismatches signal future problems for a relationship. Judah and I are currently studying this issue in a preliminary fashion. Although we think five or six mismatches may spell future trouble, only the partners can decide when the strengths of their relationship outweigh the weaknesses or vice versa. The RRP is just a tool for helping people make decisions and possibly improve their relationship.

The RRP assesses compatibility, not romantic love. The results show the areas of life where the partners are pulling in the same direction versus those where they are pulling against each other. Although the results may predict how well the partners will get along over the long haul, they do not indicate how much the partners love each other. Part of what makes relationships so complicated, I suspect, is that some people can fall in love with someone with whom they can't get along.

HAPPY COUPLE

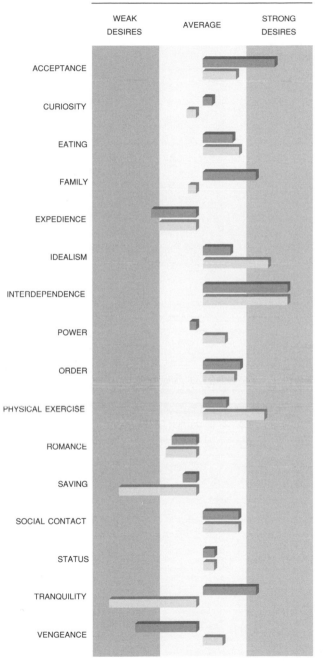

WEAK DESIRES	AVERAGE	STRONG DESIRES

ACCEPTANCE

CURIOSITY

EATING

FAMILY

EXPEDIENCE

IDEALISM

INTERDEPENDENCE

POWER

ORDER

PHYSICAL EXERCISE

ROMANCE

SAVING

SOCIAL CONTACT

STATUS

TRANQUILITY

VENGEANCE

Figure 8.1. The Basic desires of a Happy Couple (p. 117) versus an Unhappy Couple (p. 118).

UNHAPPY COUPLE

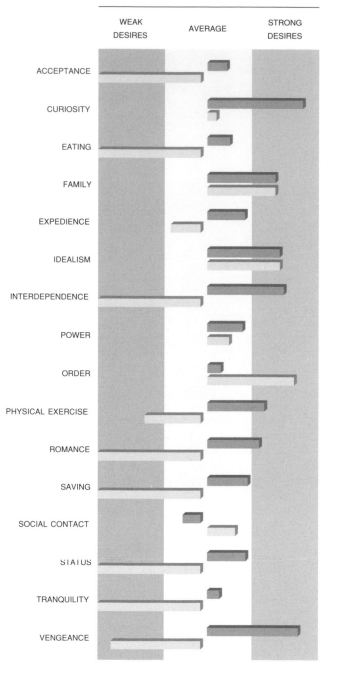

Table 8.1. RRP for Janice and Mike*			
Matched (4)	Nearly matched (1)	Nearly mismatched (1)	Mismatched (1)
Strong Family Strong Honor Strong Idealism Weak Saving	Weak Tranquility	Curiosity	Romance

* Incompatibility Index = 14.6 (average).

Compatible Couples

We will review the RRP of a number of couples, beginning with two compatible couples. Table 8.1 shows the RRP for Janice and Mike, a happily married, middle-aged couple living in Kansas. Janice is a homemaker, and Mike is in human resources.

Both Janice and Mike admire each other's character (which falls under the matched basic desire for honor). As Mike put it, they "stick to their values." They are careful to pay their taxes without cutting corners, for example, because they want to meet their obligations to their country. They take responsibility for their actions even when things go wrong.

They enjoy a little excitement in their lives (which falls under a weak need for tranquility). They admit to driving fast and like to take skiing trips together. Mike climbs mountains for the challenge and thrill.

They admire each other's commitment to social causes (which falls under matched idealism). Mike is proud of Janice's interest in helping orphans, and Janice admires Mike's work in human services. They give generously to charities that promote family values or address the interests of children.

The main source of frustration in their relationship is that Mike has a significantly higher sex drive than does Janice. Mike wanted sex more frequently than did Janice. As they grew older, however, Mike's sex drive lessened, and so did the conflict.

The RRP also suggested that Mike has an average need for intellectual curiosity but that Janice has a weak need. Mike may want to converse with Janice at dinner or when driving in a car, but Janice may prefer to limit conversation to what is going on in their lives.

Mary and Bill are happily married with three grown children – on the RRP, their incompatibility score was a low 9.6. As shown in Table 8.2, they were matched or nearly matched on four basic desires compared with being mismatched or nearly mismatched on only one. They are both religious and attend church together every Sunday. Bill is committed to making the world a better place through volunteerism

Table 8.2. RRP for Mary and Bill*

Matched (2)	Nearly matched (2)	Nearly mismatched (0)	Mismatched (1)
Strong Honor	Strong Social Contact		Tranquility
Weak Independence	Weak Acceptance		

* Incompatibility Index = 9.6 (low).

and support for charities; Mary admires Bill's participation in these activities but is less involved.

People who meet them can see their loving relationship. During a recent dinner at a friend's house, for example, they were fascinated with each other. The friend noticed that they sometimes stared at each other.

Mary and Bill support each other in a loving relationship (which falls under a weak-intensity basic desire for independence). They make decisions as a family and keep up with each other's activities. They entertain friends as a couple and belong to a number of groups. The only significant motivational difference between them is that Bill is much more cautious than is Mary.

Troubled Marriages

Kathy and Jerry, who are raising two children in Houston, Texas, had drifted apart. In counseling sessions she complained that he comes home late from work, exercises after dinner, and stays up late without talking with her. She goes to bed earlier than he does. At the time they sought counseling, they had not had sex for months.

Table 8.3 shows the results of the RRP for Kathy and Jerry. They were matched or nearly matched on three basic desires, compared with twelve on which they were mismatched or nearly mismatched. The Incompatibility Index was 28.8,

Table 8.3. RRP for Kathy and Jerry*

Matched (2)	Nearly matched (1)	Nearly mismatched (6)	Mismatched (6)
Strong Family	Weak Tranquility	Acceptance	Independence
Strong Idealism		Curiosity	Physical Activity
		Eating	Romance
		Honor	Saving
		Order	Status
		Tranquility	Vengeance

* Incompatibility Index = 28.8 (high).

Table 8.4. RRP for Susan and Andrew*			
Matched (0)	Nearly matched (2)	Nearly mismatched (4)	Mismatched (2)
	Strong Physical Activity	Family	Honor
	Strong Status	Idealism	Romance
		Saving	
		Social Contact	

* Incompatibility Index = 16.43 (average).

indicating significant incompatibility of values and desires. This couple may have little in common.

A shared interest in raising a family was the bond holding this couple together. They stayed together for the sake of their young children even though neither partner was happy. They entered counseling hoping they could improve their relationship.

Kathy complained to the counselor that Jerry does not give her enough emotional support. Kathy has a high need for support (which falls under a weak basic desire for independence), but Jerry is reluctant to provide emotional support because he is uncomfortable being close (which falls under a strong basic desire for independence). She needs more emotional support than most people, but he provides less comfort than does the average person. No wonder she is unhappy with the emotional support he gives her.

Kathy has a strong basic desire for vengeance, suggesting that she was motivated to get back at Jerry for the heartache he had caused her. Her need for vengeance may explain why she neglected her household chores when she started to feel that Jerry was not treating her right. On the other hand, Jerry has a strong basic desire for romance, but Kathy has a weak desire. Not surprisingly, he complained to the counselor that she does not give him enough sex.

The counselor worked out a compromise. Jerry will come home earlier so they can spend time together and talk. She will make an effort to have sex at least once every weekend. The counselor is optimistic about the compromise, but the RRP shows so much incompatibility I have my doubts.

Susan and Andrew live in Denver and sought marriage counseling when Andrew had an affair with a household assistant. As show in Table 8.4, the RRP Incompatibility Index was 16.43, which is within the average range. They had only two mismatched basic desires, but the specific nature of the mismatches was troublesome.

On the RRP, Andrew showed a strong basic desire for romance and a weak basic desire for honor, a combination that motivates cheating. In contrast, Susan showed a weak basic desire for romance and a strong basic desire for honor, a combination that motivates fidelity. Is it any wonder they wound up in counseling over his infidelity? He wants a sex life she does not want to give him; he sees nothing wrong with cheating while she thinks cheating is a character flaw. His mistake, he thinks, was getting caught.

When asked about his situational ethics, Andrew replied that this is how it is in the business world. When top corporate management asked Andrew, "How are you doing," he figured it was unwise to tell them about the problems he was having. Truthful businesspeople, Andrew believes, get sacked. As a savvy businessman, Andrew was proud of his expedience.

What attracted Susan and Andrew to each other? The results of the RRP showed no matches, but there was a near match on the basic desire for status. Andrew is a successful businessman, and Susan values success and money. She considered him a good provider, which was important to her.

Susan gave Andrew another chance because she wanted to hold the family together for the sake of the children. The couple has only average incompatibility, but his cheating is likely to remain a significant source of distancing in their relationship.

Premarital Counseling

It is better to marry the right person than to need counselors to teach you how to get along with somebody else. Couples who are considering marriage can use the RRP to anticipate the strengths and weaknesses of their relationships and, in some cases, perhaps break off their engagement. I realize that couples who are in love are unlikely to change their minds based on the results of a psychological assessment, but when combined with counseling, the RRP can help a couple with second thoughts decide whether or not they want to proceed with marriage.

Principle 6. Better to marry the right person to begin with than to need counselors to teach you how to get along with somebody else.

Some psychologists view premarital counseling as an opportunity to teach sound relationship skills (Stahmann & Heibert, 1987). Frankly, I would prefer to see relationship skills taught only after a firm decision has been made to marry or a couple already is married and has decided to stay together. At the premarital stage, I favor advising people with weak relationships to postpone their decision to marry. My first rule of helping people is to get them into situations where they can be successful and out of situations where events can go very badly for them.

Table 8.5. RRP for Kevin and Shelly*			
Matched (2)	Nearly matched (2)	Nearly mismatched (6)	Mismatched (3)
Weak Idealism	Weak Social Contact	Curiosity	Acceptance
Weak Independence	Strong Vengeance	Honor	Order
		Physical Activity	Tranquility
		Romance	
		Saving	
		Status	

* Incompatibility Index = 22.2 (high).

This means teaching people to marry compatible partners and to postpone or terminate plans to marry potentially incompatible partners.

If you are an intellectual, you should marry someone who is curious and not rely on counselors to teach you how to get along with someone who is incurious. If you are ambitious, you should marry someone who shares your ambitions and not rely on counselors to teach you how to get along with a laid-back partner. Relationships between compatible people can have many bumps as the years pass, so why start off with two strikes against you? Some engaged persons need to be told that people rarely change after marriage – if anything, personality conflicts intensify as the novelty and sexual passion decline.

Look at the RRP results presented in this chapter. The differences in compatibility between happy couples and those in counseling are like night and day! The happy couples have mostly matched desires and low Incompatibility Index scores; the troubled couples have mostly mismatched desires and high Incompatibility Index scores. Dating services such as e-harmony.com are on the right track in matching people for dates based on personality. Compatibility is essential (necessary but not sufficient) for a happy marriage.

Kevin and Shelly were considering marrying and moving away to the city where he planned to attend business school. At first she gladly accepted his marriage proposal, but then she got cold feet. She wondered how much she would like moving to a new city, and she dreaded the thought of having to make new friends and find a new job. The more she doubted whether or not she wanted to move, the more she doubted her love for Kevin. The couple sought the advice of a premarriage counselor.

Table 8.5 shows the RRP for Kevin and Shelly. Please notice the high degree of incompatibility. Kevin and Shelly showed only two matches – weak idealism and weak independence – against mismatches for acceptance, order, and tranquility. Additionally, Table 8.5 shows two near matches on social contact and vengeance against six near mismatches on curiosity, honor, physical activity, romance, status, and saving. The total Incompatibility Index score was a high 22.2, suggesting that Kevin and Shelly have significantly different values that may relentlessly pull them in different directions over the course of their lives.

Kevin wanted to go ahead with the marriage because he was confident they could work out their differences, but Shelly was much less confident. This difference in attitude may have been motivated by their differences in the basic desire for acceptance. Shelly has a strong basic desire for acceptance, suggesting that she may lack self-confidence and be afraid of failure. This may explain why Shelly had a change of heart and started to doubt her love. In contrast, Kevin's weak need for acceptance makes him a self-confident individual ready to charge ahead with optimism that events will work out to his favor.

Shelly's strong basic desire for tranquility makes her a cautious person who may be afraid to move away from home. In contrast, Kevin has a more adventurous nature. Shelly's strong basic desire for tranquility may explain why she is nervous about following Kevin to another city and leaving her familiar surroundings.

Since each partner has a higher-than-average need for psychological support, both may be sensitive to the needs and feelings of the other. Each may appreciate the other for being a sensitive individual.

Shelly's strong basic desire for order motivates her to dislike change, yet Kevin is asking Shelly to marry, move to another city, make new friends, and get a new job. That is a great deal of change for anyone to manage.

This couple has the potential for future conflict should they marry. Over time, he may become impatient with her insecurities, timidity, and nonadventurous spirit. She may become alienated by his self-confidence (which she may come to see as arrogance), risk taking, and adventuresome ways. They also have potential to quarrel over money, especially his desire to spend. They decided to postpone their plans to marry.

Conclusion

Since human beings are naturally intolerant of people with significantly different values and pursuits (see Chapter 7), successful marriages are almost always between people with similar values and pursuits. I developed the Reiss Relationship Profile as a tool for assessing similarity and dissimilarity of values and pursuits between any two people. The results reveal matched basic desires, mismatched basic desires, and a single score indicating the degree of overall incompatibility. Dr. Stephen Judah (2006), an experienced marriage counselor in Columbus, Ohio, is successfully demonstrating the usefulness of the RRP.

The long-term success or failure of a marriage may be largely determined at the time the couple chooses each other. If you marry somebody whose values are different from yours, you will have difficulty getting along especially as the years pass. If you marry somebody who shares your values, you have the potential for a mutually rewarding marriage that lasts a lifetime. Divorce is often a result of unwise selections, not personality deficiencies of one of the partners.

Marriage counseling and relationship-skills training can promote compatibility, but I think it is hard to overcome pervasive incompatibility. Young people should not marry thinking their partner will change. At the premarital stage, the RRP can help couples with second thoughts decide if they should postpone marriage and give the question a second look.

For married couples having problems, the RRP can help evaluate some of the reasons for the conflict. The lower the incompatibility score, the better may be the opportunity for counseling and skills training to be successful. Judah (2006) has been experimenting with ways to integrate the RRP into marriage counseling and skills training. I discussed general principles of motivation marriage counseling in my previous book, *Who Am I* (Reiss, 2000a).

9 Reinterpretation of Myers-Briggs Personality Types

The most widely used assessment of normal personality traits is the Myers-Briggs Type Indicator (MBTI). In this chapter, I compare the RMP with the MBTI. I put forth the following four hypotheses relevant to both scientific and professional interests.

Hypothesis 1. The MBTI is a valid measure of a narrow range of human motivation and is not a measure of "preferred ways of perception and judgment" as commonly claimed (Myers et al., 1998).

Hypothesis 2. The MBTI's four personality dimensions are too few in number to provide a comprehensive explanation of personality type.

Hypothesis 3. The RMP of sixteen basic desires can validly assess all of the personality traits assessed by the MBTI without paying any attention to MBTI type theory or to Jung's theory. In contrast, the MBTI cannot validly explain all of the personality traits assessed by the RMP.

Hypothesis 4. In leadership training and human development workshops, the joint use of the MBTI and the RMP stimulates the self-discovery process more fully than when only one instrument is used.

Historical Background

Galen (A.D. 129–A.D. 200) held that combinations of four humors – black bile (melancholic), yellow bile (sanguine), blood (choleric), and phlegm (phlegmatic) – determine our personalities. Galen hypothesized that individuals produce different amounts of each humor – your personality, for example, depends on the relative amounts of each humor specific to your body. Galen's theory of humors dominated personality typing from about A.D. 200 until the nineteenth century. Despite its significant popularity, the theory was invalid because humors do not exist.

Sigmund Freud developed his psychoanalytic theory of personality at the beginning of the twentieth century. In 1906 Carl Jung began a correspondence with Freud that led to Jung's becoming Freud's heir-apparent. Jung and Freud, however, had a falling out in 1914 and went their separate ways.

In the 1940s Isabel Briggs Myers and Katherine Briggs developed the MBTI as a measure of personality type. Myers and Briggs developed part of the MBTI prior to having discovered Jung's work, but the remaining part was based on their interpretation of Jung's theory. Myers-Briggs theory posits sixteen personality types formed by innate preferences for extraversion versus introversion, thinking versus feeling, sensing versus intuition, and judging versus perceiving. The MBTI assesses which of sixteen personality types best applies to any individual.

Historically, the MBTI represented a significant break with psychodynamic personality theory. Psychodynamic theorists have assessed personality from the standpoint of mental illness and psychological disorder, often seeing little difference between personality traits and symptoms of mild disorders. In contrast, the MBTI assessed the normal personality. The RMP benefits from the MBTI's having made the normal personality a topic worthy of scientific study.

Today the MBTI has multiple versions and various add-ons. The discussion in this chapter is based on the "MBTI Self-Scorable Form M" I purchased from the publisher in 2004 and again in 2006. The M form provides an assessment of personality type based on the four innate preferences of MBTI theory. Subsequently, a "level II" scoring system was developed to refine the analysis further. It is beyond the scope of this chapter to consider how my remarks might be affected by "level II." Perhaps I will offer expanded comments in a future publication.

Reinterpreting the MBTI Items

Hypothesis 1 is that the MBTI is an assessment of a narrow range of motives as opposed to an assessment of perception and judgment. In order to evaluate Hypothesis 1, I examined each of the ninety-three items on the MBTI Self-Scorable Form M. I rated these items into eighteen categories: those assessing one of the sixteen basic desires; those posing an invalid choice (meaning that the alternatives were not opposites); and those assessing nonmotivational traits unrelated to the sixteen basic desires. After I had made my ratings, I asked Jim Wiltz, who is familiar with my theory of sixteen basic desires, to do the same. Wiltz did so independently and without having discussed the items with me. The inter-rater agreement was 79.5%, indicating substantial reliability of judgment.

As shown in Table 9.1, I rated forty-nine of the ninety-three items (52.6 percent) as assessments of one of three basic desires. Included are nineteen items (20.4 percent) assessing the basic desire for order; seventeen items (18.3 percent)

Table 9.1. Motivational Analysis of MBTI Test Items

Part I	9 items assessing basic desire for order: Items 1, 2, 7, 9, 10, 11, 17, 20, 21
	7 items assessing basic desire for social contact: Items 4, 8, 12, 18, 19, 22, 23
	5 items assessing basic desire for curiosity: Items 3, 5, 13, 15, 24
	5 nonmotivational items: Items 6, 14, 16, 25, 26
	4 items assessing basic desire for order: Items 28, 36, 41, 49
Part II	5 items assessing basic desire for social contact: Items 27, 35, 42, 48, 54
	6 items assessing basic desire for curiosity: Items 29, 32, 40, 44, 47, 55
	1 item assessing basic desire for vengeance: Item 30
	6 nonmotivational items: Items 33, 46, 50, 52, 57, 58
	10 items choices not opposites: Items 31, 34, 37, 38, 39, 43, 45, 51, 53, 56
	6 items assessing basic desire for order: Items 59, 65, 68, 70, 71, 76
Part III	5 items assessing basic desire for social contact: Items 60, 66, 67, 72, 77
	1 item assessing basic desire for curiosity: Item 63
	1 item assessing basic desire for independence: Item 61
	1 item assessing basic desire for power: Item 62
	1 nonmotivational item: Item 78
	5 items choices not opposites: Items 64, 69, 73, 74, 75
	2 items assessing basic desire for vengeance: Items 80, 84
Part IV	1 item assessing basic desire for curiosity: Item 90
	1 nonmotivational item: Item 85
	11 items choices not opposites: Items 81, 82, 83, 85, 86, 87, 88, 89, 91, 92, 93

assessing the basic desire for social contact; and thirteen items (13.8 percent) assessing the basic desire for intellectual curiosity (need for cognition). I rated an additional five items as assessments of the basic desires for independence ($n = 1$), power ($n = 1$), and vengeance ($n = 3$). In total, I rated fifty-four of the ninety-three (58.1 percent) items as assessing a narrow range of motivational traits.

I suspect that MBTI Form M is a valid assessment of orderliness, intellectual curiosity, sociability, and perhaps little else.

- The forty-nine items (52.6 percent) assessing the three motives are well worded and appear to be valid. These items are similar to those used in many other scales assessing orderliness, friendliness, and need for cognition.
- The five motivational items assessing vengeance, power, and independence are too few in number to be valid. A valid assessment requires at least six to eight items for each of these basic desires. The RMP has forty items assessing vengeance, power, and independence.

- At least twenty-six items (27.9 percent) appear to have significant construct validity problems because the choices they pose are not between opposite traits. These items ask people to choose the trait that best applies to them, but both or neither trait can apply. Item number 81, for example, asks people if they are fair-minded versus caring. These are not opposites: People with a strong basic desire for idealism, for example, are both fair-minded and caring. Item number 53, moreover, invalidly assumes that preferences for building versus inventing are opposites.
- The remaining thirteen items appear to assess Jungian or MBTI type theory constructs of perception and judgment. These items encompass only 14 percent of the MBTI Form M.

The MBTI items omit many important areas of personality functioning. Few or no items pertain to topics such as need for status, materialism, saving, romance, need for physical activity, community service, risk taking, caution, self-confidence, appetite, achievement, and competitive spirit. The MBTI's assessment of these traits is at best indirect, inferring them from interactions among the four MBTI personality dimensions. The MBTI items do not seem to provide a comprehensive assessment of the normal personality.

MBTI advocates might retort that Jung's theory permits them to project the four personality types into many other areas of personality. Since the scientific community overwhelmingly rejects Jung's theory, I doubt personality theorists would agree that motives like materialism can be inferred from theoretical projections of Jung's theory. The simple fact is that the MBTI items ask repeatedly about orderliness, sociability, and intellectual curiosity, but the items ask very little or nothing about many other important aspects of personality such as materialism.

Some of the items on the MBTI seem to be based on invalid, stereotypic conceptions of personality. Item number 89, for example, seems to be based on the stereotypic conception of strong-willed, ambitious people as emotionally insensitive. Yet in reality a person can be both ambitious and emotionally sensitive.

Researchers should evaluate Hypothesis 1. If we take out the items assessing orderliness, sociability, and intellectual curiosity, is anything left that is valid? I suspect that the answer is mostly negative. Therefore, I would not describe the MBTI Form M as an assessment of Jung's personality theory or even the four personality dimensions of Myers-Briggs. Instead, I would describe the MBTI as a valid personality tool focused on the assessment of orderliness, sociability, and intellectual curiosity. In the 1950s, the MBTI was a significant step forward in the study of the normal personality, but today many scales assess orderliness, sociability, and need for cognition more efficiently than does the MBTI.

Reinterpreting the MBTI Bipolar Preferences

The MBTI describes the normal personality in terms of the following four bipolar psychological dimensions.

EXTROVERSION (E) VERSUS INTROVERSION (I). Jung (1923) distinguished between orientations to the outer (extraversion) versus the subjective world (introversion). Examples of extraversion include interest in other people, achievement motivation, and adventurous nature. Examples of introversion are reticence and becoming absorbed in one's own thoughts.

From a scientific standpoint, extraversion implies that socializing, adventurism, and ambition share a common property called "orientation to reality." I question the validity of such a proposition. Arguably, these traits are so diverse that nothing is common to them. The construct of extraversion on the MBTI seems to be too global to be valid. The RMP does not assess global E/I but instead assesses separately sociable/private (which falls under the basic desire for social contact), confident/insecure (which falls under the basic desire for acceptance), willful/nondirective (which falls under the basic desire for power), and fearful/calm (which falls under the basic desire for tranquility).

Usually when people talk about extroverts, they are referring to people who are sociable. The MBTI E/I items, moreover, basically assess how sociable a person is. Why define extraversion as a means of deriving energy from the outer world, when the MBTI is really assessing how sociable someone is? Why the overgeneralization, rather than scientific precision? Wouldn't it be more precise to define extraversion as sociability?

SENSING (S) VERSUS INTUITING (N). Plato (1966/360 B.C.E.) distinguished between sensory information and the essence of reality. A man chained to a cave wall can only see the shadows of people who pass by, not the people themselves (Plato, 1966/360 B.C.E., p. 227–35). Analogous to the man in the cave, we can perceive only the images reality creates on our senses, not the reality itself. Plato claimed there is a reality of changeless ideas and forms beyond what we can perceive with our five senses. This changeless reality is the essence of all things.

Theologians expressed similar ideas when they debated whether God can be known through logic and senses versus revelation. Our knowledge of God, they concluded, is acquired because God reveals himself to our soul, bypassing our senses and intellect.

Thus Western philosophers and theologians developed the doctrine of two kinds of knowledge – that which is revealed through the senses versus that which is revealed through the soul. Jung's distinction between sensing and intuiting fused Platonic epistemology with Freud's distinction between conscious versus unconscious ego functions (see Hall & Lindzey, 1957, pp. 86–7). The result is a conceptual muddle that implies the validity of mystical experience. Jung thought some people were born to be sensory-oriented and others to be mystics.

In MBTI theory, sensing is a preference for making decisions based on factual information obtained through the five senses, whereas intuiting is a preference for making decisions based on unconscious associations with the stimulus object, intuition, and mysticism. I suggest we redescribe the S/N distinction more clearly as an assessment of how much an individual values mystical experience. Sensing indicates a low valuation of mysticism, and a high valuation of intellectual curiosity. On the RMP, mysticism is evaluated by a desire for oneness (which falls under a weak basic desire for independence) rather than by a metaphysical theory of knowledge revealed to the soul. In making S/N one of only four MBTI scales, the MBTI exaggerates the role of mysticism in personality functioning.

THINKING (T) VERSUS FEELING (F). Jung distinguished between people whose values are based on intellectual knowledge versus those whose values are based on feelings of pleasure and pain. The MBTI assumes that "thinkers" are logical, interested in cause and effect, and impersonal. This analysis would seem to deny the possibility of a passionate or compassionate thinker. Is "Give me liberty or give me death" an example of thinking, feeling, or as I would argue, passionate thinking? The RMP distinguishes between intellectually curious versus incurious people and avoids stereotyping intellectuals as unfeeling.

JUDGING (J) VERSUS PERCEIVING (P). In theory, this MBTI scale evaluates the individual's preference for closure versus openness when interacting with the world. In reality, the J/P dimension is a straightforward measure of orderliness. Individuals the MBTI classifies as J are organized people who value stability and predictability, whereas those the MBTI classifies as P value spontaneity. The MBTI judging/perceiving dimension is an unremarkable but valid effort at measuring orderliness.

CONCLUSION. Hypothesis 2 is that the MBTI has too few psychological scales to provide a comprehensive analysis of the normal personality. The RMP uses sixteen psychological scales to describe the normal personality; the MBTI has only four psychological scales or dimensions to accomplish the same end. The E/I scale is a valid measure of social contact; the J/P scale is a valid measure of orderliness. The other two MBTI scales seem conceptually confused, especially the S/N scale, which represents a fusion of Platonic epistemology with Freudian metatheory about consciousness and seems to assess intellectual curiosity.

Reinterpreting the MBTI Personality Traits

Hypothesis 3 is that the RMP can validly assess all of the personality traits assessed by the MBTI without paying any attention to MBTI-type theory or to Jung's theory. Whereas the MBTI explains personality traits in terms of Jung's theory, the RMP explains all of these personality traits plus more in terms of sixteen basic desires. The validity of Hypothesis 3 is suggested in Table 9.2. Here is how to read Table 9.2.

- The personality trait "adaptable" is one of the possible results of the MBTI. The MBTI holds that two inherited personality types, type INFP and type ESTP, are characterized in part by adaptable behavior. In contrast, the RMP holds that a weak basic desire for order motivates people to be adaptable as a means of experiencing a high degree of spontaneity.
- The personality trait "ambitious" is one of the possible results of the MBTI. The MBTI holds that an inherited personality type, type ENTJ, is characterized in part by ambitious behavior. In contrast, the RMP holds that a strong basic desire for power motivates people to be ambitious as a means of experiencing a high degrees of willfulness and influence.

Case Vignettes of Joint Use

Hypothesis 4 is that the joint use of the MBTI and the RMP stimulates the self-discovery process more fully than when only one instrument is used. Presenting people with the results of two different assessments permits them to pick and choose the results most meaningful to them and to look at themselves from multiple perspectives. In order to evaluate this idea in a preliminary fashion, I administered the RMP and the MBTI to an undergraduate psychology class and then asked the students to write a report comparing their results.

Johnny was an undergraduate college student who completed both instruments at about the same time. The results of the MBTI classified him as an ENTJ. People with this personality type are take-charge individuals who have little tolerance for inefficient procedures in getting things done. They are logical, analytical, objectively critical, not likely to be convinced by anything but reasoning, energetic, fun-loving, and gregarious people who live life to its fullest.

The results of Johnny's RMP only partially supported the results of his MBTI. The RMP showed a strong basic desire for social contact, which supported the MBTI finding of gregariousness, and a strong basic desire for curiosity, which supported the MBTI results regarding Johnny's analytic nature.

The RMP results suggested that Johnny has a weak basic desire for independence, which is inconsistent with the MBTI's finding that he is resourceful

Table 9.2. Comparison of MBTI and RMP Explanations of Personality Traits

Personality trait	MBTI explanation	RMP explanation
Adaptable	Type INFP	Weak desire/order
	Type ESTP	
Ambitious	Type ENTJ	Strong desire/power
Analytical	Type ENTJ	Strong desire/curiosity
	Type INTP	
Aspires to do best	Type ENTJ	Strong desire/power
Belittles others	Type ISFP	Strong desire/vengeance
Bored by routine	Type INTP	Weak desire/order
Bored by theories	Type ESTP	Weak desire/curiosity
"By the book"	Type ISTJ	Strong desire/order
Cares about learning	Type INFP	Strong desire/curiosity
Commonsense	Type ESFP	Weak desire/curiosity
Compassionate	Type ISFP	Strong desire/idealism
Concerned with feelings of others	Type ISFJ	Weak desire/independence
Confident	Type ENTJ	Weak desire/acceptance
	Type ESTP	
Conflict avoidant	Type ESFJ	Weak desire/vengeance
	Type ENFJ	
	Type ISFP	
Conscientious	Type ISTJ	Strong desire/honor
	Type ISFJ	
	Type INFJ	
Considerate	Type ENFJ	Strong desire/social contact
Cooperative	Type ESFJ	Weak desire/vengeance
Curious	Type INFP	Strong desire/curiosity
Decisive	Type ESTJ	Weak desire/acceptance, Strong desire/power, Strong desire/independence
Determined	Type INFJ	Strong desire/power
Difficulty showing appreciation	Type INTP	Strong desire/independence
Direct	Type ESTJ	Strong desire/power
Dislikes rules	Type ISTP	Weak desire/order
	Type INFP	
Doesn't worry	Type ESTP	Weak desire/tranquility
Does things differently each time	Type INTP	Weak desire/order
Down-to-earth	Type ESFJ	Weak desire/status

(continued)

Table 9.2 *(continued)*

Personality trait	MBTI explanation	RMP explanation
Driven	Type INTJ	Strong desire/power
Dutiful	Type ISFP	Strong desire/honor
Empathetic	Type ENFJ	Weak desire/vengeance
		Weak desire/independence
Engaging	Type ESFJ	Strong desire/social contact
Flexible	Type ISTP	Weak desire/order
	Type ISFP	
	Type ESFP	
Follower	Type ISFP	Weak desire/power
Friendly	Type ENFJ	Strong desire/social contact
	Type ESFP	
Gentle	Type ISFP	Weak desire/vengeance
Gregarious	Type ENTJ	Strong desire/social contact
	Type ESTP	
Hardworking	Type ESTJ	Strong desire/power
	Type ISTJ	
Helpful	Type ENFJ	Strong desire/idealism
	Type ENFP	
High standards	Type INTJ	Strong desire/power
Humanitarian	Type INFJ	Strong desire/idealism
Idealistic	Type INFP	Strong desire/idealism
Improvises	Type ENFP	Weak desire/order
Independent	Type INFP	Strong desire/independence
	Type INTJ	
Insensitive	Type ESTJ	Weak desire/social contact
Inspires others	Type ENFJ	Strong desire/idealism
Ivory tower	Type INTP	Strong desire/curiosity
Leader	Type INTJ	Strong desire/power
Learns best by doing	Type ESTP	Weak desire/curiosity
Likes being in charge	Type ESTJ	Strong desire/power
	Type ENTJ	
Likes organizing	Type ESTJ	Strong desire/order
	Type ENFJ	
	Type INTJ	
Likes own space	Type ISFP	Weak desire/social contact
Likes sports	Type ESTP	Strong desire/physical activity
	Type ESFP	
Logical	Type ENTJ	Strong desire/curiosity
	Type ENTP	

Personality trait	MBTI explanation	RMP explanation
Loyal	Type ESFJ Type ENFJ Type ISFP Type INFP Type ISFJ	Strong desire. honor
Kind	Type ESFJ Type ISFP	Weak desire/vengeance
Materialistic	Type ESTP	Strong desire/status
Matter-of-fact	Type ESTJ	Weak desire/curiosity
Modest	Type ISFP	Weak desire/status, Weak desire/independence
Needs affirmation from others	Type ENFP	Strong desire/acceptance
Nonconformist	Type INTP	Strong desire/independence, Weak desire/status
Not concerned with possessions	Type INFP	Weak desire/status
Onlooker	Type ISTP	Weak desire/power
Outgoing	Type ESFP	Strong desire/social contact
Outspoken	Type INTP	Strong desire/power
Perceptive	Type ISFJ	Weak desire/independence, Strong desire /social contact
Persistent	Type INFJ	Strong desire/power
Personable	Type ESFJ	Strong desire /social contact
Popular	Type ESFJ	Strong desire/social contact
Practical	Type ESTJ Type ESFJ Type ESFP Type ISTJ	Weak desire/curiosity
Prefers facts to theory	Type ESFP	Weak desire/curiosity
Puts off decisions	Type ISTP	Strong desire/acceptance, Weak desire/power
Pragmatic	Type ESTP	Weak desire/idealism, Weak desire/honor
Quiet	Type ISTP Type INTP Type ISTJ Type INTJ	Weak desire/power, Weak desire/social contact, Weak desire/tranquility
Realistic	Type ESTP	Weak desire/idealism
Relaxed about getting things done	Type ISFP	Weak desire/power

(continued)

Table 9.2 *(continued)*

Personality trait	MBTI explanation	RMP explanation
Reserved	Type ISTP	Weak desire/social contact
	Type INTP	
	Type ISTJ	
Resourceful	Type ENTJ	Strong desire/independence
	Type INTP	
Responsible	Type ESTJ	Strong desire/honor
	Type ENFJ	
Results oriented	Type ESTJ	Strong desire/power
Self-determined	Type ENTJ	Strong desire/independence
Serious	Type ISTJ	Weak desire/social contact
	Type INTJ	
Skeptical	Type INTJ	Strong desire/independence
Spontaneous	Type ESTP	Weak desire/order
	Type ESFP	
	Type ENFP	
Stimulating	Type ENTP	Strong desire/curiosity
Stubborn	Type INFP	Strong desire/independence
	Type INTJ	
Thorough	Type ISFJ	Strong desire/order
Trustworthy	Type ESFJ	Strong desire/honor
Warm	Type ESFJ	Strong desire/social contact
	Type ENFP	

and self-determined. The results of the RMP also revealed that Johnny has a weak basic desire for tranquility, implying that he is a risktaker, dare devil, or adventurer.

Johnny agreed with the MBTI results that he is well-informed, enjoys expanding knowledge, and is quick to see illogical and inefficient procedures. "But the rest of the [MBTI's] description," he wrote, "only describes me sometimes and is not the dominating part of my personality. I believe I am more in the middle of those descriptions. Moreover, I believe the Reiss [RMP] description is an accurate profile of my characteristics."

Stephen was a student in the same class as Johnny who thought he might have made a mistake taking a course on the normal personality. The results of his MBTI indicated that he was an ENTP. Stephen agreed that he is a knowledge seeker and disorganized, which are two of the dominant traits of ENTP. He wrote that the MBTI description of him was valid as far as it went, but wondered, "What's next? The MBTI does not say anything more."

On the RMP, Stephen scored very low for honor, high for family, and high for status. The results of the RMP addressed areas of personality that were not commented on in the MBTI results. Stephen indicated that his RMP results were valid.

Kim was an ESFJ college student who completed both the MBTI and the RMP. ESFJ's are trustworthy, loyal, cooperative, warm, down-to-earth, and practical. She wrote, "I do feel that I am an extroverted person: in terms of when I am happy I am around others. I do feel that I am a sensing person: I focus on the present and make decisions from concrete information. I do feel that I am a feeling person: I do make decisions with my heart. Last I do feel that I am a judging person: I like to have an organized and planned approach to life." Although Kim agreed that she has the personality traits of an ESFJ, she felt that the MBTI provided only vague explanations for why she has such traits.

The results of the RMP revealed that Kim has a strong basic desire for social contact, which supported the MBTI results that she is warm, engaging, and personable. Kim scored at the low end of the average range on status, which is consistent with the MBTI result that she is down-to-earth. She scored at the high end of the average range for order, which is consistent with the MBTI finding that she is organized.

On the RMP, Kim had a low score for honor but a high score for idealism. This means that she was disloyal to the people in her everyday life but loyal to social causes and the downtrodden. The MBTI does not distinguish between honor and idealism.

Kim thought that the MBTI described her more validly. She thought she was more ethical and loyal than what was suggested by the RMP.

Jean was an INFP college student who completed both the MBTI and the RMP. INFPs are loyal, ethical, idealistic, independent, curious, and somewhat disorganized.

Jean's highest score on the RMP was for independence, which is consistent with an INFP personality. She agreed with this result, commenting, "I have always seen self-reliance as my defining characteristic . . . I am a very independent person who is strongly motivated by not wanting or having to depend on others. I thoroughly agree with the Reiss [Motivation] Profile that my strongest striving is for independence."

Jean also agreed with her high score for vengeance, saying she has a competitive nature. The MBTI does not assess the competitive spirit and, thus, did not reveal her competitive nature.

The results of Jean's RMP indicated that her curiosity is average. Jean wrote, "I seem to agree more with Myers-Briggs that I am curious and quick to see possibilities. Overall, I think both personality tests did a pretty good job of reporting my true self."

Michael was an ENTP. The MBTI described him as a knowledge-seeker who is good at reading people and an outspoken nonconformist. The MBTI also attributed to him traits of a disorganized person.

The results of Michael's RMP quantified the MBTI's results. His score for curiosity was 0.9 standard deviations above the norm, which is high but not high enough to suggest that knowledge and intellectualism are the strongest motives in his life.

The results of the RMP indicated that Michael is independent-minded. This finding supported the MBTI results that Michael can be a stubborn nonconformist.

On the RMP, Michael scored very low for honor and idealism, suggesting that he is expedient and realistic. In his class report, he acknowledged the validity of these results. He wrote, "I cut corners in some of my responsibilities and tasks. I can be manipulative." Michael's MBTI results did not mention anything about his expediency; the MBTI has few items assessing honor and expedience.

Michael's RMP results indicated a low score for saving. "Throughout college I have pretty much blown all my money," he explained. Michael's MBTI results did not mention his spendthrift ways.

The RMP results also suggested a high score on need for acceptance, implying a tendency to be insecure and lacking in self-confidence. Michael acknowledged that he seeks approval. "I feel better about myself when people who I respect and admire show positive approval of me."

Jim was an INFJ. According to the MBTI, INFJs are principled, conscientious, interested in the common good, and succeed by perseverance.

The RMP results indicated a strong need for honor but only an average need for idealism. Jim is concerned with the moral rules but not necessarily with humanitarian or altruistic endeavors. This finding supported the MBTI's description of Jim as conscientious, but it contradicted the MBTI result that Jim is interested in the common good.

The RMP indicated that Jim is insecure (which falls under a strong basic desire for acceptance) and a worrier (which falls under a strong basic desire for tranquility). Jim agreed that these traits validly described him and observed that nothing in his MBTI results indicated his insecurity.

Another disagreement between the results of the two tests was that the MBTI described Jim as determined, whereas the RMP described Jim as average or below average regarding this trait. Jim wrote, "At first when I got the results back, I thought independence meant . . . to do things by yourself. [Now I realize that] independence is more like proud or autonomous, which is your way of doing things. I . . . have a totally weak striving [for independence]." Jim observed, for example, that he practices Christian humility.

On the RMP Jim scored low for status, power, and vengeance. He later explained, "Status is something I do not think is important for many reasons." Jim says he is down-to-earth and humble. The MBTI results did not mention Jim's humble, peaceful, and nondirective nature.

Similarities and Dissimilarities

The RMP and the MBTI have the following five significant similarities.

- **Emphasis on Normal Personality**. Both the MBTI and the RMP assess many normal personality traits not relevant to mental illness. Neither assessment is based on psychodynamic, Freudian constructs.

- **Recognition of Opposite Traits**. Both the MBTI and the RMP recognize opposite personality traits. The MBTI, for example, has a bipolar scale of extraversion versus introversion. The RMP has a scale anchored at the extremes by social contact versus solitude.

- **Plain Language Results**. You do not need a degree in psychology in order to understand the results of the MBTI and the RMP. Any educated person attending an MBTI one-day workshop, for example, can readily understand their results on the MBTI. The results of the RMP are stated in plain language (no technical jargon whatsoever).

- **Human Development Applications**. Both tools have human development applications such as self-discovery and leadership training. Both instruments can be used to resolve interpersonal conflicts in a work setting; both can be used in job coaching.

- **Tolerance of Diverse Personalities**. Both the MBTI and the RMP teach tolerance of diverse personalities at work. Such training helps people work together as a team. Prior to the RMP, Myers and Briggs were the only influential personality theorists who embraced tolerance of all kinds of personalities.

The RMP and the MBTI have the following five significant dissimilarities.

- **Personality Dimensions versus Psychological Needs**. The MBTI reduces all normal personality traits to combinations of four personality dimensions. In contrast, the RMP reduces all personality traits to combinations of sixteen basic desires or psychological needs.

- **Comprehensive versus Narrow Assessment of Personality Traits**. The RMP assesses many more personality traits than does the MBTI. The

RMP but not the MBTI, for example, assesses competitive spirit, romantic nature, and spending habits.

- **Categorical versus Quantified Results**. The MBTI is scored into either/or, black/white personality categories, whereas the RMP has shades of gray or "in between" categories. The MBTI, for example, types every person on the planet as an extrovert (E) or an introvert (I). In contrast, the RMP assesses 20 percent of the population as having a strong basic desire for social contact (sociable/extroverted), 20 percent of the population as having a weak basic desire for social contact (private, loner/introverted), and the remaining 60 percent of the population as showing mixed introverted and extroverted traits.

- **Established versus Recent Psychometric Tool**. The RMP is a recently introduced psychometric instrument with about 25,000 administrations to date. The MBTI is a well-established tool with more than five million administrations to date.

- **Minimum versus Maximum Differentiation**. For maximum psychometric differentiation among personalities, each of the sixteen MBTI types should represent about one-sixteenth of the population. Yet some types are common, whereas others are rare. The MBTI assesses about 17.8 percent of the male population as Type ISTJ, for example, but only 1.7 percent as type ISFP (Fitzgerald & Kirby, 1997). This is a significant psychometric flaw in the MBTI.

MBTI experts are simply wrong in concluding that human nature has distributed the sixteen personality types with different frequencies. What has really happened is that the specific questions used on the MBTI vary haphazardly in the intensities of personality traits assessed. In other words, the prevalence of the sixteen MBTI personality types has everything to do with how the questions are worded and very little to do with human nature. Consider the following hypothetical example of the prevalence of a Romantic Personality Type. If we ask people, "Do you enjoy sex," we would classify about 99 percent of the population as having a Romantic Personality Type. If we ask people, "Is sex essential to your happiness," we would classify about 50 percent of the population as having a Romantic Personality. If we ask people, "Would you be willing to sacrifice your life in exchange for a night with your favorite Hollywood star," we would classify less than 1 percent of the population as having a Romantic Personality.

Human nature does not include many more Type ISTJs than ISFPs. The differences are consequences of how the questions are worded on the MBTI measurement instruments. The MBTI type ISTJ assesses more average intensity values than those assessed by the ISFP, producing the illusion of widely different prevalence rates. The MBTI should be reworded so that all sixteen types are about equally prevalent.

In contrast, the RMP questions were deliberately worded to provide maximum psychometric differentiation. On the RMP, all sixteen strong desires are equally common with all sixteen weak desires. "Strong" is always 20 percent of the population, "weak" is a different 20 percent of the population, and "average" is always 60 percent of the population.

Conclusion

The MBTI is a valid measure of a narrow range of motivational personality traits, especially orderliness, sociability, and intellectual curiosity. The MBTI lacks comprehensiveness because it has no or few items regarding a number of relevant aspects of personality such as parenting, status, romance, physical activity, achievement, competitiveness, and saving. The MBTI's theoretical foundation is based on too few personality dimensions to provide a detailed explanation of the normal personality.

The MBTI can be reinterpreted in terms of motivation theory. All of the traits on the MBTI can be assessed by the RMP without paying any attention to Jungian or MBTI theory. The normal personality may be a result of sixteen motivational forces rather than the MBTI's four psychological dimensions of perception and judgment.

The MBTI and the RMP are compatible instruments. Both instruments are embedded in a message of tolerance of all kinds of personalities, which is so important for teamwork and relationships. Both teach self-awareness. The joint use of the two instruments seems to facilitate the self-discovery process by stimulating people to think more deeply about who they are. When the two instruments are used together, individuals can compare their results and pick and choose which ones they think best describe them. Although this may not be scientifically valid, it seems to work in educational settings by stimulating the thought process.

Historically, the MBTI focused attention on inherited traits and pioneered the study of normal personality types. Yet many behavioral scientists have questioned the scientific status of the MBTI (e.g., Hunsley, Lee, & Wood, 2004). My own view is that the MBTI is a valid measure of a narrow range of personality and that the scientific criticisms are overblown. Nevertheless, I think future scientific research is needed on the motivational basis of the MBTI. Researchers should study the motives underlying each of the MBTI items. They should evaluate scientifically the extent to which Jungian traits versus sixteen basic desires explain normal personality traits. There is a need to strengthen some of the MBTI dimensional constructs, which lack clarity and rigor. Nevertheless, the MBTI should be recognized as a historically significant break with the psychodynamic tendency to confuse individuality with abnormality. The MBTI replaced Freud's construct of psychopathology of everyday life, which has promoted intolerance and overdiagnosis, with the construct of natural individual differences, which has promoted tolerance and understanding. In its day, the MBTI was an enormously important advance in thinking about personality from a normal perspective.

10 The Sixteen Principles of Motivation

The following principles formally present the tenets of motivation analysis and summarize some of the content of this book.

> **Principle I.** Basic desires, also called *psychological needs*, predict behavior in natural environments. (See Chapter 1 for details.)

If you want to predict what somebody is likely to do in real-life situations, you should find out what the individual wants, and then predict that he or she will try to get it. If you know somebody is motivated by ambition, for example, you can predict that the individual will spend long hours trying to get ahead. If you know somebody is motivated by status, you can predict that the individual will wear stylish clothes.

I recommend a two-step analysis when predicting behavior in natural environments. This strategy does not work every time, but it works much better than what behavioral experts are doing now. In Step 1, the motivation analyst determines the individual's intrinsically valued goals. In Step 2, the motivation analyst estimates the most likely way the individual will pursue his or her goals. Many factors can be taken into account in Step 2 including the individual's habits, cognitions, information-processing skills, and abilities. Consideration also should be given to behavioral contexts, environments, and situations.

Suppose two individuals – one interpersonally skilled and the other unskilled – have a strong-intensity basic desire for power. The skilled individual might pursue leadership or achievement opportunities; in contrast, the unskilled person might become bossy, pushy, controlling, or domineering. The prediction is simply the most likely way each individual can experience influence of will.

> **Principle II.** Motivation is the assertion of deeply held values, not the discharge of psychic energy. (See Chapter 2 for details.)

I read a newspaper story on the supposed rebirth of interest in Freud. The experts who were interviewed for the story acknowledged that Freud's analysis of motivation was flawed, but they went on to say that Freud was right about many other issues. They regarded Freud's errors on motivation as a trifle, or something not integral to psychoanalysis as a whole.

Psychoanalysts consider motivation as "psychic energy" that lights up personality structures the way electricity lights up bulbs. They think Freud erred in believing that sex and aggression are the only two sources of such energy. Today, many psychodynamic theorists acknowledge sources of psychic energy other than sex and aggression, but they still credit Freud for validly describing the personality structures psychic energy lights up.

I disagree with the idea that motivation is psychic energy. I think motivation is about purpose, values, and the meaning of life. The construct of psychic energy implies that life is about getting it over with (that is, discharging energy/tension until none is left). Yet when I was very ill and thought I might die soon, I did not say to myself, "Great! I finally discharged all that tension and psychic energy!" I said to myself, "I will continue to be true to my values. Even if my life and death were insignificant in a vast universe of infinite space and time, I will continue to assert my values until I no longer can do so."

We are a species motivated to assert our values. People act for no reason other than to express their values. *Behavior has purpose and meaning not captured by constructs such as "psychic energy."*

Many people seem to express their values even when doing so leads to personal pain, sacrifice, or disadvantage. Soldiers who highly value their honor may sacrifice their lives when that is what duty requires. Many parents forego personal happiness for the benefit of their children.

Motives and values are closely connected qualities of a person – if you know one, you can guess the other. A person with a strong basic desire for curiosity, for example, values ideas, whereas a person with a weak basic desire for curiosity values deeds. A person with a strong basic desire for vengeance values winning, whereas a person with a weak basic desire for vengeance values compromise. For centuries, the scholarly analysis of motivation was classified as ethical philosophy.

Principle III. We can distinguish between means and ends. Only ends can explain personality and behavior.

Aristotle (1953/330 B.C.E.) divided motives into *means* and *ends*. Ends are what we intrinsically desire, whereas means are the methods of obtaining ends. When we eat food, for example, the meal is the means and sustenance is the end. When a child plays ball for the fun of it, ball playing is the means and exercise is the end. When a child is rewarded for drawing, we have two means–ends processes: The reward is a means for experiencing the end goal of status, and the drawing is the means for experiencing the end goal of competence (which falls under the basic desire for power).

Social psychologists have misunderstood the ancient distinction between means and ends. They have discussed Aristotelian means as a separate source of motivation called "extrinsic motivation" (e.g., Deci & Ryan, 1985). This is an error in logic because extrinsic motivation is always derived from an intrinsic source and, thus, is never independent of intrinsic motivation: *Without ends (sometimes called "intrinsic motivation"), means (sometimes called rewards or "extrinsic" incentives) would not be motivational.* Were it not for hunger, we would not be motivated to eat meals. Were it not for the need for status, we would not be motivated by material rewards.

Motivation analysis embraces Aristotelian constructs. Activities or behaviors are means, whereas needs are motivating ends. The sixteen basic desires are ends, implying that they potentially explain behavior.

Principle IV. Human motivation is multifaceted and cannot be reduced to just two or three kinds. Sixteen basic desires (psychological needs) drive the human psyche. (See Chapter 2 for details.)

Throughout history scholars have debated the possibility of reducing human motives to a small number of kinds (Reiss, 2004a). The ancient Greek philosophers, for example, recognized motives representing mind, body, and soul. Hedonists divided motives into pleasure-seeking versus pain-avoidance. Freud held that all human motives are about sex or aggression. Social psychologists have classified motives into just two kinds, intrinsic and extrinsic motivation.

In contrast, psychological need theorists have recognized a number of genetically distinct motives that cannot be reduced to just two or three kinds. William James (1918/1890), William McDougall (2003/1908), and Henry Murray (1938), for example, held that human nature shows a variety of genetically distinct, universal motives. The theory of sixteen basic desires is an example of multifaceted theory. Although the sixteen basic desires can combine and act in concert, they cannot be reduced to just two or three kinds.

UCLA social psychologist Bernard Weiner (1995) prefers two categories of motivation, intrinsic and extrinsic motivation. He has criticized me for studying psychological needs because previous multifaceted approaches did not work. Past taxonomies were not scientifically validated, whereas the taxonomy presented herein has been extensively validated (see Chapter 2). Past taxonomies were based on psychodynamic theory or anecdotal observations, whereas the taxonomy presented in this book is based on scientifically valid surveys of what people say motivates them (Reiss & Havercamp, 1998). Chemists had put forth invalid taxonomies of the physical universe for nearly 3,000 years before they developed the Periodic Chart. If chemists can take 3,000 years to develop a valid taxonomy of elements, why can't psychologists take 100 years to develop a valid taxonomy of psychological needs?

The sixteen basic desires have been validated in scientific studies and real-world applications. As of this writing, more than 25,000 people have been evaluated on the RMP. Large numbers of people have reported that the instrument was helpful. In addition to testimonial support – sometimes called "social validity" or "validity people can see" – researchers have reported studies repeatedly demonstrating the scientific standards of factorial validity, internal reliability, and test–retest reliability. Researchers have shown that each of the sixteen basic desires significantly predicts the results of various personality tests or significant real-world behavior. *The validation of the sixteen basic desires calls into question the validity of efforts to recognize only two kinds of motives such as intrinsic and extrinsic.*

Principle V. Basic desires have two significant characteristics, called *intrinsically valued goal* and *satiating intensity*. The intrinsically valued goal is the aim of a basic desire. The satiating intensity is the desired amount, frequency, or intensity of the intrinsically valued goal. (See Chapter 3 for details.)

What people want from life is determined by human nature, whereas how much they want is revealed by individuality. It is human nature to desire food, but some individuals eat more than others. It is human nature to confront those who offend, but some individuals value winning more than others. It is human nature to achieve, but some individuals work much harder than others. The sixteen basic desires show the universal, intrinsically desired goals of humankind. These are the motivating aims of behavior, or the "what" in "what people want." The results of an individual's RMP estimate how much experience the person desires with each intrinsically valued goal.

Many scholars have discussed motivation with little thought paid to satiating intensities. Educational philosophers, for example, have discussed the joy of learning as if it were a potentially unlimited, infinite joy. They have argued that since learning is a joy, everybody is born with the potential to flourish in school. It rarely occurred to these philosophers to quantify the joy of learning/education and identify satiating intensities. I would argue, for example, that education is a natural joy for the first half hour or so, after which it becomes naturally frustrating for many students.

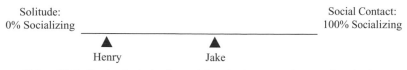

Figure 10.1. The basic desire for social contact as a continuum of motivation

---

Principle VI. Each of the sixteen basic desires can be considered as a continuum of motivation. The points on these continua represent different intensities of motivation. A "sensitivity" or "Aristotelian mean" or "satiating intensity" is the desired point of temporary balance (satiation). (See Chapter 3 for details.)

As Aristotle (1953/330 B.C.E.) observed, people are motivated to avoid the twin displeasures of "too little" and "too much" of their intrinsically valued experiences. How much is "too much" or "too little" depends on the individual's values. Figure 10.1, for example, shows that Henry and Jake differ in how much social contact they desire. Henry seeks companionship about 10 percent of his waking hours, whereas Jake seeks companionship about 50 percent of his waking hours. When the amount of social contact Henry or Jake experiences is less than they desire, they are motivated to socialize. When the amount of social contact they experience is about what they desire, they are satiated. When the amount of social contact is more than they desire, they are motivated to be alone.

Suppose that Henry and Jake attend a party that lasts five hours. Henry enjoys the party at first, but after a while the continued demand to socialize drains his energy. Jake, on the other hand, is full of pep when the party ends. After the party, Henry goes home, while Jake and friends go to the nearest bar to keep the party rolling.

People regulate, moderate, and balance their intrinsically valued experiences. The regulatory processes are imprecise and approximate. A person might balance food intake to approximately 2,500 calories per day, but on any given day or week the individual may eat substantially more or less than 2,500 per day. Similarly, people who value work–life balance might go through a period of weeks or even months of working long hours. Motivation analysis is focused on our efforts to balance our experiences over the long haul; motivation analysis does not predict short-term variations in rates of consumption of intrinsically valued goals.

Principle VII. The sixteen basic desires make us individuals. Everybody embraces the sixteen basic desires, but to different extents. The satiating intensities with which an individual experiences the sixteen basic desires reveal his/her normal personality traits. (See Chapters 3 and 4 for details.)

Behaviors that gratify average-intensity basic desires are not distinctive; these behaviors do not mark you as noticeably different from others. All you need to do to gratify average-intensity basic desires is go about your business, and the desires will be gratified *en passant*. People who have strong or weak basic desires, however, need to be proactive about gratifying their needs. Personality traits are habits people acquire to regulate and balance their strong-intensity or weak-intensity basic desires.

Consider the example of Henry and Jake shown in Figure 10.1. Whether they become introverts or extroverts may depend on the normative desires of the society in which they live. Suppose that Henry and Jake were raised in a society in which the average person spends 70 percent of his or her time socializing. In such a society, everyday life would provide many more social experiences than either Henry or Jake can tolerate. Both would be introverts in such a society because their goal would be to discourage others from interacting with them. On the other hand, suppose that Henry and Jake were raised in a society in which the average person spends only 5 percent of his or her time socializing. In such a society, everyday life would provide less social contact than either Henry or Jake desire. Both would be extroverts in such a society because they would learn habits that attract other people.

If the normative (average) desire for social contact were to fall between 10 percent and 50 percent, Henry would be an introvert, and Jake would be an extrovert. They would learn these personality traits as efficient means of regulating their social contact to their desired levels.

Some personality traits gratify two or more basic desires. The trait of being adventuresome, for example, may gratify both a weak-intensity basic desire for acceptance and a weak-intensity basic desire for tranquility. In other words, adventuresome people are both self-confident and daring (enjoy exposure to moderate danger).

The "Dictionary of Normal Personality Traits" (DNP, Appendix A) appended to this book provides a theoretical account of the strong or weak basic desires motivating the personality traits listed in a thesaurus. The DNP is a theoretical statement that can be evaluated scientifically.

Principle VIII. Strong satiating intensities motivate interest in multiple gratification objects.

As was noted in Chapter 8, the number of different gratification objects a person typically seeks is positively correlated with the intensity of the relevant basic desires. People with a strong-intensity basic desire for curiosity, for example, tend to be interested in learning about many topics, not just one or two subjects. People with a strong-intensity basic desire for status tend to be interested in owning many material things, not just an expensive car or home. People with a strong-intensity basic desire for eating tend to eat many different foods.

> **Principle IX.** Self-report often is a valid method for learning somebody's basic desires and psychological needs. (See Chapter 2 for details.)

Ever since Freud realized that one of his hysterical patients had duped him into believing she had been raped – she only imagined being raped – psychologists have been suspicious of what people tell them (called *self-report* data). Studies have shown that when people are asked about themselves, they can become defensive, exaggerate their good qualities, and underestimate their socially undesirable qualities (e.g., Crowne & Marlowe, 1960; Kagan, 2005).

Motivational assessments should arouse significantly less defensiveness than do assessments of abilities or behavior. If you want to be smart but unconsciously think you fall short, you might become defensive when asked about your intellectual abilities. Yet you should not become defensive when asked how smart you want to be. If you want to be honest but cheated on a test, you might become defensive when asked how honest you are. Yet you would not become defensive when asked how honest you want to be. On a test of what you want, you can get any result you want. Since the RMP is an assessment of motives and values, people tend to get the results they value.

Generally, self-report data are most likely to be invalid when people are suspicious of how the information will be used. When an individual is taking a personality test as part of a job interview, for example, he or she will tend to self-report desirable traits. I know a man, for example, who completed an online personality test for a job with two psychologists sitting next to him advising him how to respond. When an individual takes a motivational assessment for self-discovery purposes, however, he or she has no incentive to distort answers.

Havercamp and Reiss (2003) used the Marlowe-Crowne Social Desirability Scale (Crowne & Marlowe, 1960) to evaluate the tendency of the RMP to elicit answers people think make them look good. The results showed an average correlation of only .03, suggesting little social desirability bias to the instrument.

> **Principle X.** People should learn how to make smart choices that gratify basic desires. (See Chapters 5 and 6 for details.)

When I first heard Socrates's famous saying, "Know thyself," I tried to look inside myself to gain insight into who I am. I took the ancient philosopher's advice so seriously I set aside time one evening to introspect and discover the true me.

After I sat down in my chair, I realized I had no idea how to go about knowing myself. "Know thyself" sounds great, but it has little practical value absent some method. In my first effort to "know thyself," I sat in my chair for insights that never came. I had hoped some revelations would bubble up from my inner self so I could better understand who I am, but nothing happened. "Know thyself" is easy to say, but hard to do.

Motivation analysis provides a method for gaining self-awareness of one's strong and weak desires. Assessing ourselves on the sixteen basic desires is a first step toward gaining insight into who we are. When we learn our strong and weak basic desires, we can notice how those basic desires are expressed in our personality and behavior. We can learn how to make smart choices in terms of career, partner, and leisure. "Smart" choices are those that lead to the gratification and expression of our values. "Not-so-smart" choices are those that lead to frustration of wants and to conflicts of values.

Principle XI. Analyses of childhood feelings and experiences are often of little help in resolving an adolescent's or adult's personal problems.

Experts have said that resolving childhood feelings toward parents is important for overcoming adult problems (e.g., Fenichel, 1945; Freud, 1963/1916). Their advice is based on the following assumptions:

Hypothesis I. Motivation is "psychic energy."

Hypothesis II. "Psychic energy" can become "fixated" in childhood trauma and pleasures.

Hypothesis III. Fixated energy can cause personal troubles such as workaholism, perfectionism, and divorce.

Hypothesis IV. "Insight" into the possible childhood origins of one's troubles releases fixated psychic energy-producing catharsis.

Hypothesis V. An effective way to gain therapeutic insight is to reexperience childhood feelings toward parents.

If just one of these hypotheses is invalid – and all are scientifically unsubstantiated and debatable – the door is wide open for skeptics to question the value of analyzing childhood in order to resolve adult problems (Bandura, 1969; Ellis, 1973).

Please keep in mind that I am not calling for an end to psychodynamic therapy with people who have a mental illness. Instead, *I am saying that "normal" people who have personal troubles should learn how to solve those problems rather than how to blame them on their parents or upbringing.* Motivation analysis is potentially a more effective approach to personal troubles than is analyzing childhood, and it is much less expensive and time-consuming.

> **Principle XII.** We have a natural tendency to assume that our values are best, not just for us, but potentially for everyone. Such "self-hugging" motivates (1) personal blind spots; (2) intolerance of people with different values; and (3) a tendency to confuse individuality with abnormality. (See Chapter 7 for details.)

When we learn something about ourselves, we sometimes think we have learned something about human nature. We tend to confuse our nature for human nature because we underestimate individuality and trust our own experiences above all else. The intellectual, for example, discovers that he or she enjoys thinking and concludes that everybody should be a life-long learner. The executive discovers that he or she likes being in charge and then gives corporate seminars extolling the superior virtues of leadership. The psychologist who discovers that he or she is independent-minded claims that "autonomy" is a sign of mental health, but being in need of people (dependency) is a sign of mental illness.

Blind spots occur when we expect to be judged in accordance with our values, but others judge us instead in accordance with *their* values. We are slow to realize when people are judging us by values very different from our own.

We are an intolerant species because we are motivated to assert our own values. We have a tendency to think that something must be wrong with people whose values are significantly different from our own. We cannot comprehend how anybody can freely choose to pursue goals we intrinsically devalue because all of our experiences with those goals have been unpleasant.

> **Principle XIII.** People bond to those with similar values and separate from those with opposite values. (See Chapter 8 for details.)

When two people are matched on a basic desire – both strongly value (or both strongly devalue) the same goal – they bond with respect to that basic desire (Wiltz & Reiss, 2003). Two people with a strong basic desire for status, for example, share materialistic values, with each feeling that the other understands his or her need to be a "Very Important Person." They have the potential to form a partnership to get wealthy together. Two people with a weak basic desire for status share nonmaterialistic values, and each feels that the other understands his or her down-to-earth nature. They have the potential to form a partnership based on a modest lifestyle.

When two people are mismatched on a basic desire, however, they tend to separate on issues related to that need. They have opposite aims and pull in opposite directions. Each tends to feel misunderstood by the other. Since each is motivated to express his or her values, they have the potential to quarrel repeatedly. Two people mismatched on the basic desire for status, for example, hold incompatible values. One wants to pursue wealth or possibly fame, but the other believes that the best things in life are free. Each embraces pursuits the other does not care about or devalues.

We lose respect for people who have values very different from our own. Independent people, for example, tend to mark down interdependent people, thinking they lack pride; interdependent people tend to mark down independent people, thinking they are stubborn. Risktakers tend to mark down cautious people, thinking they are cowards; cautious people tend to mark down risktakers, thinking they are reckless.

> **Principle XIV.** People pay attention to stimuli relevant to their basic desires and tend to ignore stimuli irrelevant to their basic desires (Reiss & Wiltz, 2004).

A person motivated by a strong basic desire for social contact, for example, often looks for opportunities to socialize, whereas a person motivated by a weak basic desire for social contact may not even know who is holding a party over the weekend. A person with a strong basic desire for order may notice when somebody leaves ashes in a cigarette tray, whereas a person with a weak basic desire for order may not even notice when dirty dishes are left in the sink. A person with a strong basic desire for status may notice where everybody at work falls on the organization chart, whereas a person with a weak basic desire for status may not know who's who at work.

> **Principle XV.** Positive and negative emotions signal the temporary satiation or frustration of an intrinsically desired goal. (See Chapter 2 for details).

When an intrinsically desired goal is temporarily satiated, people experience a joy. A different joy is experienced depending on which basic goal is satiated. Vitality, for example, is the joy people experience when they temporarily satiate their need for physical activity. Fun and safety, respectively, are the joys people experience when they temporarily satiate their needs for social contact and tranquility.

When an intrinsically desired goal is temporarily frustrated, people experience a negative feeling. A different negative feeling is experienced depending on the specific basic desire that is temporarily frustrated. People experience chaos, loneliness, sluggishness, and fear, respectively, when their needs for order, social contact, physical activity, and tranquility are frustrated.

Hedonistic psychologists have argued that people are motivated to maximize pleasure and to minimize pain, but this viewpoint is technically invalid. Most people actually spend little time pursuing pleasure: Pleasure-seeking is not even one of the sixteen basic desires of life. As nineteenth-century philosopher John S. Mill (1964/1873) observed, people aim to obtain their goals (e.g., food, knowledge, status, vindication) and take pleasure *en passant*. The goals provide the motivation; the pleasure is usually a nonmotivating by-product of goal obtainment. Pleasure is nature's way of signaling that we have obtained what we want, but pleasure itself is not what we want.

Principle XVI. The sixteen basic desires potentially motivate vicarious experiences, including preferences for plays, movies, and stories.

Ever since Albert Bandura (1969) published his influential modeling studies in the 1960s, research psychologists have tended to deny the phenomenon of vicarious satisfaction of psychological needs. In the Bandura studies, some children watched a film of models hitting a 'Bobo doll," but other children watched a film of cooperative play with the Bobo doll (Bandura & Walters, 1963). After viewing the film, the children were taken to a room with the same Bobo doll and tended to repeat the behavior they saw on the film. The children who watched the aggressive models were more likely to attack and hit the Bobo doll compared to the children who had watched the cooperative models.

The Bandura modeling studies produced results opposite to those predicted by psychodynamic theory's frustration–aggression hypothesis (Dollard et al., 1939). If viewing aggressive models releases aggressive energy, as predicted by the frustration–aggression hypothesis, then the children who watched models attack the Bobo doll should have been less aggressive when they later encountered the real Bobo doll. Bandura disconfirmed this psychodynamic prediction. He showed that viewing aggressive models actually increased the children's aggressive behavior.

Psychodynamics is based on a "psychic energy" model of motivation, whereas motivation analysis is based on a value-assertion model. Motivation analysis does not predict that viewing aggressive models for brief periods of time lessens subsequent aggressive behavior. Instead, motivation analysis predicts that those children with a history of aggressive behavior will enjoy watching aggressive models more than do children with a history of nonaggressive behavior. The Bandura studies did not evaluate this prediction. The Bandura modeling studies demonstrated that aggression can be imitated, but the results did not refute the possibility that strong and weak basic desires motivate vicarious pleasures.

Motivation analysis predicts that aggressive people like to watch aggressive plays, movies, and television programs because choosing such programs is a means of asserting one's values. The results of the relevant research studies support the hypothesis that aggressive people prefer aggressive movies and television shows (e.g., Freedman, 1984).

Jim Wiltz and I conducted a study (Reiss & Wiltz, 2004) on why people watched the first reality television shows such as *Survivor* and *Big Brother*. We found that people with a strong basic desire for status tended to watch these shows. These individuals valued wealth and celebrity status, which were frequent themes of the early reality television shows.

Human beings have the potential to reexperience past joys by recalling the experiences that produced them. The sixteen basic desires motivate us to recall certain experiences. When we recall our achievements, for example, we can reexperience a sense of competence. When we reflect on our children, we can reexperience our love for them. Motivation analysis predicts that ambitious people devote more time to reminiscing about their achievements than do nonambitious people.

Dictionary of Normal Personality Traits

This dictionary shows the basic desires motivating more than 500 personality traits. If you cannot find the trait you are looking for, search for a synonym. The following chart shows the personality themes used to generate the dictionary.

Basic desire	Personality themes*
Acceptance (ACP)	↑ : Fear of criticism, insecure, pessimism, maladjusted, needy behavior ↓ : Self-confidence, optimism, adventure
Curiosity (CUR)	↑ : Thinking, learning, intellectual aspects of life, ideas ↓ : Practical, anti-intellectual, unthinking
Eating	↑ : Appetite, overweight, sensuality ↓ : Fussy eater, thin
Family	↑ : Enjoys parenting, raising children, values children ↓ : Dislikes parenting, taking care of children
Honor (HON)	↑ : Character, ethics, guilt, loyalty, patriotism, self-discipline ↓ : Expedient, unethical, lacks character, disloyal, unreliable
Idealism (IDL)	↑ : Just, involved, compassionate, altruism, fair, high road, higher calling ↓ : Realistic, hard-nosed, pragmatic, unfair, tolerates injustice
Independence (IND)	↑ : Individuality, autonomy, self-reliance, freedom, stubborn, difficult ↓ : Mysticism, religious humility, oneness, trusting, needs others, touchy-feely
Order (ORD)	↑ : Organization, structure, stability, details, planning, rituals, clean, prepared ↓ : Disorganized, spontaneous, imaginative, change, unstable, unprepared
Physical Activity (ACT)	↑ : Athleticism, exercise, strength, vitality, energy, fit ↓ : Lack of energy, unfit, lazy
Power (POW)	↑ : Assertion of will, achievement, dominance, influence, competence/mastery ↓ : Nonassertion of will, easygoing, laid-back, onlooker, submissive
Romance (ROM)	↑ : Romantic, strong sex drive, sensuality, appreciates beauty ↓ : Weak sex drive, avoids sex, tolerates plainness
Saving	↑ : Collecting, thrift, mends things, tightwad ↓ : Throws things away, wasteful, extravagant
Social Contact (SOC)	↑ : Attracts/embraces people, fun, polite, friendly, belonging ↓ : Repels/avoids people, serious, alone, humorless, rude, unfriendly
Status (STA)	↑ : Important, seeks attention, snobbery, wealth, reputation, proper, upper class ↓ : Disrespects status, vulgar, improper, lower class, unimportant
Tranquility (TNQ)	↑ : Fear, anxiety, worry, shy, avoids risk ↓ : Excitement, thrills, unafraid, cool, brave, seeks danger
Vengeance (VEN)	↑ : Aggression, hostility, conflict, confrontation, opposition, competition, violent, cruel ↓ : Cooperation, peace, kind, conflict avoidance, meek, forgiving

* **How to read:** A strong (↑) basic desire for acceptance motivates personality traits expressing fear of criticism, insecurity, pessimism, maladjustment, or needy behavior. A weak (↓) basic desire for acceptance motivates personality traits expressing self-confidence, optimism, or adventure.

Personality trait	Probable motive(s)	Personality theme
Abrasive	↓ SOC + ↑ VEN	repels people
Absent parent	↓ family	dislikes parenting
Abstemious	↑ honor	self-discipline
Academic	↑ curiosity	intellectual
Accepting of others	↓ acceptance	self-confidence
Accumulator	↑ saving	collecting
Acrimonious	↑ vengeance	hostility
Action-oriented	↓ curiosity	practical
Active	↑ physical activity	vitality
Adaptable	↓ order	change
Adventurer	↓ TNQ + ↓ ACP	unafraid and self-confident
Advocate	↑ power	influence
Aesthetic	↑ romance	beauty
Affable	↑ social contact	attracts people
Afraid	↑ tranquility	fear
Aggressive	↑ vengeance	conflict
Agonizing	↑ tranquility	worry
Agreeable	↑ social contact	attracts people
Aimless	↓ order	spontaneous
Aloof	↓ social contact	repels/avoids people
Altruistic	↑ idealism	helping others
Ambitious	↑ power	assertion of will
Amorous	↑ romance	strong sex drive
Analytical	↑ curiosity	thinking
Angry	↑ vengeance	anger
Animated	↑ physical activity	energy
Anxious	↑ tranquility	anxiety
Appeasing	↓ vengeance	conflict avoidance
Apprehensive	↑ tranquility	worry, fear
Approachable	↑ social contact	attracts people
Arbitrary	↓ idealism	unfair
Argumentative	↑ vengeance	conflict
Aristocratic	↑ status	social class
Arrogant	↑ IND or ↑ STA or ↑ POW	pride or conceit or snobbery
Ascetic	↑ honor	self-discipline
Aspiring	↑ power	achievement
Assertive	↑ power	assertion of will
Athletic	↑ physical activity	athleticism
Audacious	↑ power	assertion of will
Austere	↓ status	(absence of) wealth
Authoritarian	↑ power	assertion of will

(continued)

Personality trait	Probable motive(s)	Personality theme
Autonomous	↑ independence	self-reliant
Avoidant	↓ social contact	alone
Barbaric	↓ status or ↑ vengeance	low social class or violent
Bashful	↓ SOC + ↑ ACP	private, insecure
Belligerent	↑ vengeance	anger
Benevolent	↑ idealism	compassionate
Bitter	↑ vengeance	anger
Bigoted	↓ idealism	unfair
Blasé	↓ power	nonassertion of will
Boastful	↑ IND or ↑ STA or ↑ POW	pride or conceit or snobbery
Boisterous	↑ power + ↓ status	self-assertion, low class
Bold	↑ power	assertion of will
Boorish	↓ social contact	repels people
Braggart	↑ IND or ↑ STA or ↑ POW	pride or conceit or snobbery
Brash	↑ POW + ↓ STA	improper self-assertion
Brave	↓ tranquility	courageous
Breaks promises	↓ honor	lacks ethics
Brusque	↓ social contact	repels people
Brutal	↑ vengeance	cruelty
Buffoon	↑ social contact	fun
Cad	↓ honor	lacks character
Calculating	↑ curiosity + ↓ honor	expedient thinking
Callous	↓ idealism	lacks compassion
Calm	↓ tranquility	lacks anxiety
Cantankerous	↑ VEN + ↑ IND	irritable and difficult
Capricious	↓ honor	unreliable
Casual	↓ status	informal
Careful	↑ order	detailed
Catty	↓ honor	lacks character
Cautious	↑ tranquility	avoids risk
Cavalier	↑ status	superior, dismissive
Celibate	↓ romance	avoids sex
Chaotic	↓ order	disorganized
Changes mind often	↓ order	spontaneous
Charitable	↑ idealism	compassionate
Charming	↑ social contact	attracts people
Chaste	↓ romance	weak sex drive
Cheater	↓ honor	lacks character
Cheerful	↑ social contact	attracts people
Chummy	↑ social contact	attracts people
Churlish	↓ social contact	rude
Clannish	↑ FAM or ↑ SOC	family, belonging

Personality trait	Probable motive(s)	Personality theme
Clean	↑ order	cleanliness
Coarse	↓ status	low social class (unrefined)
Cocky	↓ acceptance	overconfidence
Cold	↓ social contact	repels people
Cold blooded	↑ vengeance	cruel
Collector	↑ saving	collector
Combative	↑ vengeance	opposition
Commoner	↓ status	low social class
Compassionate	↑ idealism	compassion
Competitor	↑ vengeance	opposition
Compliant	↓ vengeance	cooperation
Composed	↓ tranquility	calm
Compulsive	↑ order	rituals
Conceited	↑ IND or ↑ STA or ↑ POW	pride or conceit or snobbery
Conciliatory	↓ vengeance	cooperation
Condescending	↑status	superiority
Conflict-avoidant	↓ vengeance	cooperation
Confident	↓ acceptance	self-confidence
Conformist	↓ IND or ↑ STA or ↓ VEN	oneness, formal, compliant
Conscientious	↑ honor	character
Considerate	↑ social contact	attracts people
Contemplative	↑ curiosity	thinking
Contrary	↑ vengeance	opposition
Convivial	↑ social contact	attracts people
Cool	↓ tranquility	calm
Cooperative	↓ vengeance	cooperative
Coquettish	↑ romance	courting behavior
Corrupt	↓ honor	lacks character
Courageous	↓ tranquility + ↑ honor	fearless, character
Courteous	↑ social contact	attracts people
Cowardly	↑ tranquility + ↓ honor	fear + expedience
Crabby	↓ SOC + ↑ VEN	complaining, repels people
Crass	↓ social contact	repels people
Creative	↑ POW + ↑IND + ↓ ORD	power, change, individual
Credulous	↓ IND or ↓ CUR	trusting, unthinking
Critical of others	↑ vengeance	opposition
Cross	↑ vengeance	anger
Crude	↓ status	low social class
Cruel	↑ vengeance	cruelty
Cunning	↓ honor	pragmatic
Curiosity	↑ curiosity	thinking

(continued)

Personality trait	Probable motive(s)	Personality theme
Cynical	↓ honor	lacks character
Daring	↓ tranquility	seeks danger
Dashing	↑ romance	sex, courting
Debonair	↑ status	social class, formal
Deceitful	↓ honor	lacks character
Decent	↑ social contact	polite
Decisive	↑ POW + ↓ ACP + ↑ IND	assertive, confident, self-reliant
Deep	↑ curiosity	thinking
Defensive	↑ acceptance	fears criticism, rejection
Defiant	↑ vengeance	opposition
Demure	↓ IND + ↓ VEN	modesty, meek
Dependent	↓ IND + ↑ ACP	needs other, insecure
Dependable	↑ honor	character
Despot	↑ power	dominance
Detached	↓ social contact	repels people
Determined	↑ power	assertion of will
Devious	↓ honor	lacks character
Devoted	↑ honor	loyal
Diffident	↑ ACP + ↓ POW	insecure, nonassertive
Dignified	↑ status	formal
Diplomatic	↑ status + ↓ vengeance	formal, conflict avoidance
Disagreeable	↓ SOC	repels people
Disarming	↑ social contact	attracts people
Disciplined	↑ honor	character
Discreet	↑ STA + ↑ SOC	concern for reputation
Disdainful	↑ status	superiority
Disgraced	↓ honor	unethical, lacks character
Disingenuous	↓ honor	lacks character
Disloyal	↓ honor	lacks character
Disorganized	↓ order	no plan
Disrespectful	↓ status or ↓ honor	rejects status, disloyal
Distant	↓ social contact	avoids people
Distrustful	↑ independent + ↓ honor	self-reliant, disloyal
Docile	↓ vengeance	cooperation
Dogged	↑ power	assertion of will
Do-gooder	↑ idealism	altruism
Domestic	↑ family	spends time at home
Domineering	↑ power	dominance
Dopey	↓ curiosity	no thinking
Downbeat	↑ acceptance	insecure
Down-to-earth	↓ status	informal
Dreamer	↑ idealism	altruism

Personality trait	Probable motive(s)	Personality theme
Driven	↑ power	assertion of will
Dutiful	↑ honor	character
Easygoing	↓ power	easygoing
Eccentric	↑ independence + ↓ status	indifferent to reputation
Egalitarian	↓ status	egalitarian
Egotistical	↓ ACP or ↑ POW or ↑ STA	confident, conceit, or snobbery
Efficient	↑ order	organized
Empathic	↓ independence	touchy-feely
Energetic	↑ physical activity	muscle exercise
Engaging	↑ social contact	attracts people
Enterprising	↓ ACP + ↑ POW + ↑ IND	self-confident and ambitious
Envious	↑ vengeance	hostility
Epicure	↑ eating	appetite
Exact	↑ order	details
Excitable	↑ tranquility	anxious
Expedient	↓ honor	lacks character
Explorer	↓ TNQ + ↓ ACC	seeks danger, self-confident
Extravagant	↓ saving	extravagant
Extroverted	↑ social contact	attracts people
Fair	↑ idealism	just, fair
Family person	↑ family	children
Fatalistic	↓ power	onlooker
Fatherly	↑ family	children
Fearful	↑ tranquility	fear
Fearless	↓ tranquility	unafraid
Fickle	↓ honor	lacks character
Fidgety	↑ tranquility	anxiety
Fiend	↓ honor	lacks character
Fighter	↑ vengeance	confrontation
Fit	↑ physical activity	energy
Flamboyant	↑ status	seeks attention
Flatterer	↓ honor	expedient
Flexible	↓ order	change
Flirtatious	↑ romance	sex
Focused	↑ power	assertion of will
Follows nose	↓ order	spontaneity
Foolhardy	↓ tranquility	embraces risk
Forceful	↑ power	assertion of will
Formal	↑ status	formal
Forward	↑ power	assertion of will

(continued)

Personality trait	Probable motive(s)	Personality theme
Foxy	↑ romance	sex
Free-spirited	↑ independence	individualism
Friendly	↑ social contact	attracts people
Frigid	↓ romance	dislikes sex
Frugal	↑ saving	thrift
Fun-loving	↑ social contact	fun
Fussy	↑ order	details
Fussy eater	↓ eating	fussy eater
Gambler	↓ tranquility + ↓ order	risk + spontaneity
Game	↓ acceptance	self-confident
Garrulous	↑ social contact	attracts people
Generous	↑ idealism or ↓ vengeance	altruism or kindness
Gentle	↓ vengeance	peace
Genuine	↑ honor	character
Gossip	↑ social contact	embraces people
Gluttonous	↑ eating	appetite
Gourmand	↑ eating	appetite
Gracious	↑ social contact	attracts people
Greedy	↑ status	wealth (materialistic)
Gregarious	↑ social contact	attracts people
Grouchy	↑ VEN or ↑ IND	irritable or difficult
Gruff	↓ social contact	repels people
Gutless	↑ tranquility	fear
Happy	↓ acceptance	self-confidence, optimism
Hardworking	↑ power	assertion of will
Hardy	↑ physical activity	vitality
Hateful	↑ vengeance	anger
Haughty	↑ status	superiority
Headstrong	↑ power	assertion of will
Heartless	↓ idealism	hard-nosed
Hedonist	↑ romance or ↑ eating	sensual person
Helpful	↑ social contact or ↑ idealism	attracts people or altruism
Helpless	↑ ACC or ↓ independence	insecure or needs people
Hermit	↓ social contact	avoids people
High-strung	↑ tranquility	anxiety
Hoarder	↑ saving	collecting
Honest	↑ honor	character
Hot	↑ romance	sex
Humanitarian	↑ idealism	involved
Humble	↓ IND + ↓ STA	humility, unassuming
Humorless	↓ social contact	repels people
Hygienic	↑ order	cleanliness
Hypocritical	↓ honor	lacks character

Personality trait	Probable motive(s)	Personality theme
Idealist	↑ idealism	social justice
Ignorant	↓ curiosity	dislikes thinking
Imaginative	↓ independence	mysticism (not factual)
Immaculate	↑ order	cleanliness
Immature	↑ acceptance	insecurity
Impartial	↑ idealism	justice
Impersonal	↓ social contact	repels people
Impertinent	↓ status	disrespects status
Impetuous	↓ curiosity	unthinking
Impotent	↓ romance	sexual inactivity
Impudent	↓ status + ↑ power	disrespectful boldness
Impulsive	↓ curiosity	unthinking
Inactive	↓ physical activity	lacks energy
Inconsiderate	↓ social contact	repels people
Inconsistent	↑ acceptance	fear of criticism/failure
Indecisive	↑ ACP or ↑ ORD	self-doubting or obsessive
Independent	↑ independence	autonomy
Individualistic	↑ independence	autonomy
Indomitable	↑ power	assertion of will
Inefficient	↓ order	disorganized
Infamous	↓ honor	lacks character
Inflexible	↑ order	stability
Influential	↑ power	assertion of will
Informal	↓ status	modest
Ingratiating	↑ social contact or ↑ status	attracts or flatters people
Inhibited	↑ tranquility	worry, fear
Inquisitive	↑ curiosity	learning
Insecure	↑ acceptance	fear of criticism
Insensitive	↓ SOC	repels people
Insider	↑ status	standing
Insolent	↓ status	disrespectful
Insubordinate	↑ vengeance	opposition/conflict
Insulting	↑ vengeance	conflict
Insurgent	↑ vengeance	opposition/conflict
Integrity	↑ honor	character
Intellectual	↑ curiosity	thinking
Interdependent	↓ independence	oneness
Introvert	↓ social contact	enjoys time alone
Intuitive	↓ independence	mysticism
Involved	↑ idealism	involved
Irrepressible	↑ power	assertion of will

(continued)

Personality trait	Probable motive(s)	Personality theme
Irreverent	↓ status	disrespectful
Irritable	↑ vengeance	anger
Jealous	↑ vengeance	competition
Jovial	↑ social contact	fun
Juvenile	↑ acceptance	insecurity
Kind	↓ vengeance	kind
Knowledgeable	↑ curiosity	learning
Lackadaisical	↓ physical activity	lacks energy
Laid-back	↓ power	laid-back
Lazy	↓ physical activity	dislikes exercise
Leader	↑ power	dominance
Learner	↑ curiosity	learning
Lethargic	↓ physical energy	lacks energy
Liar	↓ honor	lacks character
Licentious	↑ romance	sex
Likeable	↑ social contact	attracts people
Listless	↓ physical energy	lacks energy
Lively	↑ physical activity	vitality
Loafer	↓ physical activity	lack of energy
Lofty	↑ status	upper class
Logical	↑ curiosity	thinking
Looks the other way	↓ idealism	tolerates injustice
Lover	↑ romance	sex
Loyal	↑ honor	character
Magical	↓ independence	mysticism
Magnanimous	↑ idealism	high road
Malevolent	↑ vengeance	cruelty
Malicious	↑ vengeance	cruelty
Martyr	↑ idealism	higher calling
Maternal	↑ family	raising children
Mean	↑ vengeance	cruelty
Meek	↓ vengeance	conflict avoidance
Melancholy	↑ acceptance	insecure, pessimism
Merciful	↓ vengeance	forgiving
Merciless	↑ vengeance	cruelty
Messy	↓ order	disorganized
Methodical	↑ order	organized
Militant	↑ vengeance or ↑ honor	opposition, disciplined
Mischievous	↓ honor	bad conduct
Miserly	↑ saving	collecting
Modest	↓ IND + ↓ STA	humility, unassuming
Mollifying	↓ vengeance	peace
Monastic	↓ social contact	avoids people
Motherly	↑ family	children

Personality trait	Probable motive(s)	Personality theme
Mystic	↓ independence	mysticism
Nasty	↑ vengeance	cruelty
Neat	↑ order	organized
Needy	↑ acceptance	insecure
Nefarious	↓ honor	lacks character
Neglectful	↓ honor	unreliable
Nervy	↓ tranquility	unafraid
Neurotic	↑ tranquility	anxiety
Never home	↓ family	dislikes parenting
Nice	↓ vengeance	kind, conflict avoidance
Noble	↑ status	upper class
Nonaggressive	↓ vengeance	conflict avoidance
Nonassertive	↓ leadership	lacks will
Nonchalant	↓ tranquility	unafraid, cool
Nonconformist	↑ independence + ↓ status	individuality, reputation
Nondirective	↓ leadership	laid-back
Nonintellectual	↓ curiosity	unthinking
Noninvolved	↓ idealism	unmoved by injustice
No-nonsense	↓ social contact	humorless
Nonviolent	↓ vengeance	conflict avoidance
Nurturance	↑ family	raising children
Nymph	↑ romance	sex
Obedient	↓ power	submissive
Obnoxious	↓ social contact	repels people
Obstinate	↑ independence	stubborn
Oddball	↑ independence + ↓ status	individuality, reputation
Oily	↓ honor	lacks character
Opinionated	↑ independence	individuality
Oppositional	↑ vengeance	opposition
Optimist	↓ acceptance	optimism
Ordinary	↓ status	unimportant
Organized	↑ order	structure
Ostentatious	↑ status	commands attention
Outdoorsy	↑ physical activity	exercise
Outgoing	↑ social contact	attracts people
Outsider	↓ status or ↓ social contact	low standing, avoids people
Outspoken	↑ power	assertion of will
Overconfident	↓ acceptance	self-confidence
Overeater	↑ eating	appetite
Oversexed	↑ romance	strong sex drive
Pack rat	↑ saving	collecting
Panicky	↑ tranquility	anxiety

(continued)

Personality trait	Probable motive(s)	Personality theme
Passionate	↑ romance	sex
Paternal	↑ family	raising children
Patient	↓ tranquility	not anxious
Patrician	↑ status	social class
Peacemaker	↓ vengeance	conflict avoidance
Pedantic	↑ order	details
Peevish	↑ vengeance	anger
Peppy	↑ physical activity	vitality
Perceptive	↑ SOC or ↓ IND	attracts people, touchy-feely
Perky	↑ physical activity	vitality
Persistent	↑ power	assertion of will
Persuasive	↑ power	assertion of will
Pessimist	↑ acceptance	fear of failure
Philanthropic	↑ idealism	compassionate
Philosophical	↑ curiosity	thinking
Phobic	↑ tranquility	fear
Picky	↑ order	details
Pigheaded	↑ independence	stubborn
Pious	↑ honor	self-discipline
Pitiless	↑ vengeance	cruelty
Planner	↑ order	prepared
Platonic	↓ romance	without sex
Playful	↑ social contact	fun
Pleasant	↑ social contact	attracts people
Plebian	↓ status	lower class
Polite	↑ social contact	attracts people
Pompous	↑ status	seeks attention
Positive	↓ acceptance	optimism
Powerful	↑ power	assertion of will
Practical	↓ curiosity	practical
Pragmatic	↓ idealism	realistic
Prankster	↑ social contact	fun
Precise	↑ order	details
Predictable	↑ order	stable
Prepared	↑ order	planning
Presumptuous	↑ status	overestimates due
Principled	↑ honor	character
Private	↓ social contact	avoids people
Prodigal	↓ saving	wasteful
Professional	↑ power	competence
Profligate	↓ saving	extravagant
Promiscuous	↑ romance	sex

Personality trait	Probable motive(s)	Personality theme
Proper	↑ status	formal
Proud	↑ independence	individuality
Provocative	↑ vengeance	conflict
Prudent	↑ saving or ↑ tranquility	thrift
Prudish	↓ romance	dislikes sex
Pugnacious	↑ vengeance	opposition
Punctual	↑ order	plans, details
Purist	↑ order	details
Puritanical	↓ romance	dislikes sex
Purposeful	↑ power	assertion of will
Pushy	↑ power	influence, power
Quarrelsome	↑ vengeance	opposition
Quiet	↓ TNQ or ↓ POW or ↓ SOC	calm, nonassertive, shy
Realistic	↓ idealism	realistic
Rebel	↑ vengeance	conflict
Reckless	↓ tranquility	seeks excitement
Reclusive	↓ social contact	avoids people
Refined	↑ status	social class
Reflective	↑ curiosity	thinking
Regular	↓ status	Informal
Relentless	↑ power	assertion of will
Remorseful	↑ acceptance	pessimism
Resentful	↑ vengeance	conflict
Resourceful	↑ Independence	self-reliant
Respectful	↑ status or ↑ honor	loyal
Responsible	↑ honor	character
Reticent	↓ SOC or ↑ ACP	private, insecure
Rigid	↑ order	stability
Risktaker	↓ tranquility	risk
Rogue	↓ honor	lacks character
Romantic	↑ romance	sex
Rotten	↓ honor	lacks character
Rude	↓ social contact	repels people
Ruthless	↑ vengeance	cruelty
Sanctimonious	↑ honor	ethics
Saucy	↑ romance	sex
Saver	↑ saving	collecting
Scholar	↑ curiosity	thinking
Scoundrel	↓ honor + ↓ idealism	lacks character + unfair
Scrupulous	↑ honor	ethics
Secure	↓ acceptance	self-confidence

(continued)

Personality trait	Probable motive(s)	Personality theme
Sedate	↓ tranquility	calm
Sedentary	↓ physical activity	lacks energy
Seductress	↑ romance	sex
Self-assured	↓ acceptance	secure
Self-confident	↓ acceptance	secure
Self-conscious	↑ acceptance	fear of criticism
Self-determined	↑ independence	individuality
Self-doubter	↑ acceptance	insecure
Self-interest	↓ honor	expedient
Selfish	↓ IDL or ↓ SOC	unfair or unfriendly
Self-righteous	↑ honor	ethics/morality
Sensitive	↑ acceptance	fear of criticism
Sensual	↑ romance	sex, beauty
Sentimental	↑ romance	romance
Serene	↓ tranquility	calm
Serious	↓ social contact	humorless
Shabby	↓ status	lower class
Shameless	↓ honor	expedient
Showoff	↑ status	seeks attention
Shrewd	↑ CUR + ↓ IDL	hard-nosed thinking
Shy	↓ SOC or ↑ ACP	private, insecure
Sincere	↑ honor	ethics/morality
Single-minded	↑ power	assertion of will
Skeptical	↑ IND or ↑ CUR	self-reliant thinker
Smug	↑ status	superiority
Sneaky	↓ honor	lacks character
Snobbish	↑ status	superiority
Sociable	↑ social contact	attracts people
Sophisticated	↑ status	social class
Spineless	↑ tranquility	fear
Spirited	↓ acceptance	self-confident
Spiteful	↑ vengeance	anger
Spontaneous	↓ order	unplanned
Spotless	↑ order	cleanliness
Standoffish	↓ social contact	repels people
Steadfast	↑ honor	character
Stingy	↑ saving	thrift
Stoic	↑ honor + ↓ social contact	self-discipline, serious
Strange	↓ status	indifference to reputation
Strident	↑ vengeance	conflict, opposition
Strong-willed	↑ power	assertion of will
Studious	↑ curiosity	thinking
Suave	↑ status	social class

Personality trait	Probable motive(s)	Personality theme
Submissive	↓ power	submissive
Superior	↑ status	superiority
Suspicious	↑ acceptance	insecurity
Sweet	↑ social contact	attracts people
Swindler	↓ honor	lacks character
Taciturn	↓ SOC or ↑ ACP	private, insecure
Tactful	↑ status + ↓ vengeance	conflict avoidance
Tactless	↓ status or ↑ vengeance	disrespects status
Tame	↓ power	easy to control
Tardy	↓ order	spontaneous
Theatrical	↑ status	seeks attention
Thin	↓ eating	thin
Thorough	↑ order	details
Thoughtful	↑ curiosity	thinking
Thrifty	↑ saving	thrift
Tidy	↑ order	organized
Tight	↑ saving	tightwad
Timid	↑ tranquility	fearful, cautious
Tolerant	↑ idealism	fair
Traitor	↓ honor	disloyal
Transcendental	↓ independence	mysticism
Treacherous	↓ honor	lacks character
Tricky	↓ honor	lacks character
Trustworthy	↑ honor	character
Truthful	↑ honor	character
Tyrant	↑ power	dominance
Unambitious	↓ power	nonassertion of will
Unapproachable	↓ social contact	repels people
Unassuming	↓ status	informal
Unceremonious	↓ status	informal
Uncompromising	↑ independence	stubborn
Unconfident	↑ acceptance	insecurity
Undersexed	↓ romance	weak sex drive
Unemotional	↓ tranquility	calm
Unethical	↓ honor	character
Unflappable	↓ tranquility	calm
Unfriendly	↓ social contact	repels people
Uninhibited	↓ tranquility	unafraid
Unkind	↑ vengeance	cruel
Unpleasant	↓ social contact	repels people
Unprepared	↓ order	spontaneous

(continued)

Personality trait	Probable motive(s)	Personality theme
Unpretentious	↓ status	informal
Unreasonable	↑ independence	stubborn
Unscrupulous	↓ honor	lacks character
Unthinking	↓ curiosity	unthinking
Untidy	↓ order	disorderly
Untrustworthy	↓ honor	lacks character
Unyielding	↑ independence	stubborn
Upbeat	↓ acceptance	optimism
Upright	↑ honor	character
Uptight	↑ tranquility	anxious
Vain	↑ IND or ↑ STA or ↑ POW	pride or conceit or snobbery
Valiant	↓ tranquility	brave
Vengeful	↑ vengeance	conflict, anger
Venturesome	↓ acceptance + ↓ tranquility	self-confident and unafraid
Vicious	↑ vengeance	cruel
Vigorous	↑ physical activity	vitality
Virile	↑ romance	sex
Virtuous	↑ honor	character
Visionary	↑ idealism	higher calling
Vivacious	↑ social contact	attracts people
Volunteer	↑ idealism	altruism
Voracious	↑ eating	food
Warm	↑ social contact	attracts people
Wasteful	↓ saving	waste
Weak eater	↓ eating	not interested in food
Weak-willed	↓ power	nonassertion of will
Well-prepared	↑ order	planning
Whiz	↑ power	competence, achieving
Wicked	↓ honor	lacks character
Wild	↓ tranquility	thrills
Willful	↑ power	assertion of will
Winner	↑ vengeance	competition
Withdrawn	↓ social contact	alone
Workaholic	↑ power	assertion of will
Worrier	↑ tranquility	worry
Yellow	↑ tranquility	fear

Reiss Motivation Profile Estimator

Instructions: This worksheet is a self-discovery method for estimating your strong and weak basic desires, but the results are not scientifically valid. Place ✓ next to the items that *definitely* describe you. Enter the estimated result in the table and consult Chapter 3 to interpret your estimated results.

Strong basic desires	Average basic desires	Weak basic desires

ACCEPTANCE

Strong Acceptance

_____ 1. You are noticeably more insecure than most people are.
_____ 2. You have more difficulty than most people handling criticism.
_____ 3. You have a reputation for being inconsistent in your performance.

Weak Acceptance

_____ 4. You are self-confident.
_____ 5. You have a reputation for consistency in your performances.
_____ 6. You have a "can do" attitude.
_____ 7. Enter the total number of checkmarks for Strong Acceptance. _____
_____ 8. Enter the total number of checkmarks for Weak Acceptance. _____
_____ 9. Subtract 8 from 7. _____

If the number on line 9 is +2 or +3, you may have strong Acceptance.
If the number on line 9 is −2 or −3, you may have weak Acceptance.
If the number on line 9 is −1, 0, or +1, you may have average Acceptance.

CURIOSITY

Strong Curiosity

_____ 1. You have a reputation for being analytical or thoughtful.
_____ 2. Your ideas are very important to you.
_____ 3. You have a reputation as a thinker.

Weak Curiosity

_____ 4. You have a reputation for being a practical person.
_____ 5. You rarely think about theories you cannot put to use.
_____ 6. School bored you.
_____ 7. Enter the total number of checkmarks for Strong Curiosity. _____
_____ 8. Enter the total number of checkmarks for Weak Curiosity. _____
_____ 9. Subtract 8 from 7. _____

If the number on line 9 is +2 or +3, you may have strong Curiosity.
If the number on line 9 is −2 or −3, you may have weak Curiosity.
If the number on line 9 is −1, 0, or +1, you may have average Curiosity.

EATING

Strong Eating

_____ 1. You derive a lot of pleasure from eating.
_____ 2. You have a tendency to be overweight.
_____ 3. You know a lot about gourmet foods.

Weak Eating

_____ 4. You have a reputation for being a fussy eater.
_____ 5. You have a tendency to be underweight.
_____ 6. You rarely look forward to meals.
           7. Enter the total number of checkmarks for Strong Eating.   _____
           8. Enter the total number of checkmarks for Weak Eating.   _____
           9. Subtract 8 from 7.   _____
If the number on line 9 is +2 or +3, you may have strong Eating.
If the number on line 9 is −2 or −3, you may have weak Eating.
If the number on line 9 is −1, 0, or +1, you may have average Eating.

FAMILY

Strong Family

_____ 1. Your children are everything to you.
_____ 2. You like to be around children.
_____ 3. You spend a lot of time with your family.

Weak Family

_____ 4. Children bore you.
_____ 5. When you were a young adult, you did not want children.
_____ 6. You often are too busy to spend time with your family.
           7. Enter the total number of checkmarks for Strong Family.   _____
           8. Enter the total number of checkmarks for Weak Family.   _____
           9. Subtract 8 from 7.   _____
If the number on line 9 is +2 or +3, you may have strong Family.
If the number on line 9 is −2 or −3, you may have weak Family.
If the number on line 9 is −1, 0, or +1, you may have average Family.

HONOR

Strong Honor

_____ 1. You make it a point to do your duty.
_____ 2. You have a reputation for loyalty.
_____ 3. Your word is your bond.

Weak Honor

_____ 4. You will tell lies if it means keeping your job.
_____ 5. You might break prior commitments when circumstances change.
_____ 6. You have a reputation for being opportunistic.
7. Enter the total number of checkmarks for Strong Honor.   _____
8. Enter the total number of checkmarks for Weak Honor.   _____
9. Subtract 8 from 7.   _____
If the number on line 9 is $+2$ or $+3$, you may have strong Honor.
If the number on line 9 is -2 or -3, you may have weak Honor.
If the number on line 9 is -1, 0, or $+1$, you may have average Honor.

IDEALISM

Strong Idealism

_____ 1. You have compassion for poor and sick people.
_____ 2. You admire people whose work benefits humanity or the needy.
_____ 3. You give generously to charities.

Weak Idealism

_____ 4. You believe it is not your responsibility to help the downtrodden.
_____ 5. You "look the other way" rather than get involved in other people's troubles.
_____ 6. Social injustice rarely outrages you.
7. Enter the total number of checkmarks for Strong Idealism.   _____
8. Enter the total number of checkmarks for Weak Idealism.   _____
9. Subtract 8 from 7.   _____
If the number on line 9 is $+2$ or $+3$, you may have strong Idealism.
If the number on line 9 is -2 or -3, you may have weak Idealism.
If the number on line 9 is -1, 0, or $+1$, you may have average Idealism.

INDEPENDENCE

Strong Independence

_____ 1. It is very important to you to be self-reliant.
_____ 2. You have a reputation for being stubborn.
_____ 3. You have a reputation for doing things your way.

Weak Independence

_____ 4. You value "touchy-feely" experiences.
_____ 5. You are more of a conformist than most people you know.
_____ 6. You feel comfortable relying on family or spouse for support.
7. Enter the total number of checkmarks for Strong Independence._____
8. Enter the total number of checkmarks for Weak Independence._____
9. Subtract 8 from 7.   _____

If the number on line 9 is +2 or +3, you may have strong Independence.
If the number on line 9 is −2 or −3, you may have weak Independence.
If the number on line 9 is −1, 0, or +1, you may have average Independence.

ORDER

Strong Order

_____ 1. You have a reputation for being well organized.
_____ 2. Your have a reputation for cleanliness.
_____ 3. You have difficulty adapting to change.

Weak Order

_____ 4. You have a reputation for being disorganized.
_____ 5. You like to do things on the spur of the moment.
_____ 6. You tend to have several balls in the air at once.
7. Enter the total number of checkmarks for Strong Order.   _____
8. Enter the total number of checkmarks for Weak Order.   _____
9. Subtract 8 from 7.   _____

If the number on line 9 is +2 or +3, you may have strong Order.
If the number on line 9 is −2 or −3, you may have weak Order.
If the number on line 9 is −1, 0, or +1, you may have average Order.

PHYSICAL ACTIVITY

Strong Physical Activity

_____ 1. Working out is important to your happiness.
_____ 2. Twice you made an athletic team (high school plus college combined).
_____ 3. Being fit is very important to you.

Weak Physical Activity

_____ 4. You have a reputation for being lazy physically.
_____ 5. You tend to avoid physically rigorous activities.
_____ 6. You are unfit.
7. Enter the total number of checkmarks for Strong Physical
Activity.   _____
8. Enter the total number of checkmarks for Weak Physical Activity._____
9. Subtract 8 from 7.   _____
If the number on line 9 is +2 or +3, you may have strong Physical Activity.
If the number on line 9 is −2 or −3, you may have weak Physical Activity.
If the number on line 9 is −1, 0, or +1, you may have average Physical Activity.

POWER

Strong Power

_____ 1. You have a reputation as a self-starter.
_____ 2. You seek leadership roles.
_____ 3. You have a tendency to give others unsolicited advice.

Weak Power

_____ 4. You avoid challenges.
_____ 5. You dislike telling others what they should do.
_____ 6. You have a reputation for being laid back.
7. Enter the total number of checkmarks for Strong Power.   _____
8. Enter the total number of checkmarks for Weak Power.   _____
9. Subtract 8 from 7.   _____
If the number on line 9 is +2 or +3, you may have strong Power.
If the number on line 9 is −2 or −3, you may have weak Power.
If the number on line 9 is −1, 0, or +1, you may have average Power.

ROMANCE

Strong Romance

_____ 1. You dress attractively almost every day.
_____ 2. Sex is essential to your happiness.
_____ 3. People who attract many sex partners impress you.

Weak Romance

_____ 4. You rarely have sex (significantly less than once a week).
_____ 5. You lack confidence in your sexual skills.
_____ 6. You rarely think about romance/sex during your average day.
     7. Enter the total number of checkmarks for Strong Romance. _____
     8. Enter the total number of checkmarks for Weak Romance. _____
     9. Subtract 8 from 7. _____

If the number on line 9 is +2 or +3, you may have strong Romance.
If the number on line 9 is −2 or −3, you may have weak Romance.
If the number on line 9 is −1, 0, or +1, you may have average Romance.

SAVING

Strong Saving

_____ 1. You mend old rather than buy new replacements.
_____ 2. You hate throwing things away.
_____ 3. You have a reputation for being frugal.

Weak Saving

_____ 4. You do not take care of the things you own.
_____ 5. You often bust your monthly budget.
_____ 6. You have a reputation for being wasteful.
     7. Enter the total number of checkmarks for Strong Saving. _____
     8. Enter the total number of checkmarks for Weak Saving. _____
     9. Subtract 8 from 7. _____

If the number on line 9 is +2 or +3, you may have strong Saving.
If the number on line 9 is −2 or −3, you may have weak Saving.
If the number on line 9 is −1, 0, or +1, you may have average Saving.

SOCIAL CONTACT

Strong Social Contact

_____ 1. You are good at social networking.
_____ 2. You have a reputation for being friendly.
_____ 3. You have a more active social life than most people you know.

Weak Social Contact

_____ 4. You have a reputation for being unapproachable.
_____ 5. You spend a lot of time alone (more than most people you know).
_____ 6. You have difficulty making "small talk."
7. Enter the total number of checkmarks for Strong Social Contact._____
8. Enter the total number of checkmarks for Weak Social Contact._____
9. Subtract 8 from 7.   _____

If the number on line 9 is +2 or +3, you may have strong Social Contact.
If the number on line 9 is −2 or −3, you may have weak Social Contact.
If the number on line 9 is −1, 0, or +1, you may have average Social Contact.

STATUS

Strong Status

_____ 1. You have a reputation for being a formal person.
_____ 2. You usually buy the most prestigious items you can afford.
_____ 3. You are impressed with wealthy people.

Weak Status

_____ 4. You are unimpressed with celebrities.
_____ 5. You are an informal person.
_____ 6. You pay little attention to what other people think of you.
7. Enter the total number of checkmarks for Strong Status.   _____
8. Enter the total number of checkmarks for Weak Status.   _____
9. Subtract 8 from 7.   _____

If the number on line 9 is +2 or +3, you may have strong Status.
If the number on line 9 is −2 or −3, you may have weak Status.
If the number on line 9 is −1, 0, or +1, you may have average Status.

TRANQUILITY

Strong Tranquility

_____ 1. You are a worrier.
_____ 2. You have panic attacks.
_____ 3. You have little tolerance for pain.

Weak Tranquility

_____ 4. You have a reputation for being cool under pressure.
_____ 5. You are a dare-devil.
_____ 6. You have a reputation for being brave in the face of danger.
        7. Enter the total number of checkmarks for Strong Tranquility.   _____
        8. Enter the total number of checkmarks for Weak Tranquility.   _____
        9. Subtract 8 from 7.   _____

If the number on line 9 is +2 or +3, you may have strong Tranquility.
If the number on line 9 is −2 or −3, you may have weak Tranquility.
If the number on line 9 is −1, 0, or +1, you may have average Tranquility.

VENGEANCE

Strong Vengeance

_____ 1. You get into many quarrels, arguments, or fights.
_____ 2. You have a reputation for being a competitor or a fighter.
_____ 3. Winning is very important to you.

Weak Vengeance

_____ 4. You have a reputation for being a peacekeeper.
_____ 5. You go out of your way to avoid confrontation.
_____ 6. You are turned off by violence.
        7. Enter the total number of checkmarks for Strong Vengeance.   _____
        8. Enter the total number of checkmarks for Weak Vengeance.   _____
        9. Subtract 8 from 7.   _____

If the number on line 9 is +2 or +3, you may have strong Vengeance.
If the number on line 9 is −2 or −3, you may have weak Vengeance.
If the number on line 9 is −1, 0, or +1, you may have average Vengeance.

The Sixteen Basic Desires at a Glance

Basic desire	Goal	Survival benefit	Intrinsic value	Personality traits	
				Strong desire	Weak desire
Acceptance	Avoid criticism	Avoid suicide	Self	Self-doubting	Self-confident
Curiosity	Thinking	Learning	Knowledge	Intellectual	Practical
Eating	Sustenance	Biological need	Refined taste	Overeater	Fussy eater
Family	Raise children	Perpetuation of species	Children	Devoted parent	Childless or Absent parent
Honor	Moral behavior	Safety in numbers	Character	Principled, upright	Expedient, opportunistic
Idealism	Better world	World peace and health	Social causes	Humanitarian, idealistic	Looks other way
Independence	Self-reliance	Spreads search for food to new areas	Individuality	Proud, stubborn	Interdependent, humble
Order	Structure	Efficiency, cleanliness	Stability	Organized, methodical	Flexible, disorganized
Physical Activity	Muscle movement	Eats/mates first	Fitness	Energetic	Lackadaisical
Power	Influence	Dominance	Competence, achievement	Take-charge, willful	Laid-back, nondirective
Romance	Sex	Reproduction	Passion	Romantic	Platonic
Saving	Collection	Hoards food and essentials	Frugality	Collector	Extravagant
Social Contact	Peer companionship	Safety in numbers	Friendship	Affable, extroverted	Reserved, introverted
Status	Social standing	Privileged	Social class	Formal	Informal
Tranquility	Safety	Flees danger	Caution	Timid	Brave
Vengeance	Get even	Self-defense	Winning	Competitor	Peacemaker

How to read: The basic desire of "Acceptance" motivates people to avoid criticism from others (GOAL), not commit suicide (SURVIVAL BENEFIT), and to VALUE the self. People who have a habitually strong-intensity psychological need for acceptance develop the personality traits of self-doubting. People who have a habitually weak-intensity psychological need for acceptance develop the personality traits of self-confident. Reiss's "Dictionary of Normal Personality Traits" shows the theoretical connections between strong and weak versions of the sixteen basic desires and every personality trait in a thesaurus.

 **Notes**

Overview

1. Here is a partial list of what I mean by "personal troubles": abrupt, arrogant, attention-seeking, bossy, career burnout, combative, dependent (needs people), dishonest, disloyal, disorganized, divorce, elitist, hates school, insecure, lack of self-confidence, lazy, loner, marital conflict, moody, never home, nonassertive, overconfident, overeats, oversensitive, overspends, perfectionist, rebellious, risky behavior, socially awkward, show-off, stubborn, stuffed shirt, temper, timid, troubled marriage, underachieves, unfit, unhappy, unpopular, work–life imbalance (workaholism), and worrier. Excluded from my list of "personal troubles" are the well-recognized "Axis I" mental disorders such as Schizophrenia, Panic Disorder, and Major Depression (American Psychiatric Association, 1994).

Chapter 3. Intensity of Basic Motivation

1. The formal name for the RMP is the Reiss Profile of Fundamental Goals and Motivational Sensitivities (Reiss & Havercamp, 1998).
2. The basic desires for status and power are correlated perhaps because of a common origin. Unlike animals, human beings can gain dominance in two ways: merit versus inheritance. People can become VIPs through great achievement or high birth. Some people feel important because of their achievements (which falls under the basic desire for power), whereas others feel important because of their high birth, wealth, good looks, or fame (which falls under the basic desire for status). Achievers look down on royals as undeserving of great respect, whereas royals look down on achievers because they needed to work to become important. Royals pride themselves in their idleness precisely to make the point that they are so important they do not have to work.
3. The RMP does not recognize a general motive for attention-seeking. Instead, the RMP analyzes what a person wants others to pay attention to. Seeking the attention of a caregiver, for example, can be motivated by hunger or discomfort.

Calling attention to one's achievements is motivated by the basic desire for power, whereas calling attention to one's wealth or social class is motivated by status.

Attitudes toward attention-seeking can vary depending on "old" versus "new" money. Some people with new money may brag about their wealth or display it in "vulgar" ways. Some people with old money may shun bragging in order to distinguish themselves from people with new money. They are thinking, "We were born and bred for high society. We do not have to engage in vulgar displays of wealth or become braggarts so people will learn of our importance."

Chapter 6. Six Reasons for Adolescent Underachievement

1. Social psychologists have offered a second line of argument to blame under-achievement on competition for grades. According to these psychologists, more than 100 scientific studies prove that the use of rewards in experimental laboratories can briefly undermine intrinsic curiosity (Deci, Koestner, & Ryan, 1999). Other experts who have carefully examined the same evidence have concluded that rewards do not undermine intrinsic motivation (Eisenberger & Cameron, 1996). In my scholarly work I identified multiple flaws in the relevant scientific studies, including multiple errors in formal logic (Reiss, 2005a; Reiss & Sushin-sky, 1975). We should avoid drawing any conclusions from studies on intrinsic and extrinsic motivation. The whole idea that there are but two kinds of motives, called intrinsic and extrinsic, is invalid and inconsistent with the data presented in Chapter 2 validating sixteen kinds of motives.

Chapter 8. Relationships

1. On the RRP, a "match" occurs either when both partners score strong intensity on the same desire, or when both partners score weak intensity on the same desire. A "mismatch" occurs when one partner scores strong intensity on a particular desire and the other scores weak intensity on the same desire. A "near match" can occur in two ways: (1) when one partner has a strong-intensity desire and the other has an above-average intensity desire; (2) when one partner has a weak-intensity desire and the other has a below-averagec intensity desire. A "near mismatch" can occur in two ways: (1) when one partner has a strong-intensity desire and the other has a below-average intensity desire; (2) when one partner has a weak-intensity desire and the other has an above-average intensity desire.

References

Adler, A. (1964). *The practice and theory of individual psychology.* New York: Harcourt, Brace, Jovanovich. (Originally published in 1927.)

Allport, G. W. (1961). *The individual and his religion.* New York: Macmillan.

American Psychiatric Association (1994). *Diagnostic and statistical manual of mental disorders (4th ed.).* Washington, D.C.: American Psychiatric Association.

Anastasi, A. (1988). *Psychological testing (6th ed.).* New York; Macmillan.

Aristotle (1953). *The Nichomachean ethics* (trans. J. A. K. Thompson). New York: Penguin Books. (Original work created about 330 B.C.E.)

Atkinson, J. W., & Feather, N. T. (1966). *A theory of achievement motivation.* New York: John Wiley & Sons.

Aureli, F., & de Waal, F. B. M. (2000). *Natural conflict resolution.* Berkeley: University of California Press.

Baker, H. S. (1979). The conquering hero quits: Narcissistic factors in underachievement and failure. *American Journal of Psychotherapy, 33,* 418–427.

Bandura, A. (1969). *Principles of behavior modification.* New York: Holt, Rinehart, & Winston.

Bandura, A., & Walters, R. H. (1963). *Social learning and personality development.* New York: Holt, Rinehart & Winston.

Baron, R. (1998). *What type am I?* New York: Penguin books.

Berger, P. (2000). *Knight fall: The truth behind America's most controversial coach.* New York: Pinnacle/Kensington.

Blood, R. O., Jr. (1969). *Marriage.* New York: The Free Press.

Bruno, F. J. (1993). *Psychological symptoms.* New York: Wiley.

Buss, D. M. (1994). *The evolution of desire: Strategies of human mating.* New York: Basic Books.

Butcher, J. N., Dahlstrom, W. G., Graham, J. R., Tellegen, A., & Kaemmer, B. (1989). *MMPI-2: Minnesota Multiphasic Personality Inventory-2.* Minneapolis: University of Minnesota.

Cacioppo, J. T., Petty, R. E., Feinstein, J. A., & Jarvis, W. B. (1996). Dispositional differences in cognitive motivation: The life and times of individuals varying in need for cognition. *Psychological Bulletin, 119*, 197–253.

Cameron, N. (1963). *Personality development and psychopathology: A dynamic approach.* Boston: Houghton Mifflin.

Carey, J. C., Hamilton, D. L., & Shanklin, G. (1986). Does personality similarity affect male roommates' satisfaction? *Journal of College Student Personnel, 27*, 65–69.

Carli, L. L., Ganley, R., & Pierce-Otay, A. (1991). Similarity and satisfaction in roommate relationships. *Personality and Social Psychology Bulletin, 17*, 419–426.

Carnegie, D. (1981). *How to win friends and influence people.* New York: Simon and Schuster. (Originally published in 1936.)

Claridge, G., & Davis, C. (2003). *Personality and psychological disorders.* New York: Oxford University Press.

Crowne, D. P., & Marlowe, D. (1960). A new scale of social desirability independent of psychopathology. *Journal of Consulting Psychology, 24*, 349–354.

Csikszenthmihalyi, M. (2000). Happiness, flow, and human economic equality. *American Psychologist, 35*, 1163–1164.

Darwin, C. (1859). *The Origin of Species.* London: Murray.

  (1965). *The expression of the emotions in man and animals.* Chicago: The University of Chicago Press. (Original work published in 1872.)

Deci, E. L., & Ryan, R. M. (1985). *Intrinsic motivation and self-determination in human behavior.* New York: Plenum.

Deci, E. L., Koestner, R., & Ryan, R. M. (1999). A meta-analytic review of experiments examining the effects of extrinsic rewards on intrinsic motivation. *Psychological Bulletin, 125*, 627–668.

Dolan-Sewell, R. T., Krueger, R. F., & Shea, M. T. (2001). Co-occurrence with syndrome disorders. In W. J. Livesley (Ed.), *Handbook of personality disorders: Theory, research, and treatment.* New York: Guilford.

Dollard, J., Doob, L. W., Miller, N. E., Mowrer, O. H., & Sears, R. R. (1939). *Frustration and aggression.* New Haven, Conn.: Yale University Press.

Dunlap, K. (1919). Are there any instincts? *Journal of Abnormal Psychology, 14*, 307–311.

Dykens, E. M., & Rosner, B. A. (1999). Redefining behavioral phenotypes: Personality-motivation in Williams and Prader-Willi syndromes. *American Journal of Mental Retardation, 104*, 158–169.

Eisenberger, R., & Cameron, J. (1996). The detrimental effects of reward: Myth or reality. *American Psychologist, 51*, 1153–1166.

Ellis, A. (1973). *Reason and emotion in psychotherapy.* Secaucus, N.J.: Lyle Stuart. (Originally copyrighted in 1962.)

Engel, G., Olson, K. R., & Patrick, C. (2002). The personality of love: Fundamental motives and traits related to components of love. *Personality and Individual Differences, 32*, 839–853.

Erikson, E. H. (1963). *Childhood and society.* New York: W. W. Norton. (Originally published in 1950.)

Eron, L. D., & Huesmann, L. R. (1990). The stability of aggressive behavior – Even unto the third generation. In M. Lewis and S. M. Miller (Eds.), *Handbook of developmental psychology* (pp. 147–156). New York: Plenum.

Fenichel, O. (1945). *The psychoanalytic theory of neurosis.* New York: Norton.

Fish, T. R., Rabidoux, P., Ober, J., & Graff, V. L. (2006). Community literacy and friendship models for people with intellectual disabilities. *Mental Retardation, 44*, 443–446.

Fitzgerald, C. & Kirby, L. K. (1997). *Developing leaders: Research and applications in psychological type and leadership development.* Palo Alto, Calif.: Davies-Black.

Flugel, J. C. (1961). *Man, morals, and society.* New York: The Viking Press.

Freedman, J. L. (1984). Effect of television on aggressiveness. *Psychological Bulletin, 96*, 227–246.

Freeman, K. A., Anderson, C. M., Azer, R. H., Girolami, P. A., & Scotti, J. A. (1998). Why functional assessment is enough: A response to Reiss and Havercamp. *American Journal of Mental Retardation, 103*, 80–91.

Freud, S. (1951). *Psychopathology of everyday life.* New York: New American Library. (Originally published in 1901.)

(1963). *Introductory lectures on psychoanalysis.* London: Hogarth Press. (Original work published in 1916.)

Garb, H. N., Lilienfeld, S. O., & Wood, J. M. (2003). In M. Hersen (2004). *Comprehensive handbook of psychological assessment.* (pp. 453–469) Hoboken, N.J.: Wiley.

Gill, A. (2002). *Art lover: A biography of Peggy Guggenheim.* New York: Harper Collins.

Gimpel, G. A., Collett, B. R., Veeder, M. A., Gifford, J. A., Sneddon, P., Bushman, B., Hughes, K., & Odell, J. D. (2005). *Clinical Pediatrics, 44*, 405–411.

Gleick, J. (2003). *Issac Newton.* New York: Pantheon Books.

Gordon, E. M., & Sarason, S. B. (1955). The relationship between "test anxiety" and "other anxieties." *Journal of Personality, 23*, 317.

Gottman, J. M., & Silver, N. (1999). *The seven principles for making marriage work.* New York: Crown.

Gray, J. (1992). *Men are from Mars, women are from Venus.* New York: Harpercollins.

Haimowitz, M. L., & Haimowitz, N. R. (1966). The evil eye: Fear of success. In M. L. Haimowitz and N. R. Haimowitz (Eds.), *Human development: Selected readings.* New York: Cromwell.

Hall, C. S.. & Lindzey, G. (1957). *Theories of personality.* New York: Wiley.

Harding, W. R. (1965). *The days of Henry Thoreau.* New York: Knopf.

Hathaway, S. R., & McKinley, J. C. (1943). *The Minnesota Multiphasic Personality Inventory (rev. ed.)* Minneapolis: University of Minnesota Press.

Havercamp, S. H. (1988). *The Resis Profile of Motivation Sensitivity: Reliability, validity, and social desirability.* Columbus: Ohio State University.

Havercamp, S. H., & Reiss, S. (2003). A comprehensive assessment of human striving: Reliability and validity of the Reiss Profile. *Journal of Personality Assessment, 81*, 123–132.

Hilgard, E. R., & Atkinson, R. C. (1967). *Introduction to psychology (5th ed.)*. New York: Harcourt.

Hill, K. T. (1972). Anxiety in the evaluative context. In W. W. Hartup (Ed.), *The young child: Review of research* (vol. 2, pp. 225–263). Washington, D.C.: National Association for the Education of Young Children.

Hinton, R. J. (1968). *John Brown and his men*. New York: Arno Press.

Horney, K. (1939). *New ways in psychoanalysis*. New York: Norton.

Hunsley, J., Lee, C. M., & Wood, J. M. (2004). Controversial and questionable assessment techniques. In S. O. Lilienfeld and S. J. Lynn (Eds.), *Science and pseudoscience in clinical psychology*. New York: Guildford.

Irwin, T. (1995). *Plato's ethics*. New York: Oxford University Press.

Jackson, D. N. (1984). *Personality Research Form manual*. Port Huron, Mich.: Research Psychologists Press.

James, W. (1918). *The principles of psychology (vol. 2)*. New York: Dover. (Original work published in 1890.)

Jones, L. M., McCaa, B. B., & Martecchini, C. A. (1980). Roommate satisfaction as a function of similarity. *Journal of College Student Personnel, 21*, 229–234.

Judah, S. M. (2006). *Staying together when an affair pulls you apart*. Downers Grove, Il.: IVP Books.

Jung, C. (1923). *Psychological types*. New York: Harcourt.

Kagan, J. (2003). A time for specificity. *Journal of Personality Assessment, 85*, 125–127.

Kavanaugh, P., & Reiss, S. (2003). *Why high school students get poor grades*. Unpublished manuscript, The Ohio State University Nisonger Center.

Keyes, R. (1985). *Chancing it: Why we take risks*. Boston: Little, Brown.

Kline, P. (1972). *Fact and fantasy in Freudian theory*. Edinburgh: T & A Constable.

Kohn, A. (1993). *Punished by rewards*. Boston: Houghton Mifflin Company.

Lapidus, J., Green, S. K., & Baruh, E. (1985). Factors related to roommate compatibility in the residence hall: A review. *Journal of College Student Personnel, 26*, 420–434.

Lecavalier, L., & Tasse, M. J. (2002). Sensitivity theory of motivation and psychopathology: An exploratory study. *American Journal of Mental Retardation, 107*, 105–115.

Lepper, M. R., Corpus, J., & Lyengar, S. S. (2005). Intrinsic and extrinsic motivational orientations in the classroom: Age differences and academic correlates. *Journal of Educational Psychology, 97*, 184–196.

Maller, R., & Reiss, S. (1992). Anxiety sensitivity in 1984 and panic attacks in 1987. *Journal of Anxiety Disorders, 6*, 241–247.

Mandel, H. P. (1997). *Conduct disorder and underachievement: Risk factors, assessments, treatments, and prevention*. New York: Wiley.

Mandel, H. P., & Marcus, S. I. (1995). *"Could do better": Why children underachieve and what to do about it*. New York: J. Wiley.

Maslow, A. H. (1943). A theory of motivation. *Psychological Review, 50*, 370–396.
  (1954). *Motivation and personality.* New York: Harper & Row.
Maw, W. H., & Maw, E. W. (1964). *An exploratory study into the measurement of curiosity in elementary school children.* Project no. 801 (SAE 8519). United States Office of Education, Department of Health, Education, and Welfare.
May, R. (1969). *Love and will.* New York: Dell.
McCann, J. (1958). *Saint Benedict.* Garden City, N.Y.: Image Books.
McClelland, D. C. (1961). *The achieving society.* Princeton, N.J.: Van Nostrand.
McDougall, W. (2003). *An introduction to social psychology.* Mineola, N.Y.: Dover. (Originally published in 1908.)
McNally, R. J. (2002). Anxiety sensitivity and panic disorder. *Biological Psychiatry, 52*, 938–946.
Menninger, K. (1938). *Man against himself.* New York: Harcourt, Brace, & World.
Mill, J. S. (1964). *Autobiography of John Stuart Mill.* New York: New American Library. (Originally published in 1873.)
Millon, T., & Davis, R. (2000). *Personality disorders in modern life.* New York: John Wiley & Sons.
Murphy, G. (1929). *An historical introduction to modern psychology.* New York: Harcourt, Brace and Company.
Murray, H. A. (1938). *Explorations in personality: A clinical and experimental study of fifty men of college age.* New York: Oxford University Press.
  (1943). *Thematic Apperception Test.* Cambridge, Mass.: Harvard University Press.
Myers, I. B., and McCaulley, M. H. (1985). *Manual, a guide to the development and use of the Myers-Briggs Type Indicator.* Palo Alto, Calif.: Consulting Psychological Press.
Myers, I. B., McCaulley, M. H., Quenk, N. L., & Hammer, A. L. (1998). *MBTI Manual (3rd ed.).* Palo Alto, Calif.: Consulting Psychological Press.
Olson, K. R., & Chapin, B. (in press). Relation of fundamental motives and psychological needs to well being and motivation. In *Psychology of Motivation.* New York: Nova Science Publishers.
Olson, K. R., & Webber, D. (2004). Relations between big five traits and fundamental motives. *Psychological Reports, 95*, 795–802.
Pedersen, L. E. (1993). *Sixteen men: Understanding masculine personality types.* Boston: Shambhala.
Pfohl, B. (1996). Obsessiveness. In G. Costello (Ed.), *Personality characteristics of the personality disordered.* New York: Wiley, 276–88.
Plain Dealer (2006). College athlete depression. *The Plain Dealer,* August 27.
Plato (1966). *The Republic of Plato* (trans. F. M. Cornford). New York: Oxford University Press. (Orginally written in about 360 B.C.E.)
Preyer, W. (1995). *The mind of the child.* London: Routledge/Thoemmes Press. (Originally published in 1880.)
Quenk, N. L. (2002). *Was that really me?* Palo Alto, Calif.: Davies-Black.

Rafalovich, A. (2005). Exploring clinician uncertainty in the diagnosis and treatment of attention-deficit hyperactivity disorder. *Sociology of Health and Illness, 27*, 305–323.

Ramsay, G. (1843). *An inquiry into the principle of human happiness and human duty.* London: William Pickering.

Randsdell, P. (1989). *The queen of mean.* New York: Bantam.

Rapoport, J. L. (1990). *The boy who couldn't stop washing.* New York: Plume.

Reiss, S. (1997). Trait anxiety: It's not what you think it is. *Journal of Anxiety Disorders, 11*, 201–214.

   (2000a). *Who am I? The 16 basic desires that motivate our actions and define our personalities.* New York: Tarcher/Putnum.

   (2000b). Human individuality, happiness, and flow. *American Psychologist, 55*, 1161–1162.

   (2001). Secrets of happiness. *Psychology Today*, 50–56.

   (2004a). Multifaceted nature of intrinsic motivation: The theory of 16 basic desires. *Review of General Psychology, 8*, 179–193.

   (2004b). The 16 strivings for God. *Zygon, 39*, 303–320.

   (2005). Extrinsic and intrinsic motivation at 30: Unresolved scientific issues. *Behavior Analyst, 28*, 1–14.

Reiss, S., & Crouch, T. (2005). *Why people become aorgan donors? Paper presented at 133rd meeting of the American Public Health Assocaitian.* Philadelphia.

Reiss, S., & Havercamp, S. M. (1997). The sensitivity theory of aberrant motivation: Why functional analysis is not enough. *American Journal of Mental Retardation, 101*, 553–566.

   (1998). Toward a comprehensive assessment of fundamental motivation. *Psychological Assessment, 10*, 97–106.

   (1999). Sensitivity, functional analysis, and behavior genetics: A response to Freeman et al. *American Journal on Mental Retardation, 104*, 289–293.

   (2005). Motivation in a developmental context: Test of Maslow's theory of self-actualization. *Journal of Humanistic Psychology. 45*, 41–53.

Reiss, S., & McNally, R. J. (1985). Expectancy model of fear. In S. Reiss & R. R. Bootzin (Eds.), *Theoretical issues in behavior therapy.* New York: Academic Press, 107–121.

Reiss, S., & Reiss, M. (2004). Curiosity and mental retardation: Beyond IQ. *Mental Retardation, 42*, 77–81.

Reiss, S., & Sushinsky, L. W. (1975). Overjustification, competing responses, and the acquisition of intrinsic interest. *Journal of Personality and Social Psychology, 31*, 1116–1125.

Reiss, S., Peterson, R. A., Gursky, D. M., & McNally, R. J. (1986). Anxiety sensitivity, anxiety frequency, and the prediction of fearfulness. *Behavior Research and Therapy, 24*, 1–8.

   (2001). Trait motivational correlates of athleticism. *Journal of Personality and Individual Differences, 30*, 1139–1145.

   (2004). Why people watch reality TV? *Media Psychology, 6*, 363–378.

Rimm, S. B. (1986). *Underachievement syndrome: Causes and cures*. Vancouver, B.C.: Apple Publishing Company.

Russell, B. (1972). *A history of western philosophy*. New York: Simon & Shuster. (Originally published in 1945.)

Sarason, I. G. (1978). The test anxiety scale: Concept and research. In C. D. Speilberger & I. G. Sarason (Eds.), *Stress and Anxiety* (vol. 5, pp. 193–216). Washington, D.C.: Hemisphere.

Schmidt, N., Lerew, D., & Jackson, R. (1997). The role of anxiety sensitivity in the pathogenesis of panic. *Journal of Abnormal Psychology, 106*, 355–364.

Schwartz, S. H. (1994). Are there universal aspects in the structure and contents of human values? *Journal of Social Issues, 50*, 19–45.

Snyder, C. R., & Lopez, S. J. (2002). *Handbook of positive psychology*. New York: Oxford University Press.

Speilberger, C. D., Gonzales, H. P., Taylor, C. J., Algaze, B., & Anton, W. D. (1978). Examination stress and test anxiety. In C. D. Speilberger & I. G. Sarason (Eds.), *Stress and Anxiety* (vol. 5, pp. 167–189)). Washington, D.C.: Hemisphere.

Stahmann, R. F., & Hiebert, W. J. (1987). *Premarital counseling*. Lextington, Mass.: Lexington Books.

Strean, H. S. (1985). *Resolving marital conflicts: A Psychodynamic perspective*. New York: Wiley.

Thorman, G. (1996). *Marriage counseling handbook: A guide to practice*. Springfield, Il.: Charles C. Thomas.

Thorndike, E. L. (1913). *Educational psychology* (vol 1). New York: Columbia University.

Tressler, I. D. (1937). *How to lose friends and alienate people*. New York: Stackpole sons.

Weiner, B. (1995). Intrinsic motivation. In A. Manstead, M. Hewstone, S. Fiske, M. Hoggs, H. Reis, & G. Samlin (Eds.) *The Blackwell encyclopedia of social psychology*. Cambridge, U.K.: Blackwell.

White, R. W. (1959). Motivation reconsidered: The concept of competence. *Psychological Review, 66*, 297–333.

White, R. W., & Watt, N. F. (1973). *The abnormal personality*. New York: The Ronald Press.

Whiting, J. M., & Child, I. J. (1953). *Child training and personality*. New Haven: Yale University Press.

Wiltz, J., & Reiss, S. (2003). Compatibility of housemates with mental retardation. *American Journal of Mental Retardation, 108*, 173–180.

Woodworth, R. S. (1918). *Dynamic psychology*. New York: Columbia University Press.

Zubin, J., Eron, L. D., & Schumer, F. (1965). *An experimental approach to projective techniques*. New York: Wiley.

Index